Some Birding Places of P

California Birds

A Photographic Journey and Guide

Tim Stanley

California Birds: A Photographic Journey and Guide

© 2021, 2022 Joseph Timothy Stanley
Front cover photo: Jerry Ting
Back cover photo: Jeff Bleam

All rights reserved. No part of this book may be reproduced in any manner or stored in a retrieval system of any kind without prior written permission from the publisher. Photographs belong to the person whose name appears on them; if no name appears, they were taken by and belong to the author.

ISBN 978-0-9842391-8-4
Library of Congress Control Number: 2020922311
First printing, October 2022

2 Timothy Publishing
P.O. Box 53783
Irvine, CA 92619-3783
USA
www.2timothypublishing.com

Printed in Korea

For a copy of this book by mail, order online or send a check or money order for $37.00 to the P.O. Box above. Shipping and handling are included in the amount stated. California mailing addresses, add $2.40 sales tax.

See website for discounts on bulk purchases.

With thanks to the One who gives us richly all things to enjoy.

Contents

Preface — x
    About the Photographs — xi
    The Molt — xii
    Terms and Descriptions Used — xii
    Plant Names — xii
    Bird-Watching Tips — xiii
    How to Use this Book — xiii
    Key Identifying Features of Birds — xiv
    A Few Notes about Migration — xv

Seabirds — 1
    Duck-Like Seabirds — 3
    Albatrosses — 11
    Gull-Like Seabirds — 13
    Very Small Seabirds — 19

Moving Closer to Shore — 22
    Gulls — 25
    Terns and Skimmers — 42
    Pelicans — 53
    Cormorants — 57

Waterfowl — 65
    Swans and Geese — 66
    Ducks — 75
    Grebes — 101
    Mergansers — 108
    Loons — 112

Shorebirds — 116
    Plovers — 117
    Oystercatchers — 122
    Avocets and Stilts — 123
    Sandpipers and Sandpiper-Like Birds — 127
    Turnstones — 153
    Phalaropes — 155

Coots, Gallinules, and Rails — 161

The Heron Family: Herons, Egrets, and Bitterns — 166
    Herons — 166
    Egrets — 172
    Bitterns — 177

Other Birds of the Wetlands — 179
- Ibis and Cranes — 179
- Kingfishers — 182

Hawks and Hawk-Like Birds — 183
- Falcons — 183
- Accipiters, or Bird Hawks — 191
- Buteos, or Stocky, Soaring Hawks — 199
- Ospreys — 211
- Kites — 213
- Eagles — 215
- Vultures and Condors — 219

Owls — 221

Nighthawks and Poorwills — 235

Gamebirds — 239
- Doves and Pigeons — 239
- Quail and Grouse — 247
- Turkeys and Pheasants — 255

Cuckoos and Roadrunners — 257

Crows, Jays, and Allies — 259
- Crows and Ravens — 259
- Magpies — 261
- Jays and Nutcrackers — 263
- Grackles — 268

Hummingbirds — 269

Woodpeckers and Sapsuckers — 279

Swallows and Swifts — 297

Songbirds I: Thick-Billed Birds — 314
- Sparrows and Juncos — 314
- Towhees — 343
- Finches — 347
- Goldfinches and Siskins — 353
- Grosbeaks — 359
- Buntings — 367
- Crossbills — 369
- Tanagers — 371

Songbirds II: Thin-Billed Birds — 375
- Bluebirds, Robins, and Thrushes — 375
- Thrashers, Mockingbirds, and Shrikes — 384
- Wrens, Wrentits, and Titmice — 393
- Kinglets and Vireos — 403
- Nuthatches, Creepers, and Chickadees — 411
- Warblers — 419
- Gnatcatchers — 441
- Flycatchers and Kingbirds — 445
- Bushtits and Verdin — 461
- Pipits and Dippers — 464
- Waxwings and Phainopeplas — 467
- Meadowlarks and Horned Larks — 469
- Blackbirds, Cowbirds, and Starlings — 471
- Orioles — 481

Exotic Imported Species — 487

Appendixes
- Epilogue — 493
- Appendix 1: Molting Photos — 495
- Appendix 2: Helpful Silhouettes — 499
- Appendix 3: Uncommon Variants — 501
- Appendix 4: Fledglings and Juveniles — 503
- Appendix 5: More Photos with Interesting Stories — 507
- The Value of Birds — 508

Glossary — 509

Bibliography — 511

Acknowledgments — 513

Author's Apology — 516

Voices Index — 520

Index — 530

Preface

This book is an invitation to go birding with me.

Watching birds is fascinating. On any day you never know what birds are going to show up or what they will do. They are free to go where they wish, and that sense of freedom is shared by all who watch them. Additionally, their indescribable beauty can have an equally positive and powerful effect upon us.

I do not claim to be a bird expert and did not approach this book as if I were. Rather, the approach I've taken is that of a student of nature who has learned that with every discovery, several other discoveries await, and with every question answered, three more arise.

You are invited to join the journey I have been on, see something of what I have seen, and share my joy and the wonder of it all.

California provides a wide range of habitats, and more than 650 species of birds are on record as having at least visited our state. Of this number, about 300 species rarely come or are irregular. I have concentrated on the other 350 species that can be found in California every year. As much as is possible in a volume of this size, I will show you sufficient photographs of these birds, tell you something about them, and tell you when and where you can see them. Some are not easy to find, but persistence pays off.

Some of the birds included in this book are considered uncommon or even scarce generally but are common enough in the limited areas where they occur. Good examples are the Gray Jay, the Gray-crowned Rosy-finch, and the Gila Woodpecker.

Other species migrate through the state rather quickly or come in small numbers. I have included a few species that fit these categories and noted likely places and times where you may find them. Two examples are the Solitary Sandpiper and the White-throated Sparrow.

I do not split hairs on the identification of certain bird species. Barrels of ink have been used in bird books to describe the visual differences between dowitchers, Empidonax Flycatchers, Rufous and Allen's Hummingbirds, and certain gulls. But the fact is, only years of experience will help you discern some species, and even then, you cannot be certain a good deal of the time. As much as possible, the reader has been spared the unnecessary confusion because identification, however helpful, is not the ultimate goal. Instead, this book is a journey and provides a way to explore and consider a creation so wonderful it is impossible to fully comprehend.

Come along!

About the Photographs

The photographs in this book were selected to show birds in their natural environments and, when possible, to show them engaged in a characteristic activity. This increases our appreciation, understanding and, more importantly, our sense of awe.

Some species, such as the Steller's Jay, have only one photo because no other bird looks like them, the sexes look alike, and their plumage is consistent. The sexes of other species, such as the Vermilion Flycatcher, look different, as do juvenile birds, so more photos are included. Others, like the Western Sandpiper, require multiple photos because of seasonal plumage changes. In addition to age, sex, and seasonal differences, some hawks and seabirds have different morphs (see p. 510) and identifying them is even more complex. The Red-tailed Hawk required four pages of photos to show the species adequately and to help with identification.

People often ask, "Why is it that so many birds I see do not look like the ones in the books?" This is a good question, and there are three parts to the answer:

1. Books that cover North American birds spend about 60 percent of their space on species we don't see, or rarely see, in California. Western regional books are better, but still about 40 percent of the information in those books does not apply very much to California. By concentrating on California birds, more space is available to present the relevant information in one volume.
2. There are seasonal variations for many species, and the appearance of most birds changes as they mature. That can make identification difficult or impossible if we don't have enough pictures.
3. The photos need to show characteristic features, and they need to be large enough to show those features clearly.

I have attempted to meet these criteria as much as possible in one comfortably sized volume. Taking it a step further, I've included many photos that tell a story.

Jack and Petra Clayton

The Molt

Feathers fade and wear out, so birds molt to shed the old ones and grow the new. Some birds molt gradually, replacing their feathers almost continually. Others, including most songbirds, experience a nearly complete change of feathers in the summer after the nesting season and a partial molt in the winter or early spring before breeding. Usually, the feathers are replaced in a balanced way over a few weeks so that the bird does not become vulnerable to predators. Some of our male ducks, including mallards, are an exception in that they become nearly flightless during the summer molt.

For many bird species, the molt is a radical seasonal transformation and results in two very different looks in the same year—and a lot of variations during the process. During the molt, these birds can appear disheveled and look like just about anything. Other birds, however, such as Sanderlings, have quite a wardrobe through the year and always seem to be well dressed. Still others merely become darker or lighter.

A study of the photographs in Appendix 1 will help greatly in the identification of other species during their molt. (Molting birds aren't pretty, so their photos were not placed at the front of the book.)

So changes in how a bird looks result largely from feather wear and replacement. But feathers also fade and diet can play a big part in how a bird looks—and don't underestimate the effect of lighting. Reflection and refraction of light also influence feather color, sometimes greatly.

Terms and Descriptions Used

Measurements following the bird's name are from head to tip of tail.

Seabirds, shorebirds, songbirds, and the like, are general terms only.

Breeding, summer, winter, and *colorful* are terms used for plumage, and all have limitations. The term that fits the context best is used.

The terms *spring* and *fall* for migration are also limited. See *Notes about Migration* on page xv.

Geographical range descriptions are also, by necessity, generalized.

Voices: Many birds have a large vocabulary, many subtle differences in intonation, or both. The voicings listed are among the most common.

Abundance terms: *Common* means you'll usually see a bird, or many of them, in their season, range, and habitat; *fairly common*, that you often will; *uncommon*, that numbers will be less and they will not be seen as often; *scarce*, that they are hard to find.

Plant Names

Knowing the plants that birds prefer is often a key to finding them in season, so where space allowed, many of the plant names are supplied.

Bird-Watching Tips

1. Look and listen. (You will be amazed at what you've been missing.)
2. Find the food, find the birds.
3. Every species has boundaries, of both geography and habitat.
4. For every bird there is a season.
    a. Many birds that arrive in winter aren't seen here at other times.
    b. Ditto for other birds in their seasons.
5. Birds of a feather flock together. Usually.
6. Birds not of a feather also flock together.
    a. In a flock of any species, look for birds of other species.
7. Safety in numbers.
    a. If there are a hundred trees in a park, most of the birds will often be in just two or three of them.
8. The early birder sees the birds. Usually.
    a. Birds wake up hungry and until satisfied don't care about you; afterwards, you make them nervous.
    b. Birds are most active when the temperature is mild. During the warmer months, they are out in the early morning and early evening and rest mid-day. During cooler weather, they forage mid-day. This life pattern requires less caloric intake and is balanced by when insects and other prey are active.
9. Birds usually see you long before you see them.
    a. A bird approached frequently disappears, so stay in the shadows if possible. They can't see you there.
10. In out-of-the-way areas, a car makes a good bird blind.
    a. Position your car with the sun behind you and wait. Stay inside; the birds can't see you there—even if your window is down. This method is especially effective if you are on-site at dawn.
11. The best time to see songbirds is right after a rain when the sun comes out.
12. Taking photos enhances learning. An expensive camera is not necessary.
13. Be thankful for and consider what you are given each day. (See #1.)

How to Use This Book

1. Read the table of contents to see the titles and sequence used.
2. As you go through the book, or when you look up a bird, take special note of the introductions that are provided for some of the bird families. That information can be helpful and is not repeated for each species in the family.
3. Take it a little at a time and enjoy the journey.

Key Identifying Features of Birds

Identification of a bird requires at least a few clues and often comes down to a process of elimination. Range, habitat, and season always need to be considered. In addition, the examples below can help the birder know what to look for.

1. Size: Is the bird the size of a sparrow, a robin, a crow? (6", 10", 17"?)
2. General shape of the bird:
    a. Orioles and solitaires are slender; grosbeaks and bluebirds are heavier.
    b. The silhouettes in Appendix 2 give a good idea of what to look for.
3. Bill length and shape:
    a. A sparrow's bill is short and thick.
    b. A pipit's bill is longer and narrow.
    c. A tern's bill is shaped like a dagger, a gull's is not.
4. Head shape: Is it round, like a chickadee's, or pointed like a titmouse's?
5. Length and position of the tail:
    a. A towhee's tail is longer in proportion to the body than that of most sparrows.
    b. A wren holds its tail up; a flycatcher typically holds it down.
6. Length of legs in proportion to the body: Are they long, like an avocet's, or shorter, like a plover's?
7. Does the bird have a white ring around the eye? If so, is the eye-ring partial or full, bold or faint, or is it teardrop shaped?
8. Does the bird have contrasting color bars perpendicular to the feathers on the wing? If so, are the wing bars bold or subtle? How many are there?
9. Flight pattern. Every species has one:
    a. A finch bounces through the air.
    b. A robin flaps its wings continuously.
    c. A woodpecker flaps fast and then glides.
    d. Bluebirds fly up, not down, to a perch.
    e. Waxwing flocks fly in curves.
10. Posture. Many species have a preferred posture:
    a. A Townsend's Solitaire sits upright.
    b. A finch is as comfortable perching horizontally as vertically.
11. Personal habits:
    a. Black Phoebes and some other birds pump their tails.
    b. Hermit Thrushes have a nervous twitch.
    c. Sparrows usually stay close to or on the ground.
    d. Some warbler species like the treetops; others stay low.
12. Voice is often the best locator and identifier.

A Few Notes about Migration

1. Migration of a species is as much determined by the food available as it is by changes in the weather. Songbirds that eat both insects and seeds often don't migrate at all because they have seeds to get them through the winter. Those that eat only insects and fruits, like tanagers and orioles, must migrate to survive.
2. Migrations can be long, such as the Swainson's Hawk's journey to Argentina for the winter, or shorter, such as the Brewer's Sparrow's trip from the northern part of California to the south.
3. Certain species, such as some warblers, migrate quickly from their summer to winter homes, often flying hundreds of miles nonstop. Others species, such as many ducks, take their time on the trip, stopping along the way to molt or to enjoy food sources for as long as the supply is adequate.
4. "Fall" migration begins in midsummer for several species of songbirds, shorebirds, and others. "Spring" migration begins in January for some swallows and other birds that breed in the lowlands but not until late April for those that breed in the High Sierras.
5. Long migrations are all about fuel efficiency: Arctic breeders ride seasonal air currents south; soaring birds, including hawks, migrate mid-day, taking advantage of updrafts; other birds, including most warblers, flycatchers, and thrushes, migrate at night.
6. Birds too young or too weak to make the trip may stay all year and not leave with the migrating flocks.
7. Males, females, and juveniles of certain species migrate separately. Imagine my surprise when I looked out my window one spring day and saw 20 Hooded Orioles—all females—in the apple tree just outside my office! For some species, the females go to the breeding grounds first to begin nest building; with other species, the males go first to stake out a territory.
8. Turn-around time for some migrating birds can be quite short. They may arrive, breed, raise their young, and leave within three or four months.
9. After nesting, many migrants move farther north or to higher elevations before returning south. They are following the food supply and may be allowing their young more time before making a long trip.
10. The number of migrating birds in any year is largely dependent on rainfall. Plentiful rain yields plentiful food, which yields plentiful birds.

Roger Zachary
Sanderlings

Seabirds

On the sea, just off our coast, there awaits a whole world of birds for our discovery—the seabirds. Most of the birds in this section are seldom seen from shore, but some can frequently be observed from wharves, jetties, and headlands, especially in the north.

There are more than 100 species of seabirds in California waters. About 30 of them are common, and about the same number breed either on or just off the California coast. Three species make up the great majority of our total offshore bird population: the Sooty Shearwater, the Cassin's Auklet, and the Common Murre.

During the fall migration, a trip to a prominent headland or point along the coast can turn into an unforgettable adventure, as vast numbers of seabirds pass these places. The birds ride the storm fronts and are clustered together, so much so that it is not unusual to see thousands of birds pass by in an astonishingly short time. From Point Saint George in the far north to Point Loma in the south, when the storms roll in, the show is on for all who bring patience along.

A boat ride is another way to see these birds. There are pelagic, or open-sea, birding trips and whale-watching trips out of many harbors. The best birding trips are out of Monterey and other harbors to the north. Seabirds are attracted to the fish, and the fish congregate at the edge of the continental shelf where there is an upwelling of deep, cold, nutrient-rich water. The continental shelf is closest to shore in Monterey Bay, so that makes it the prime spot on our coast. The best time for a pelagic trip out of Monterey is from August through October.

Islands and offshore rocks along the continental shelf are another big attraction off the coast. These provide sheltered breeding areas for millions of seabirds, so sailing near them offers an opportunity to see things that cannot otherwise be observed.

The chief breeding grounds for seabirds off our coast are the Farallon Islands, located about 30 miles west of San Francisco. Eleven species and more than a half-million breeding birds can be found there during the breeding season. The Channel Islands in the south also have important breeding grounds. The islands host several species of seabirds as well as large colonies of Brown Pelicans and Western Gulls.

Rocky outcrops and hard-to-access cliffs on the mainland are also common breeding places, especially in the north. Real estate for breeding and nesting seabirds is very limited so populations are dense in the colonies. Thankfully, human access is restricted at most nesting sites, and that gives the birds a chance to survive.

In California waters, from the Oregon border to Point Conception near Lompoc, a cold ocean current comes down from the Gulf of Alaska, bringing with it an abundance of sea life. At Point Conception, the California landmass turns east and the ocean (and land) temperature is warmer, being influenced more by the tropics. Since all birds have a niche where they do well, many northern bird species rarely venture south of Point Conception, and many southern birds seldom travel north of that point. Far more seabirds are found in the north where food is plentiful. Although some species can be seen all year, most are more abundant during their migrations, typically mid-spring and late summer/early fall.

The intent of this section of the book is to give a little glimpse of the birds that are just offshore.

For all species in this section, the male and female birds look similar.

Below: Swarming shearwaters at Morro Bay.

Marlin Harms

Duck-Like Seabirds

Common Murre (17")

The Common Murre is one of the most plentiful seabirds off our coast. Many breed on the Farallon Islands, and they are year-round residents north of Point Reyes. Some winter as far south as Point Conception, decreasing in numbers as you go south. Common Murres typically stay out over the continental shelf, but when the fish come close to shore, the murres follow and are often seen from wharves and jetties along our coast. Santa Cruz is a good place to see them from late July to early May, especially from the wharf.

Awkward in flight but swift as a torpedo underwater, murres are propelled by their powerful wings. They live mostly on anchovies and smelt, and when ashore, they stand erect like penguins.

During the gold rush, Common Murre eggs were a staple food in San Francisco. Later, poultry farms were introduced and that allowed the depleted murre population to recover.

Voice: Silent at sea. In the breeding colony, a guttural urr, *often in staccato fashion.*

Below: Breeding plumage (April to August).

Jeff Bleam

Above: Colony. **Below:** Nonbreeding plumage.

Pigeon Guillemot (13.5")

Pigeon Guillemots are cold-water birds that are found on rocky coastlines north of Point Conception. Many breed on the Farallon Islands, about 30 miles west of the Golden Gate. Others breed as far north as the Arctic and as far south as Santa Cruz. They are almost always seen in flocks.

Like many other seabirds, Pigeon Guillemots swim underwater using their wings for propulsion and their feet as rudders.

Voice is a high-pitched whistle and a wavering twitter. If alarmed, they make a high-pitched buzzing sound somewhat like a referee's whistle.

Top: Breeding plumage (April to September). **Bottom left:** Nonbreeding plumage; juveniles look similar. **Right:** Adult on a nest at Santa Cruz where they are common during the breeding season.

Tufted Puffin (15–16")

In breeding plumage, Tufted Puffins are as exotic a bird as you will ever see. Many breed on the Farallon Islands; others breed much farther north. They are seldom found south of Monterey Bay.

Tufted Puffins winter at sea, often far from shore. They are shallow divers and live on fish and small squid.

Voice is a low, guttural, raspy growling that is heard only at the nest site.

Top: Breeding plumage (April to September). **Bottom:** Nonbreeding subadult.

Aaron Maizlish

Glen Tepke

Rhinoceros Auklet (15")

Rhinoceros Auklets breed on some of the Channel Islands, the Farallons, and on other islands farther north. They feed mostly on fish.

The horn and white tufts are present only during breeding season, which is April to September. At sea, Rhinoceros Auklets are usually solitary. They are occasionally seen from wharves and jetties in the north. At Santa Cruz, they are most often seen from August to October.

Voice: Typically silent at sea. At the breeding colony, they moo like a cow but more comically. The breeding colony sounds like a dairy farm where the cows have gone ape.

Top: Partial breeding plumage. **Bottom:** Full breeding plumage.

Eric Ellingson

Eric Ellingson

Cassin's Auklet (9")

The chunky little Cassin's Auklets breed on islands all along the California coast. They are very common, especially in the north, but are seldom seen from shore.

Unlike Rhinoceros Auklets, the Cassin's usually don't eat fish. Instead, they feed on krill, tiny crustaceans called copepods, and zooplankton. They are typically seen feeding in flocks.

Voice: Silent at sea. In the colony, they make a noise like the burst of steam from a carpet-cleaning machine.

Top: Breeding adults are gray. **Bottom:** Nonbreeding adults are brown. Breeding plumage is from March to September.

Jeff Bleam

Donna Pomeroy

Marbled Murrelet (10")

A strange duck (although not a duck), the Marbled Murrelet of the far north coast spends its days on the ocean and its nights in nests in the tall trees of old-growth coniferous forests. The nesting trees may be many miles inland. As long as a robin but chunky and with a shorter tail, these seabirds forage for fish and crustaceans in shallow coastal waters and bays. They are often seen in pairs.

The Marbled Murrelet's range in California extends as far south as Monterey Bay, but they are much more common in the far north. A good place to see them is at Patrick's Point. Closer to home for most of us, Waddell Beach, north of Santa Cruz, is a good place to look.

Voice is a high-pitched gull-like scream of keer! *or* peer! *At times, a drawn out, fussy, nasal squeak.*

Top: Breeding plumage (April to September). **Bottom:** A winter bird.

Eric Ellingson

Glen Tepke

Ancient Murrelet (10")

These seabirds breed in Alaska, and some are winter guests in California waters. Ancient Murrelets are usually seen in the far north out over the continental shelf and out of sight of land. Occasionally, some are spotted off rocky shores but seldom south of Monterey Bay.

The name *Ancient* refers to the bird's breeding plumage, which reminded someone of a shawl worn by an elderly woman.

Voice consists of chips and chirps, often rapidly strung together in the manner of a House Sparrow.

Top: A juvenile. **Bottom:** Breeding plumage (January to August).

Eric Ellingson

Eric Ellingson

Albatrosses

Black-Footed Albatross (32")

By far the most common albatross off California, the Black-footed Albatross is usually seen north of Monterey. It breeds mostly on the Hawaiian Islands and is found year-round in California waters, often scavenging food scraps from ships.

With a wingspan of over seven feet, these masters of flight roam the sea far and wide, sailing with ease just above the surface of the water, taking advantage of slight updrafts caused by wave action. The causes of lift in flight have mystified engineers for centuries, and recent airliner wing design changes testify we are still learning from the birds.

When not scavenging, the Black-footed Albatross's diet consists largely of flying fish, fish eggs, and squid. They rarely come close to shore.

Voice sounds like the braying of a donkey.

Jeff Bleam

Jeff Bleam

Laysan Albatross (32")

Named after one of the Hawaiian Islands, these birds breed mostly on Laysan and on the Midway Atoll. Although Laysan Albatrosses are rarely seen from land in California, these giants are sometimes spotted during pelagic trips out of San Diego, Monterey, and Marin.

Distance means nothing to these flight instructors that can glide for hours without a wingbeat. When the wind is calm, they rest on the water.

Their diet consists largely of squid, floating carrion, and discarded fish and fish scraps from fishing vessels.

Voice: Usually silent at sea.

Below: Black-footed (left) and Laysan Albatrosses.

Gull-Like Seabirds

Parasitic Jaeger (16.5")

Parasitic Jaegers breed on the Arctic tundra and winter on the ocean south of Monterey Bay. They can be seen closer to shore than most seabirds because they prey on smaller terns that frequently fish near the shore. The terns are good fishers, and the jaegers are bullies and thieves. If you see a tern flying erratically while being chased by a brown bird, the chaser is probably a Parasitic Jaeger. Since jaegers are just as likely to eat the tern, most terns will drop the fish.

The gull-like jaegers have dark, light, and intermediate color morphs (see page 510). Parasitic Jaegers are best identified by their powerful wingbeats, aggressive behavior, and falcon-like acrobatics. They are most common here from April to May and in September.

Voice is a squeaky, nasal two-syllable bark, usually repeated.

Left: Adult chasing a gull. **Top right:** Juvenile; **bottom:** light adult.

Pomarine Jaeger (19–21")

The Pomarine Jaeger breeds in the high Arctic and migrates through California waters to South America. A small number winter off our coast, mostly in the south and off the Central Coast.

Pomarine Jaegers are predators and pirates on the high seas. They make a living stealing from other birds but do not engage in acrobatic chases the way the Parasitic Jaeger does. Instead, Pomarines attack like a linebacker in football, using the brute force of their stocky bodies combined with their swift and powerful flight. The two jaegers can look very similar, but *their behavior easily identifies them*. Both will follow fishing vessels to scavenge scraps.

Voice is mid-tone nasal squawking. Some voicings are like barking.

Below: Some plumage variations. They can also be dark all over.

Tom Edell

Jeff Bleam

Roger Zachary

Northern Fulmar (18")

Built like a boxer—stocky, with a thick neck and a bull-headed appearance—the gull-like Northern Fulmar breeds in Alaska and arrives in California waters in the fall and are most common here at that time. Some years very few come.

Fulmars forage on the surface and also dive like terns. They usually stay out over the continental shelf, where they feed on a wide variety of sea life, and are well known to commercial fishermen for their scavenging.

Note the nostril-like tube on the upper bill of the bird at the top of the next page. Like many other seabirds—including albatrosses, shearwaters, petrels, and storm-petrels—fulmars are tubenoses. They are equipped with specially designed glands, or "tubes," on the top of their bills for extracting salt, which accumulates and is then sneezed out.

Voice: Usually silent in California waters.

As the photos show, Northern Fulmars may appear white, brown, gray, or anywhere in between.

Glen Tepke

Seabirds

Howard Patterson

Glen Tepke

Glen Tepke

Shearwaters

Shearwaters are long-winged, gull-like seabirds that glide effortlessly just above the surface of the waves to forage. Although they are not usually seen from land, shearwaters occasionally make grand appearances, as in the photo on page 2. Like fulmars, shearwaters are tubenoses. (See page 15 for explanation.)

Sooty Shearwater (17.5")

Sooty Shearwaters are the most abundant seabird in California waters and are often seen in very large flocks from April to October. Sootys head south in the fall to their breeding grounds in the Southern Hemisphere.

Flocks of Sooty Shearwaters are commonly joined by other shearwaters. They feed on krill and squid that come to the surface. Sootys are rarely seen from land but are common just a few miles offshore.

Voice: Usually silent at sea, even when in large flocks.

Below: Sooty Shearwaters flushed by a boat going by.

Jeff Bleam

Black-Vented Shearwater (14")

Most shearwaters range over a large expanse of ocean, but the Black-vented is an exception. They breed on islands off Baja California and winter in Southern California waters. Black-vented Shearwaters can often be seen from Point Loma in San Diego and from the Palo Verde Peninsula, near Los Angeles, from late fall to early spring. They are relatively uncommon north of Point Conception.

Voice: Silent at sea.

Below: The white belly and black feathers at the vent clearly separate this bird from the Sooty Shearwater. The vent of a bird is the opening under the tail for both excrement and egg delivery.

Glen Tepke

Very Small Seabirds

Although rarely seen from shore, birds as small as large sparrows and up to the size of a Brewer's Blackbird are also common offshore. Along the California coast, these are the storm-petrels. They are mostly night foragers that scoop up plankton from the ocean surface like a swallow getting a drink from a stream or pond. Storm-petrels are tubenoses (see page 15) and nest on rocky islands or outcroppings.

Below: Fork-tailed and Ashy Storm-petrels.

Black Storm-Petrel (9")

A warm-water bird, this largest storm-petrel in California waters is commonly seen between Baja and Monterey Bay on pelagic birding outings from spring to fall. Black Storm-petrels are usually silent but flocks may make mechanical rattling sounds while feeding.

Fork-Tailed Storm-Petrel (8.5")

The Fork-tailed Storm-petrel is a cold-water bird that is common in southeast Alaska. They can be seen all year off our far north coast but seldom south of Monterey Bay. They are usually solitary or in small groups and are often with flocks of other storm-petrels.

Like our other storm-petrels, they are usually silent at sea.

Ashy Storm-Petrel (8")

Strictly a California bird, almost all Ashy Storm-petrels breed on the Farallon Islands and gather in Monterey Bay in the fall.

Wilson's Storm-Petrel (7")

Wilson's Storm-petrels breed in the Southern Hemisphere and are found in California waters in the summer. They look similar to Leach's Storm-petrels, but their feet stick out past their tail when they fly. Wilson's Storm-petrels are the smallest storm-petrel in this collection and are the size of a large sparrow. Although uncommon, they often follow ships to feed on waste. They may peep softly while feeding.

Jeff Bleam

Leach's Storm-Petrel (8")

Like other storm-petrels, Leach's frequently feed on slicks of oil and fat on the ocean surface. Some of the oil and fat is from ocean carrion, some is ship waste, but Leach's seldom follow ships as the Wilson's do. Leach's Storm-petrels are usually seen in summer. Many California birds lack the white rump. See *Wilson's Storm-petrel* above.

Nick Pulcinella

Moving Closer to Shore

Occasionally, huge schools of small fish swim near the surface and close to shore. The result is a feeding frenzy enjoyed by all except the fish. In **the photo below** are cormorants, Brown Pelicans, gulls, shearwaters, and who knows what other birds. The **photo on the next page** was taken near Pismo Beach and shows something of the size of one of these gatherings.

Roger Zachary

Birds on Shore

Gulls

Some gulls found in California are seagulls; others are primarily inland birds. One of the best places to see a wide variety of gulls is around San Francisco Bay, especially in winter. Most gulls will eat anything, and easy food is plentiful at the many restaurants and dumps around the bay, so many gulls are there all year. Another good place to see an assortment of species from fall to spring is wherever a creek or river terminates at the coast, especially in the north.

Gull identification can be difficult. Different species commonly mingle and many species look similar. Large gulls do not achieve adult plumage until the fourth year, and each year, as they mature, their plumage changes considerably—both in winter and in summer. Also, feathers wear, fade, and are replaced, and during the molt the birds can look very different. Identification is further complicated because some species interbreed and hybrids are common. So, positive identification can be challenging, especially with immature birds. Frequently, many factors have to be taken into consideration to identify a gull, and even then . . .

A thorough treatment of gull identification would take an entire volume, so I've left that for others. The goal of this section is to increase the reader's appreciation of gulls without burdening you with confusing details. *The sexes of the gulls listed here look alike.* **The females, however, are much smaller so a size range is given for adults.**

Below: California Gulls with a first-year Glaucous-winged (brown, left), Herring (pink legs), and Ring-billed (center) near Santa Cruz in February.

Black-Legged Kittiwake (13-16.5")

In the late spring and early summer, Black-legged Kittiwakes nest in colonies on cliffs or other inaccessible areas along the coast of Alaska. The rest of the year they spend on the ocean, usually in flocks. Some stay in the north all year; others winter as far south as Baja California. They are rarely seen on shore in California except in the far north.

Like other ocean birds, kittiwakes favor places of upwellings near the continental shelf, which is closest at Humboldt and Monterey. In the winter, kittiwakes are sometimes seen with other gulls along the shore at Redwood National Park. They are also winter regulars in Monterey Bay but usually stay away from shore.

Voice: Kittiwakes are typically silent in winter, so are unlikely to be heard in California. Calls are a nasal, one-syllable bark and a three-syllable squeaking. Their name, kittiwake, *is heard on the breeding grounds.*

Top: Adults in nonbreeding plumage. **Bottom, left to right:** Breeding plumage (April to September) and a flying juvenile.

Western Gull (19-25")

Common year-round all along the West Coast, Western Gulls breed on rocky islands and outcrops and have large breeding colonies on Santa Barbara and Anacapa Islands. Naturally, they capture fish and other aquatic life on the surface of the water and on shore. Unnaturally, Western Gulls have a fondness for potato chips and anything else that is in your picnic basket. They also prey on nesting birds and are regulars at the dumps and fast-food parking lots.

In the north, Western Gulls interbreed with Glaucous-winged Gulls and hybrids are common, very common in Washington state.

Note the **pinkish legs and feet**; **sloping forehead**; large, **bulbous** bill and **darker back** than a California Gull. There are exceptions, but taken as a whole, these field marks separate Western from California Gulls.

Voice is the classic scream of a seagull. They also squeal and bark.

Below: Adult and first-year bird.

Next page, top: Breeding adult (red eye) with young, begging juveniles. **Middle, left to right:** Second-year bird; third-year bird. **Bottom:** Immature and adult.

Gulls

California Gull (17-21")

A common winter gull along the Northern California coast, the California Gull is usually found inland the rest of the year. The ones we see on the coast typically nest by the salt ponds around San Francisco Bay or on the islands of lakes from the Klamath Basin to Mono Lake. Younger, nonbreeding California Gulls may remain on the coast all year, often mingling with Western Gulls. California Gulls are not nearly as common as Western or Ring-billed Gulls in Southern California.

Note the **smaller size, yellow legs and feet**, **bill shape**, and the **red and black** marks on the bill of the adults. The **head shape** is also rounder than a Western Gull's, and the adult's **back is usually lighter** than the Western's. Young birds have **pinkish legs**.

Voice is a classic seagull scream but more scratchy than that of a Western Gull.

Below: This gull at Mono Lake was a hoot. While the other gulls sat on the water and pecked at the flies one at a time, this fellow, obviously desiring efficiency, lined himself up with the shoreline, then sprinted along it with his mouth wide open. Note the all-white head and neck, which is indicative of breeding plumage (March to September). See photo page 25.

Next page, top: February adults transitioning to breeding plumage. **Middle:** Adult in nonbreeding plumage flanked by younger birds. **Bottom, left to right:** First-year bird; second-year bird.

Jeff Bleam

Herring Gull (19-25")

Large, stout gulls with a *menacing look*, Herring Gulls breed in the Canadian Rockies and in the mountains of interior Alaska. They arrive in California, and in California waters, in September and are usually gone by the end of April. Many stay out at sea, far from land.

Herring Gulls are not as abundant as some of our other gulls and are usually found in and around Monterey Bay and to the north. They are common in season in the rice belt of the Sacramento Valley, around San Francisco Bay—especially when herring are spawning—and in the Delta, where they frequent agricultural fields, parks, and landfills.

Herring Gulls are often seen with flocks of Western and California Gulls and stand out because of their *size and lighter color*. Note their *pinkish legs* and a bill that is not as large or bulbous as the Western Gull's.

Voice: Calls include yeow! *in classic screaming seagull fashion, a high-pitched* ha-ha-ha *that is squeaky, a low-pitched* ha-ha-ha *that is scratchy, and a drawn-out* whaaa, *like a crying baby.*

Below: Adult Herring Gulls behind the much smaller but similar looking Ring-billed Gulls at the Salton Sea. Note the different bills. The legs of one Herring Gull appear as different colors due to shadow.

Next page, top: Third-winter bird. Adult nonbreeding birds are similar but less brown. **Middle:** Second-winter bird. **Bottom:** Juvenile or first-year. **Additional photo** is on page 25.

Jack and Petra Clayton

Fredric F. Petersen

Keith Carlson

Glaucous-Winged Gull (20-26")

The ***largest and lightest-colored*** gulls commonly found in California are Glaucous-winged Gulls. They nest and are often seen year-round from Alaska to Washington, but some come farther south to California during the winter. The farther north in the state, the more common they are; they are uncommon south of Monterey Bay.

Glaucous-winged Gulls typically remain on the coast and frequent the dumps of northern coastal towns. They are rarely seen farther inland.

Unlike our other gulls, the Glaucous-winged Gull's ***tail is the same color as its back.*** This applies to adults and immature birds alike, which makes both easy to identify.

Hybrids among gulls are common, and the Glaucous-winged often interbreeds with Western, Herring, and Glaucous Gulls, making some birds difficult, if not impossible, to identify.

Voices are the classic scream of a seagull and a low-pitched, nasal keow-keow-keow *that falls between a bark and a quack.*

Below: Nonbreeding adult. A breeding adult has an all-white head. Breeding plumage is usually from February to September.

Next page, top: First-winter bird. **Middle, left to right:** First-year bird turning gray; second-winter bird in giant kelp. **Bottom:** Third-winter bird.

Jeff Bleam

Jeff Bleam

Jeff Bleam

Jack and Petra Clayton

Glen Tepke

Heermann's Gull (16-19")

These gulls breed along the west coast of Mexico, and many migrate up our West Coast, timing their trip with the migration of the Brown Pelicans. Although the pelicans go farther, Heermann's Gulls are uncommon north of Eureka. Birds that travel north for the summer gather into large flocks around Monterey Bay in the fall for the trip south.

Heermann's Gulls are experts at stealing fish from Brown Pelicans. They arrive right after a catch, and if they get there before the pelican can swallow the fish, they peck mercilessly on its bill until the pelican opens it slightly, at which time possession of the fish usually changes bills.

Voice is between a cluck and a quack. A noisy flock sounds like a barnyard full of chickens and ducks.

Top: Mostly immature birds. **Bottom:** Nonbreeding and breeding adults. The breeding bird has a white head (December to August).

Above: Gulls in a thermal column just inland from Newport Bay.

Gulls and hawks are often seen in spinning columns of warm air called *thermals*. Migrating birds fly into them and are lifted higher. At a higher altitude, the birds exit and glide down toward their destination, saving precious energy. Sometimes the spinning of the air mass is much faster than at other times, occasionally slinging some birds out at high speed. At other times, the birds appear to be spinning so fast that they can't get out. The columns eventually dissipate, and the show is over. Thermals are a common sight just inland from small bays, such as upper Newport Bay, and gulls use them for commuting trips farther inland. At the end of the day, they return to the coast in droves. If they have to fly low, the droves usually number fewer than a hundred birds. If they are riding a high air mass, the numbers can be in the thousands.

Ring-Billed Gull (14-17.5")

The well-named Ring-billed Gulls are common and widespread in California, perhaps because they don't mind people. They breed in the Klamath Basin and to the north and east, and winter in the western third of the state. Ring-billed Gulls are found inland as often as they are on the coast and are probably the most common gull at our reservoirs and inland parking lots. On the coast, they are often seen dropping clams and other shellfish on rocks to break them open, a practice of many gulls that leaves piles of broken shells at suitable locations.

Note the smaller size, the yellow legs of the more mature birds, and the pink legs of the juvenile. Also note the position of the black ring around the bill for the birds of different ages.

Voice is a rising bloody-murder scream. Also a hoarse, lower-pitched ow! as if they were being hurt.

Below: Breeding adult (April to September).

Next page, top: First-winter bird. **Middle:** Light juvenile (usually not seen far from nesting areas). **Bottom:** Nonbreeding adult on surf grass. Second-year birds look similar to nonbreeding adults but are more spotted. Ring-billed Gulls achieve adult plumage in the third year. **Additional photo** of breeding adults is on page 31.

Mew Gull (13-16")

These *smaller*, less-common gulls breed in the tundra of northwestern Canada and Alaska and winter along the Pacific coast as far south as Baja.

Mew Gulls are typically in California from November to April and are seen along the shore and in mudflats, wet fields, and landfills along the coast. Small flocks are fairly common in the far north, uncommon south of Monterey Bay. Look for them in agricultural fields as they feed on worms after a heavy rain. Another good place to find them is at Arcata Bay.

Their *cuter-than-usual face* with large head, large black eyes, and *short bill* makes Mew Gulls easy to identify. The feet and legs of adult birds are green-yellow. Young birds have grayish-pink feet and legs.

Voice is a high-pitched squeal.

Below: Breeding birds in a pine tree at Santa Cruz. Birds have three eyelids: an opaque pair like ours, and a transparent membrane. They may close either to rest, as did the gull on the right.

Next page, top: Nonbreeding adult (September to April). **Middle:** First-winter bird. **Bottom:** Second-year bird. Mew Gulls mature in three years. *Juveniles are brown*, similar to the Ring-billed on page 38.

Bonaparte's Gull (11-13")

Our smallest gull, Bonaparte's Gull, was named after a French zoologist who was a distant cousin of Napoleon's, but the name is usually understood as a tongue-in-cheek poke at the emperor. They breed in Canada and Alaska and winter along the Pacific coast, usually out at sea. Spring migration is a good time to see Bonaparte's Gulls along the California coast and in our bays, marshes, and reservoirs. In April and May, they are fairly common at the Salton Sea, at the Palo Alto Baylands in the south Bay Area, and at Black Butte Reservoir near Orland.

Bonaparte's Gulls are often mistaken for terns but can be recognized at a distance by their foraging method, which is unlike that of our other gulls and terns. They dive somewhat like a tern but don't hit the water hard. They also hover and pick up food from the surface of the water, which terns do only occasionally. The Bonaparte's diet is primarily small fish and insects. They do not visit landfills.

Voice is grating, usually a short bark or squeak. Also, a tern-like buzz.

Below: A flock in mid-April with breeding (black head), nonbreeding (far left), and transitioning birds. Breeding plumage is from April to August. Bonaparte's mature in two years. The first-year bird's plumage is similar to that of a first-year Mew Gull (page 40, middle) and can be identified by the black spot at the back of the eye (below left). Juveniles are brown and are seldom seen in California. **Inset:** Note the black tail.

Jerry Ting

Jeff Bleam

Terns

Terns look somewhat like gulls but are more streamlined, and although some gulls will dive for fish, they are clumsy compared to these masters of the craft. Terns often dive from high above and strike the water with such force that it is hard to understand how the impact does not break them into pieces.

Most terns are basically coastal birds, but many also fish at marshes, ponds, and lakes farther inland. They breed in colonies and migrate in flocks but may disperse at other times.

Some tern species are famous for making long migrations every year. The Arctic Tern travels from the Arctic to the tip of South America, but the terns we see in California take much shorter journeys.

For most California species, the full black cap is indicative of a breeding bird (typically March to August); the partial cap indicates a nonbreeding bird.

The sexes of terns look alike—to us—but not to the terns.

Jerry Ting

Caspian Tern (21")

The Caspian is our largest tern and is easily identified by its size, ***thick red bill with a black tip***, and voice. They live on fish in freshwater and saltwater habitats.

Most of the Caspian Terns we see in California winter along the coast of Mexico and are here between March and September. Some breed around San Francisco Bay, at the Salton Sea, at coastal marshes in Orange and San Diego Counties, and at lakes from the Klamath Basin to Mono Lake. They will be where the fish are, either along the coast or inland.

Voice consists of raspy, nasal croaks, usually ka-rah *and* ka-rack.

Top: Colony. Breeding birds (March to September) wear a black cap; nonbreeding, dark gray. **Bottom:** First-year bird. **Add'l photo:** Page 47.

Howard Patterson

Royal Tern (20")

Royal Terns are warm-water birds that breed mostly in Mexico and seldom travel north of Point Conception. A small number can be seen year-round in the southern part of California, but they are much more common here in the winter. (How's that for a switch—these birds migrate north for the winter!)

Note the **thick, orange bill**. The Groucho Marx look is that of a nonbreeding bird. **Breeding birds have a full black cap** like the Elegant Terns on page 45. Breeding plumage is from March to June.

Voice is a grating squeak/scream.

Below: The bird in the middle of the three is a juvenile that was incessantly bugging one of his parents (at left). When the other showed up, he kept quiet. I suspect some history influenced that behavior.

Note the shorter, lighter bill and light legs of the juvenile. The juvenile also has streaking on the wings and back.

The photo was taken at Crystal Cove State Park in Orange County, where small flocks typically arrive after the first heavy rain in the fall. They follow the fish and come and go throughout the fall and winter.

Elegant Tern (17")

Elegant Terns winter in Mexico and in recent years have extended their breeding range as far north as Orange County and their post-breeding range to San Francisco Bay. They are commonly seen from late March to early October along the coast in Southern California and from July to October from Monterey Bay to San Francisco Bay.

The bill of an Elegant Tern is as long as its head. The bill is **longer and thinner** than that of the Royal Tern and differs from the Royal's in that it is **curved downward**.

Voice is typically a grating, high-pitched kar-eeek! *or* eeek! *Varies.*

Below: Part of a large breeding colony at Bolsa Chica in Huntington Beach in late March. They sounded like a bunch of frogs croaking on a summer night but were much louder. The racket could be heard from half a mile away, above the noise of the traffic on the Pacific Coast Highway. The entire scene was something to behold, with all the gyrations, antics, and pairs of birds taking off together. Everything was done at fever pitch. **Inset:** Nonbreeding adult. Note the curved bill.

Jerry Ting

Forster's Tern (14")

The *mid-sized* Forster's Tern is commonly seen all year around San Francisco Bay, in the San Diego area, and at the Salton Sea. They also breed in the Delta, in the Central Valley, and around high mountain lakes east of the Sierras. They are common breeders at Lake Tahoe. Forster's Terns winter along the coast, mostly from the Bay Area to the tip of Baja.

Forster's are nearly identical in appearance to the **Common Tern**, which breeds in the Canadian Rockies, migrates down the West Coast in relatively small numbers, and winters in southwestern Mexico. About the only visual difference between the two species is that the Forster's has a black eye patch in nonbreeding plumage, whereas the Common Tern lacks the eye patch and has a partial black cap instead.

Voice is raspy and includes a sound like a loose banjo string. When repeated rapidly, it sounds nagging. Also, check *and squeaky noises. The Common Tern's voice is quite different and lacks the banjo sound.*

Below, top: Breeding adult (March to August). Note the black tip on the bill. **Bottom:** Nonbreeding adult. Note the black bill. **Add'l:** P. 47.

Jeff Bleam

Howard Patterson

Above: Elegant, Caspian, and Forster's Terns.
These three species are often seen together, especially during breeding season.

Below: Elegant Terns. Note the even spacing, which is tighter in cold weather, greater in warm weather.

Black Tern (9.5")

Black Terns are uncommon in California, but some breed and spend the summer in the rice-growing areas of the Sacramento Valley. In the winter, Black Terns live at sea off the coasts of Central and South America. They can be seen along the migration route at lakes, ponds, and marshes, and especially at the Salton Sea in early October.

Unlike other terns, Black Terns don't dive deeply. They eat small fish and insects and feed more like a swallow, flying erratically and dipping into the water. At times, they will follow a tractor that has stirred up insects in an agricultural field. A good place to watch them from May to early September is along the Feather River south of Oroville.

Voice is a nasal, squeaky kik, *at times continuous. Also, a grating squeak, like a little dog barking.*

Top: Breeding plumage (March to August). **Bottom:** A juvenile. Adult nonbreeding birds look similar but are gray instead of brown.

Rob English

Nick Pulcinella

Least Tern (9")

Our smallest tern, the Least Tern, winters in Central America and is found from April to September on California's south coast, where they breed beside sheltered lagoons and shallow bays. Like other terns, they build their nests on the sandy ground. Least Terns are warm-water birds and are seldom seen north of San Francisco Bay.

Voice is a raspy, squeaky kreek *and squeaky* kil-up. *Also,* chit, chit, chit.

Below: Breeding adult in Sand Verbena at Bolsa Chica in Huntington Beach.

Next page, top to bottom: Bambino; young'un; and juvenile.

***

July 9, 2018
I've come out early this morning to observe a nesting colony of Least Terns. At first light, things are just starting to stir in the colony. The chicks and youngsters are wandering around, foraging on the ground while they wait for their parents to wake up and go fishing for them. Suddenly, I spot a Western Gull standing motionless in their midst, unnoticed. He must have arrived before I did, and there is no other reason for his being there other than to try to snatch a young tern for breakfast. As the adults begin to take off for the morning hunt, one spots the gull. He calls and is answered. In seconds, a few terns are strafing the gull. Quickly, the air is filled with screaming terns and gulls. The gulls seemed to have appeared from nowhere. But they must have been there on the ground, just camouflaged and not previously seen by me or by the terns.

***

Terns

Black Skimmer (18")

Skimmers are warm-water birds that are expanding their range from Mexico into California. They are usually seen south of Point Conception but now go as far north as San Francisco Bay. In the south, they come twice a year, in winter and in summer, and some have begun to breed here. Skimmers nest in colonies, often alongside terns.

A more fascinating bird you will never watch, although I suppose that that could be said about many. Skimmers were engineered to make a living by skimming the surface of the water for fish and are equally expert at gliding along a curled wave in the ocean as they are at working a pond. They scout an area from above, circle around and level off at the water's surface, submerge their longer, lower mandible (bill) slightly, and glide along steadily at about 10 mph, all the while making smooth wingbeats. When they locate a fish, they snap their top bill down to grab the prey. Exactly how skimmers locate a fish I don't know, but sometimes they make last-second adjustments in trajectory.

At a good fishing spot, skimmers often hunt two or three or more abreast. At such a location, it is not uncommon for many terns to be there diving for the same fish. Ducks and geese seem to know to stay clear of the area, and the air traffic control system must be pretty good. I have never seen a collision but have seen several last-millisecond avoidance maneuvers.

Skimmers typically fish in the early morning and late afternoon.

Voices are a nasal bark and a raspy bark.

Mick Thompson

Bottom Photo: In recent years, some skimmers have been breeding at San Joaquin Marsh in Irvine. However, most that come do not breed here.

Brown Pelican (48–50"; wingspan, 77")

Brown Pelicans nest in colonies on the Channel Islands and along the coast of Mexico. Many travel up the coast as far as British Columbia after breeding and then gather into large flocks and head south by November. Brown Pelicans are usually seen on the coast but are also common in San Francisco Bay and at the Salton Sea.

These huge birds make their living diving for fish—a spectacular demonstration of both materials design and skill. After a catch, pelicans must drain a large amount of water from their bill and then turn the fish with their tongue so they can swallow it headfirst. This takes time, and Heermann's Gulls often take advantage of that time to steal the pelican's catch (see Heermann's Gull, page 35).

Brown Pelicans are often seen gliding in the trough of a wave just above the surface of the water—a remarkable display of the laws of physics and aerodynamics.

Voice: Brown Pelicans are usually silent. Occasionally, they utter a low croak. Hungry nestlings squeal.

Below: Juvenile.

Next page, top: Breeding plumage (December to August). **Bottom:** Nonbreeding birds. The sexes look alike.

Jerry Ting

Bill Kaufman

American White Pelican (62"; wingspan, about 9')

A huge bird that has the wingspan of a California Condor but weighs a little less, the White Pelican is the second largest bird in the state.

In California, White Pelicans breed and nest on islands in lakes in the Klamath region. During winter, they inhabit bays, sloughs, marshes, ponds, and lakes from the Delta to our southern border. Many winter on the Salton Sea. White Pelicans do not dive for fish like their brown cousins. Instead, they fish while sitting on the water.

Fishing is often a communal effort that begins with the flock's forming a tight group and swimming together across a pond or lake (**next page, top**). The paddling of their feet herds the fish in front of them and brings them closer together. When the fish are close to the surface, the birds begin to gracefully and gently scoop them up one at a time, all the while continuing quietly across the pond and not breaking ranks. Sometimes this becomes a synchronized ballet: one, two, three, scoop; one, two, three, scoop. At other times, birds at the front of the flotilla slow or stop, while those at the back swing around and go ahead of the others to encircle the school of fish. The circle is drawn tighter, the command is given, and the birds go bottoms up to feed (**middle photo**). When the fish get spooked, the gentle giants lose all propriety, and mayhem breaks out. As the fish begin to disperse, the birds beat their wings against the water to try to keep the fish in the net they have formed. Eventually, the fish thin out, and the feeding stops.

And those watching the spectacle shake their heads in amazement.

Voice: Sometimes low grunts, otherwise silent.

Below: A breeding bird (February to June). The yellow parts begin to turn pale and pinkish by June and their feathers as if they've been dipped in muddy water. The juvenile looks similar to a nonbreeding bird.

Next page: A fishing party.

Cormorants

Cormorants are fast underwater swimmers and expert fishers. We have three species in California, and all are often seen with wings spread, drying out in the sun or preening, both of which are preparations for the next fishing excursion. Note the extra-wide webbed feet in some of the photos.

Like other fishing birds, cormorants swallow fish whole. They are equipped with an internal sorting system that separates the edible parts of the fish from the inedible and packages the bones, fins, and scales, wrapping them into a mucus-covered ball that the birds can regurgitate safely. The sexes of cormorants look alike.

Below: A Double-crested Cormorant. And, yes, it did swallow the fish.

Brandt's Cormorant (34")

Brandt's Cormorants are found in coastal waters and less frequently in San Francisco Bay. Although some breed at La Jolla, they are far more common in the north, where they live year-round. Brandt's Cormorants rarely venture to inland ponds and lakes as do the Double-crested.

Voice sounds like a hog.

Next page, top: Nesting birds on the bluffs at Santa Cruz. The nests are made of ice plant. Adults have a yellow patch on the jaw. Breeding birds (April to June) have a bright blue pouch under the bill. **Bottom left:** First-year bird. **Right:** Adult in full breeding regalia. The white tufts on the face are usually not visible.

Cormorants

Double-Crested Cormorant (32″)

At home in freshwater and saltwater, Double-crested Cormorants are seen on the ocean and on inland lakes and ponds and often commute between the two. Many are year-round residents near the coast, but their numbers are increased in the fall with birds that breed in the Klamath region and beyond. They nest, and often roost, in trees.

Unlike our other cormorants, Double-crested Cormorants often work in a pack, herding fish. It is a disciplined, coordinated effort. When the birds begin fishing, they sit high in the water (**next page, top photo**). Once the fish are crowded together, the cormorants start dipping their heads into the water to scoop them up, or they make shallow dives to capture them, all the while staying in the pack. Because Double-cresteds lack the waterproofing qualities of other cormorants, in less than half an hour they are water-logged, with only their necks above water, and look like snakes weaving across the pond (**next page, middle photo**).

Voice is a deep, muffled burping. When flying together, they keep up a constant soft peeping, presumably to avoid midair collisions.

Top: The crests, which can be black, show only during breeding season (March to May). **Bottom, left:** First-year bird; molting looks similar.

Jeff Bleam

Pelagic Cormorant (26–29")

Our smallest cormorant, the Pelagic Cormorant, is not well named. It is usually seen in coastal waters and rarely goes far out to sea, as the Brant's commonly does. Pelagics also venture into sloughs.

Pelagic Cormorants are cold-water birds and are much more common in the north. They follow the fish but are essentially year-round residents where they occur. Pelagics build nests similar to the Brandt's, but prefer the clefts of rocks. They are far outnumbered by Brandt's in their range. Unlike other cormorants, Pelagics are typically solitary feeders and sometimes dive a hundred feet down for their supper.

Voice is like a baby's cooing but deeper; also a rusty squeak and bark.

Photos: Note the narrow bill. Breeding birds (February to May) have a white patch on their flanks and a red face. The green is iridescence.

Jeff Bleam

Gordon F. Brown

Above: Photo taken at Santa Cruz where Pelagics are common.

Next pages: A winter day at Santa Cruz. >>>
Black Oystercatchers, Surfbirds, Black Turnstones, and Sanderlings.

Jeff Bleam

Waterfowl

Donna Pomeroy

Tundra Swan (52")

As their name implies, Tundra Swans breed on the tundra in the high Arctic. They winter from western Washington to the southern end of California's Central Valley. From November to mid-March, small flocks are often seen feeding in flooded agricultural fields in the Klamath Basin and in the Sacramento Valley. A very few go as far south as the lower Colorado River Valley.

Meriwether Lewis (of the Lewis and Clark Expedition) called them Whistling Swans because of the sound of their wings in flight. High flyers, Tundra Swans are often heard before they are seen.

Voice, on the ground, is a hollow-sounding, owl-like hoh, *sometimes with guttural cackling. In flight, the call is squeaky and somewhat like a Canada Goose's but shorter and higher-pitched.*

Below: Adults with subadult at left. Juveniles are light gray all over but have turned mostly white by December.

Jeff Bleam

Geese

Male and female geese look alike, but the females are smaller.

Canada Goose (30–43")

Large, noisy flocks of Canada Geese flying overhead in V formation during the spring and fall migrations made these majestic birds a symbol of the wilderness. But not so much anymore. They have adapted to city and suburban life, and now many are year-round residents in our city parks and on our golf courses, where they graze on nicely mowed lawns. Nevertheless, my heart still jumps when I hear a flock fly over, and what a thrill it is to see the large, wild flocks in the Sacramento-San Joaquin Delta and in the far north.

The size and tameness of these beautiful birds gives us a great opportunity to see and ponder the complexity of the structure of their various feathers. The more you look, the more you see, and the more you see, the more awe-inspiring you find them.

Note the large range in the size of these birds.

Voice in flight is much like an old-fashioned bicycle horn; hence their nickname, "Honkers." On the ground, they grunt. If provoked, they hiss.

Below: I don't know, but it looks to me like some of the neighbor kids joined this family outing.

Jeff Bleam

Above: Breast feathers of Canada Goose.

Crackling Goose (23-32")

Crackling Geese are a smaller, short-necked race of Canada Geese. Size varies considerably. Some flocks winter in the Klamath area and in the Sacramento Valley. They are not common in California.

Voice is similar to, but higher than, a Canada Goose's.

Brant (24–26")

Geese of the high Arctic during the breeding season, Brants are seen all along our coast and in our bays, estuaries, and lagoons during the winter. During migration, Brants are high flyers, often flying well above one thousand feet. They do not fly in V formations but in lines or in a lazy U formation. They migrate mostly over the ocean, sometimes far offshore.

Huge flocks of Brants winter in Humboldt Bay; large flocks farther south, particularly at Bodega and Morro Bays; and small flocks at Bolsa Chica and San Diego Bay. They begin arriving in the north by late September, in the south by mid-October, and most have left the state by late May.

Brants feed mostly on plants around the shoreline—eelgrass when they can find it.

Voice is like a stuttering, insecure honk of a Canada Goose. When a flock gets going, it sounds like they are gargling.

Below: Photo was taken at Bolsa Chica in Huntington Beach.

Ross's Goose (23")

The Ross's is to the Snow Goose what the Crackling is to the Canada Goose—a smaller goose with a shorter neck. Ross's Geese also have a rounder head and stubbier bill than the Snow Goose. (**See next page**.)

Ross's Geese are often seen mixed in with a flock of Snow Geese, and the two interbreed. Habits and habitat are the same as those of Snow Geese.

Voice is a nasal honk.

Snow Goose (25–33")

Snow Geese are high Arctic breeders that winter by the thousands in the California grain-growing areas. Huge flocks can be found in the Klamath Basin, especially at Tule Lake; in the Central Valley, especially in the Delta; and in the Imperial Valley, at the southern tip of the Salton Sea.

The Snow Geese feed on waste grain that is left over after the harvest, grain that is planted for them, and grain that was not planted for them and has not been harvested but that they enjoy equally as well.

When they first arrive, in October, the great majority are white, and they are very skittish. Thousands will take to the air if they are spooked in the least. As the weather turns warmer, the geese molt and gradually put on their bluish coats (similar to the juvenile on the **next page**). During the molt, nothing scares them and they stay grounded. *Their size and the darkness of color in the blue phase vary significantly.*

Voice is a loud, low, nasal whouk *and a high-pitched similar-sounding* squeak. *Flocks use both of these voicings at the same time, and when thousands of them let loose, it is something never forgotten.*

Next page, top: Ross's Goose in foreground, Snow Geese behind. Goose at left is a juvenile. **Next page, bottom:** White-fronted Geese in front, Snow Geese in back at Merced National Wildlife Refuge.

Gary Weller

Geese

Greater White-Fronted Goose (28")

Greater White-fronted Geese breed in the Arctic and winter in California primarily from Tule Lake in the far north to the Sacramento-San Joaquin Delta region. Some continue south into Mexico and stop at the south end of the Salton Sea in October, and a relative few winter there. White-fronts typically remain in large flocks, but individuals are sometimes seen outside their usual winter range.

The habits of White-fronted Geese are much like those of Snow and Ross's Geese, and the White-fronts also greatly appreciate the California grain growers. All these geese usually stay in tight flocks of their own kind, although they intermingle some. The tightness of the flock is important because a coyote or raptor is far more likely to prey on a straggler. And, yes, some raptors, including the Great-horned Owl, will take birds larger than they are.

Greater White-fronted Geese can be confused with some domestic barnyard geese and sometimes interbreed with them. Juvenile White-fronts are grayish-brown.

Voice is a high-pitched squeaky squawk that is quite different from the voices of our other geese.

Below: This goose looked out of place at a park near us. It likely got on the wrong flight and ended up migrating with the much more abundant Canada or Snow Geese, with which they are usually seen.

Egyptian Goose (26")

An import from you-can-guess-where, Egyptian Geese are well established in many city and county parks in Southern California. They seem to get along fine with the Canadas and graze in the same manner.

Voice is a bark-like honking that becomes faster when the goose is excited.

Bottom photo: Like the local Canada Geese, the Egyptians are quite tame. We enjoyed watching the family below for months, as the kids grew up, until they left for the summer. The parents were protective but accepted us after a while.

Ducks

Ducks can be divided into dabbling ducks, which forage on the surface of a pond and sometimes on land, and diving ducks.

Several species of ducks breed in the Klamath region of the far north, and small numbers breed at various other locations throughout the state, but most of the ducks we see in California breed somewhere north of the state and arrive with the cool heavy rains in the fall and stay until the weather turns warm in the spring. *The formula for ducks is very simple: no rain, no ducks; lots of rain, lots of ducks*.

Most migrating ducks molt and put on their colorful coats before arriving in the fall and many do not molt again until after they leave in the spring. So we see many more ducks in what is called their breeding plumage. The time required to change plumage varies and the ducks can look different during the process so additional photos are supplied for some species. *Both sexes turn duller after the breeding season.*

Juvenile ducks usually look like females.

Ducks' bills have specialized edges to help them grasp food. These vary greatly from species to species. (See p. 84.) Ducks' bills (size, shape, color) are also a major key to identification of similar-looking females.

Female ducks do most of the talking, and several species do not pass the standard duck test—they don't quack.

Unless noted otherwise, the ducks listed here are common or fairly common in California between September and May.

Dabbling Ducks

Mallard (20–23")

Mallards are the most common duck in California. Those in city parks are tame; wild mallards behave like any other wild duck.

Breeding (colorful) plumage is from October until they begin molting again in May. During the late spring molt, when they are losing their pretty colors, the males often congregate in flocks and barely move. They seem grumpy at that time, and the females leave them alone.

Voice: The female's boisterous, classic quacking is commonly heard in city parks; the male utters a subdued, hoarse yeeb.

Top: Breeding pair in a flooded cornfield. **Bottom:** Nonbreeding pair.

Jerry McFarland

Wood Duck (18–19")

Wood Ducks live in freshwater ponds and along slow-moving streams where they build their nests and roost in trees. They are uncommon in California but are most numerous in the Central Valley west of the central Sierras, especially at Cosumnes River Preserve. They typically don't migrate but if aquatic foods are scarce in winter, will visit grain fields or go to dryer areas for acorns. In the south, Wood Ducks are sometimes found in parks with a pond and mature oaks and sycamores.

Voice is a rising squeak, like pulling cellophane apart. Female is louder.

Below: Pair in breeding plumage (September to June). Nonbreeding plumage is similar but duller.

American Wigeon (19–20")

A few American Wigeons are year-round residents in the northeast corner of the state, but most that we see in California breed in Canada and Alaska. They arrive in September and are gone by the end of April. Wigeons are found in most of the state except in the deserts and high mountains.

In marshes, American Wigeons seem as gentle as any duck, and their sweet peeping voices keep a flock close together in the manner of Bushtits. It is all so cute. But when on a deepwater pond with diving ducks, wigeons show the other side of their character. American Wigeons are bullies and thieves. I once watched some American Wigeons bully a small group of Ring-necked Ducks. The Ring-necks were no match for the wigeons that snatched the Ring-necks' dinner at will as soon as they surfaced with it. Observing this stressful situation was a sobering reminder that not all is well in the animal kingdom.

Voice is a sweet peeping, similar to the first whistle of a tea kettle.

Above: Breeding pair of wigeons (October to June). Nonbreeding male looks like a female but has a black ring around his eye.

Right: Breeding males. The green on the head is from iridescence.

Below: Note the black-tipped bill.

Gadwall (19–20")

Some Gadwalls live year-round in the temperate areas of the state in marshes and reed-lined lakes where they forage in shallow water. Many others breed east of the Sierras and fly over the mountains in the fall to join them.

Voice: The female has a boisterous raspy quack similar to that of a mallard; the male has a soft, buzzy, nasal quack but is usually quiet.

Top: Transitioning plumage; photo taken April 10. Note the female's white belly, which readily distinguishes it from similar-looking female ducks. **Bottom left:** Breeding plumage is brightest Dec to March; photo taken Jan 26. Note the male's tweed jacket. **Right:** Nonbreeding male, May 5.

Jerry Ting

Ethan Winning

Northern Pintail (25–26")

Pintails are elegant ducks that hold their heads and tails high. They get their name from the male's breeding plumage. Small numbers live year-round from the Delta to the northeast corner of the state, but most that we see breed in Alaska and inland Canada and come to California in the fall. The migrating ducks begin arriving at wetlands and agricultural fields all over the state with the first heavy rain. Huge flocks can be found in the rice-growing region north of Sacramento, especially at the wildlife preserves. Migrating pintails are also found in sheltered saltwater habitats. They typically leave by the end of April.

Voice: The female has a nasal, hoarse quack and a guttural staccato. The male peeps in a quivering way.

Top and bottom: Breeding plumage (November to June). **Inset:** Nonbreeding male; female grays similarly. Photo was taken October 6.

Blue-Winged Teal (15–16")

Blue-winged Teal are warm-water ducks. Some breed in the Klamath Basin, but most that we see in California begin arriving from farther north early in September. While here, they are found primarily in the Sacramento-San Joaquin Delta wetlands and on ponds and marshes along the coast south of Mendocino. Most of these ducks continue farther south into Mexico or even as far away as South America. They may stay with us for a while or they may not, but one day they are here, and the next they are gone.

Voice: Commonly, a nasal bark/quack and high-pitched peeping.

Below: Breeding plumage (November to June). In the summer, the male looks like a female. Females look similar to other female teal but the bill readily identifies them. The Cinnamon's is largest, the Blue-winged's is mid-sized, and the Green-winged is a smaller duck with a smaller bill.

Jack and Petra Clayton

Marlin Harms

Green-Winged Teal (14-15")

Like most other ducks, the flocks of Green-winged Teal begin arriving with the first heavy rain, usually sometime in September. Although a small number can be seen year-round in the Klamath Basin, most breed in Alaska and inland Canada. The migrating ducks occupy shallow wetlands and marshes throughout the state, mostly in the Central Valley. When the weather turns warm or if it does not rain for a while, they leave.

Voice: The male's is a high-pitched peeping; the female's is a cross between hoarse laughter and a mallard's quacking.

Top: Breeding plumage (October to June). **Bottom, left:** Nonbreeding plumage; the sexes and juveniles look similar. **Right:** A breeding pair.

Cinnamon Teal (16–17")

Cinnamon Teal are warm-water ducks. Some are year-round residents in marshes in the temperate areas of western California; many more breed in the marshes of the northern and eastern parts of the state (and beyond) and join the full-time residents in the fall.

Voice: The male snorts like a pig; the female has a soft, raspy quack.

Top: Breeding plumage (brightest from late November to late April.) **Bottom left:** Nonbreeding male (July to September), wing colors are usually hidden; early November. **Right:** A pair in mid-May transitioning out of breeding plumage. **Next page, top:** Late November.

Female Cinnamon Teal can be confused with Blue-winged Teal because of the blue patch on the wing, but **the bill of the Cinnamon Teal is much larger**. Juvenile Cinnamon Teal look like pale females.

Jerry Ting

Jeff Bleam

Top photo: Teal Town—all three species.

Special Interest Note:

All ducks have specialized bills. The Long-tailed Duck, a diving duck (below left), was given a bill with a serrated edge to enable it to grasp slippery fish and underwater vegetation. The Cinnamon Teal, a dabbling duck (below right), was outfitted with delicate ridges on the sides of the bill that, in concert with the tongue, strain out tiny aquatic plants and animals. How the mud is sorted, I don't know, but I'm certain that was calculated in the equation.

Jerry Ting

Northern Shoveler (19")

The shoveler's Latin name, Spatula, is exactly what their **extra-wide bill** looks like. However, it is a highly sophisticated tool with comb-like edges inside that effectively strain out small aquatic vegetation, plankton, and tiny invertebrates as the ducks forage on the surface of a pond. (See the bottom right photo on page 84.)

Some shovelers are year-round residents of the Sacramento Valley and the Delta area; others come for the winter from as far north as Alaska and northern Canada. The migrating birds start showing up in marshes and ponds all over California in September. Departure time varies significantly, but most are gone by sometime in May.

Shovelers often work together to forage more efficiently. Sometimes a pair will swim in a tight circle, creating a vortex and causing small aquatic organisms to come to the surface. At other times, many ducks form a circle for the same purpose (**top photo on the next page**) and feed on them in the manner of white pelicans (see page 56).

Voice: Males make a hollow, nasal thuck-thuck; *females, a nasal* quack-a.

Below: A nonbreeding pair. They are duller yet in the summer. The photo was taken October 14.

Next page, top: A foraging circle. The ducks are in breeding plumage (December to May). **Bottom:** A couple of drakes fighting—I assume over a female.

Jeff Bleam

Diving Ducks

Donna Pomeroy

Bufflehead (14")

Named for their large buffalo-like heads, our smallest ducks, the Buffleheads, are quick and graceful divers—and a lot of fun to watch. They are omnivores and dine on a wide variety of aquatic life.

A few Buffleheads live year-round in the Klamath Basin, but the majority we see in the state breed in Canada and, like typical Canadians, come to California for the winter. They are found along the coast in lagoons, estuaries, and sheltered bays and also inland on shallow ponds. Less frequently, they are seen on lakes and deep ponds.

Voice is like a blend of a crow's and a female mallard's.

Below: Males are a study in iridescence, per photos. They are brightest from October to May. **Bottom, right:** Likely a mother and daughter.

Ruddy Duck (15")

The little Ruddy Duck's signature is its tail, which sticks up. They are warm-water ducks and are found on ponds year-round in most of the state except in the mountains. Many more join the locals for the winter.

This apparently lazy duck usually feeds at night so is usually seen sleeping in loose "rafts" during the day. They also migrate at night.

Voice: Ruddys are usually silent. Occasionally, soft squeaky peeping.

Top: A breeding pair (March to August). **Middle, left to right:** Nonbreeding male; male in transition. **Bottom:** Juvenile.

Ring-Necked Duck (17")

A small number of Ring-necked Ducks breed in the Klamath Basin but most that we see come from Oregon, Washington, or Canada. The migrating ducks arrive in Northern California as early as late September. In the south, they may not come until much later. Their departure times also vary considerably.

These diving ducks prefer deeper freshwater ponds and lakes in wooded areas but can also be found in water as shallow as four feet on slow-moving rivers. They are often seen in small flocks but, just as often, as lone pairs on a pond.

Ring-necked Ducks will eat just about any submerged plant or animal but usually not fish.

This duck is not well named. The chestnut-colored ring on the neck of the male in breeding plumage is due to iridescence and can only be seen when the light is just right. The color may appear in nearly any shape or location. A better way to identify the duck is by the ring around the bill, which easily distinguishes it from a scaup (p. 95). Also, note the female's white eye-ring. A female scaup lacks the eye-ring.

Voice is a half bark, half quack.

See page 77 for a story about Ring-necked Ducks and wigeons.

Below: Mid-February pair in transitioning plumage. Nonbreeding is duller. **Inset:** Dec. male in breeding plumage; brightest is Nov. to Jan.

Lesser Scaup (17")

Some Lesser Scaup live year-round in the Klamath Basin, but most spend the summer in Canada and winter farther south. They are found throughout California in many habitats but are most numerous on ponds in the Central Valley. Lesser Scaup are also common along the coast, usually in bays, lagoons, and estuaries.

The Lesser Scaup is very similar to the Greater Scaup but has a peaked head, whereas the Greater has a rounded head. However, when active, the Greater Scaup may raise its crown, making it look like a Lesser. Lesser Scaup are more common.

Scaup are frequently seen in tight rafts of many ducks.

Voice: Females bark and garble out a quack; males are usually silent.

Below: Breeding pair; breeding male; female or juvenile male. Iridescence can make the heads of male scaup appear green, purple, or black. Nonbreeding male scaup look like they've been dipped in muddy water.

Greater Scaup (18")

Greater Scaup are nearly identical to their Lesser brethren but have a rounder head. They are much less common than Lesser Scaup, prefer coastal areas, and, except for San Diego Bay, usually stay farther north when in California. They are common in San Francisco Bay. Greater Scaup also breed farther north, in Alaska and northern Canada.

The Scaup twins begin arriving in October; most leave by May. Other than latitude, habitat is the same for both species.

Voice is nearly identical to that of the Lesser Scaup.

Bottom, left to right: Male with a clam, female with a mussel. Along with veggies, both shellfish are scaup staples and are swallowed whole.

Common Goldeneye (19")

A cold-water bird, the Common Goldeneye breeds in Canadian forests and winters along our north coast and in the Central Valley. They are found in the surf, in protected bays and estuaries, and on inland lakes and ponds. Common Goldeneyes are regulars around San Francisco Bay but are infrequent south of Monterey. They are here from November to early April.

Common Goldeneyes eat insects, fish, fish eggs, crabs, mollusks, pond weeds, bulrush, and anything else any duck would eat.

Voice: The females have a low, hog-like croak and a raspy kruk. *The male's voice is much softer and higher. Their wings whistle as they fly. The sound is similar to, but softer than, that of a Mourning Dove taking off.*

Top: Males doing the neck jive to impress the lady. Nonbreeding birds are duller. **Bottom:** Female. Young males have a brown head with white spot.

Barrow's Goldeneye (18")

Unlike the Common Goldeneye, the Barrow's is scarce. They breed in western Canada and some are in California by November.

Compare the **crescent-shaped** white mark on the face of the male Barrow's with the white spot on the Common Goldeneye.

Although uncommon in California, Barrow's Goldeneyes are winter regulars at Lake Merritt in Oakland and in the Palo Alto Baylands.

Voice: The female has a nasal, raspy kuk *that she repeats a few times. The male's voice is similar but not as raspy, and he doesn't have much to say. The wings make a low whistle in flight, like that of the Common Goldeneye. Among hunters, both goldeneyes are known as whistlers.*

Below: A male and two females in breeding plumage (October to June). First-year males have a brown head like the female but also have the white crescent of the adult male on their faces. Compare the female's bill with that of the female Common Goldeneye.

Jeff Bleam

Redhead (19–20")

Small numbers of Redheads are year-round residents of the Sacramento-San Joaquin Delta and other wetter parts of the Central Valley. In the fall, migrating flocks from as far away as northern Alberta join them and also inhabit coastal lagoons, marshes, and inland lakes. Many Redheads winter as far south as southern Mexico. They are not as common as many other ducks in California.

Female Redheads frequently lay their eggs in the nests of other Redheads or of other ducks. Such brood parasitism is not uncommon among ducks, but Redheads take it to the extreme.

Voice: The female has a raspy, nasal quack; both sexes grunt. During the breeding season, the male makes a hollow, nasal siren sound.

Top: Pair in breeding plumage, which is from November to June. Photo was taken in May. **Bottom:** Nonbreeding plumage. Photo was taken in mid-August.

Jeff Bleam

Fredric F. Petersen

Canvasback (21–22")

Canvasback Ducks are the largest of our diving ducks. Some are year-round residents on lakes east of the Cascades and in the Sacramento Valley; many more winter along the coast in sheltered waters. They are fairly common in San Francisco Bay from late October to early April.

Like scaup, Canvasbacks are commonly seen in tight rafts. Note the sloping head.

Voice: Usually silent; at times, grunt. Female sounds like a crow gargling.

Top: Pair in breeding plumage (October to June). **Bottom:** Transitioning pair. Summer (nonbreeding) Canvasbacks are duller yet. Juveniles look similar to the adult female.

Jeff Deam

Jeff Bleam

Harlequin Duck (16–17")

Harlequins are small, uncommon sea ducks found in Northern California waters during winter. They breed along mountain rivers but not in California anymore. In our state, good places to look for Harlequin Ducks from late October to April are Point Saint George, Trinidad Head, and Humboldt Bay.

At a distance, Harlequin Ducks look black or gray; their colors are not evident until seen close-up and in good light. The chief identifying features at a distance are their white spots and patches. Immature males look similar to females for the first year and usually have their full colors by their third year. Females look similar to female Buffleheads but do not have the Bufflehead's white wing patches.

The name comes from an Italian comedy with a character dressed in an oddly painted costume.

Voice: Typically, a mouse-like squeak, hence their nickname: "Squeakers."

Top, from left: Two females, breeding male, two nonbreeding males.

Surf Scoter (19–20")

Surf Scoters are common ocean-going ducks that are seen both on the ocean and in lagoons where shellfish are abundant. Surf Scoters breed in Alaska but a small number remain in Northern California all year. In the winter, they are common along the north coast and in San Francisco Bay, and decrease in number as you go south. In the south, they are often in the lagoon at Bolsa Chica and at Point La Jolla. In season, they are frequently seen riding the waves just behind the breakers.

The menu for scoters is mostly small fish and submerged invertebrates, especially clams and oysters. They can hold their breath for about a minute and are fun to watch because you never know where they will surface after a dive. From an elevated vantage point, you can watch scoters working underwater to pry loose a mussel or clam. They study the situation, position themselves carefully at the right angle, then, seemingly in slow motion, apply their tool to the task, in turn using it like pliers or like a crowbar.

Voice: Usually silent.

Top: Adult males and a female. The spots on the female's face differ from Harlequin's and Bufflehead's. **Bottom:** Young female; young male.

White-Winged Scoter (21")

White-winged Scoters are winter visitors from Canada. They are cold-water ducks and are found on the ocean and in lagoons in the north. These unusual and uncommon ducks seldom go south of Monterey Bay. A good place to look for them from late October to early April is at the mouth of the Klamath River.

Habits are similar to those of the smaller Surf Scoter. When swimming underwater, these chunky ducks look like the Pillsbury Doughboy.

Voice: White-winged Scoters are usually quiet. When heard, they make a few soft sounds that may be described as a squeak, a raspy cluck, *and a nasal, bark-like quack.*

Below: Male and female. Immature male lacks the white around eye.

Black Scoter (19")

Our least common scoter, the Black Scoter, breeds in Alaska, and a small number are winter visitors in California. They are found on the ocean off rocky shores and in lagoons and bays. Black Scoters are occasionally seen as far south as Point Reyes but are much more frequent in the far north. A good place to look for them is in the harbor at Crescent City. They are cold-water ducks and are usually found here only between November and March.

The habits of Black Scoters are like those of other scoters and, when seen, they are often with Surf Scoters.

Voice is a soft wailing whistle.

Below: Male and female. Immature male is brown with two dull whitish spots on his face, similar to, but not as defined as, a female Surf Scoter's.

Glen Tepke

Fredric F. Petersen

Grebes

Grebes, like the loons and mergansers that follow them in this book, are duck-like fishing birds. They were engineered with lobed toes and legs placed farther back than those of a duck. Four of the five species of grebes in this section are commonly found in California.

Most grebes make floating nests in the marsh reeds. Their eggs often get wet, but usually hatch if tended. The sexes look alike.

Western Grebe and Clark's Grebe (25")

Western Grebes breed in the Central Valley and in the Great Basin on freshwater lakes and marshes lined with reeds and rushes. In winter, they are often seen in coastal waters and lagoons.

The courtship ritual of both grebes is spectacular. The couple becomes accustomed to each other over a few days, going on excursions around the pond. Eventually, they begin bobbing their heads up and down, swimming together with neck erect and wearing fancy hats, and performing synchronized neck gyrations. For the grand finale, called "rushing," the pair suddenly stands up straight and runs across the water together. This lasts up to eight seconds, after which the pair may or may not mate. Most of the head bobbing and even the neck gyrations do not end with the couple's rushing. But you know they are going to rush when they crouch down with their necks outstretched and stare at each other.

*Voice is a high-pitched, piercing scream—*kereep! *The youngsters scream bloody murder if they are not fed as soon as they want to be.*

Below: Western Grebes. **Next page:** Courtship.

(Text continues on page 103.)

Marlin Harms

Western Grebe and Clark's Grebe (continued)

The Clark's Grebe was recently spun off from the Western Grebe as a separate species. Compare the location of the black-to-white line at the eye of the Clark's Grebe in the top photo on this page with that of the Western Grebes on page 101. Also, the bill of the Clark's is bright ***orange***; the Western's is ***greenish yellow***. The two species interbreed. (See courtship and rushing photos on the previous page.)

Clark's Greebes breed on freshwater lakes from Tahoe to the Klamath Basin and winter both along the coast and a short distance inland.

Voice: The Clark's voice is very similar to the Western Grebe's.

Top: Clark's subadult. **Bottom:** Juvenile Western and (younger) Clark's.

Pied-Billed Grebe (13")

Pied-billed Grebes are common residents of reedy marsh ponds, lakes, and slow-moving rivers throughout California. Unlike those in colder climates, most of our Pied-billed Grebes don't migrate and rarely fly.

I took a photo nearly identical to the one below. That grebe made a beeline for the bulrushes as soon as he caught the fish. Gulls and cormorants were in the area, and he did not want to lose his catch—even if it was as long as he was. I saw him get it halfway down his gullet before he disappeared into the bulrushes.

Voice is a rapid, low, raspy pumping or grunting somewhat like a starter motor on a piece of machinery; also a high-pitched whopping.

Top: To be swallowed head-first only! **Bottom left:** A breeding bird. Note the black ring around the bill. **Right:** The fluffed bird is a juvenile.

Jack Lindahl

Eared Grebe (12–13")

Some Eared Grebes are year-round residents of the sloughs and ponds of the Sacramento-San Joaquin Delta but most breed in the Great Basin, east of the Cascades and Sierras, and winter along our coast. The migrating birds begin arriving in mid-September and are found on the ocean in shallow water, in lagoons, and on lakes. They can be seen by the thousands on Mono Lake and on the Salton Sea in the fall. Many more continue on to winter in Mexico.

Voice: Usually silent. During breeding season, the male says aaah-weetic!; *the female, a higher-pitched* a-weetic. *The* weetic *is compressed.*

Top: Breeding plumage (April to September). **Bottom, left to right:** Nonbreeding adult; subadult. Note the ***indistinct facial lines*** on the nonbreeding bird, which distinguish it from a Horned Grebe.

Horned Grebe (13–14")

Horned Grebes breed in Alaska and inland Canada and winter in the Delta and in coastal waters and lagoons as far south as central Baja. They are far more numerous in the northern part of our state, where they are also seen on lakes and reservoirs. Eared Grebes are common, Horned Grebes are not. Horned Grebes are in California from mid-October to mid-April. The yellow feathers on the breeding bird's head are sometimes raised, hence the name.

The grebe in the **bottom photo** tried to swallow that flounder for a long time. He smacked it on the water repeatedly to soften it up, but to no avail; it was just too wide to get it down the hatch. Poor guy.

Voice: Usually silent in California. On the breeding grounds, not so.

Top: Breeding plumage (April to August). **Bottom:** Nonbreeding.

Red-Necked Grebe (18–19")

Red-necked Grebes are cold-water birds that breed in Alaska and inland Canada and winter on our coast as far south as Point Conception. They are not nearly as common, either in California or elsewhere, as our other grebes. The farther north you are on the coast, the more likely you are to see a Red-necked Grebe. They are usually alone.

The Red-necked Grebes begin arriving in California in September and leave again by May. They are usually seen on the ocean, either in the surf or in bays and coves. In California, they are seldom found in lagoons or on ponds. A good place to see them, without traveling to the far north, is off Limantour Beach at Point Reyes National Seashore.

Voice: Usually silent in California. On breeding grounds, a high-pitched, hoarse, staccato peeping; burro-like sounds; and various squeaking noises.

Top: Breeding plumage (February to August). **Bottom:** Nonbreeding.

Glen Tepke

Roger Zachary

Mergansers

Mergansers are streamlined duck-like diving birds equipped with saw-edged mandibles for holding slippery fish.

Unlike grebes, the sexes of mergansers look very different during the breeding season. Nonbreeding and immature males look like females.

We have three species in the state, and all are fairly common where found.

Common Merganser (24")

Common Mergansers breed on freshwater lakes and along rivers in the Sacramento Valley and in the northern Sierras. Some live in California all year, others from farther north winter as far south as the Colorado River Valley. Although uncommon in the south, Lake Isabella is a favorite wintering site, and a few may be encountered just about anywhere there is a large body of freshwater. They are rarely found in saltwater habitats.

Voice: Gruk *if threatened. Many strange noises on the breeding grounds.*

Bottom: Pair in breeding plumage (November to July). The nonbreeding male looks similar to the female.

Red-Breasted Merganser (23")

Arctic and sub-Arctic breeders, Red-breasted Mergansers spend the winter in coastal waters, bays, and lagoons as far south as central Baja. A few can also be found on the Colorado River and on the Salton Sea.

Red-breasted Mergansers are shallow diving ducks. Watching a fishing expedition with a dozen or more working together is an unforgettable experience. Like a naval fleet, they set sail in formation across a lagoon in search of a meal (**see photos on next page**). When they find a school of fish, they try not to disturb it but gently dip into the water after them. Once the school is spooked, the tempo goes up tenfold with birds darting every which way and snagging anything and everything in sight.

Voice: Usually silent; sometimes gruk *similar to a Common Merganser's.*

Below, top: Male in breeding plumage (November to May). **Bottom:** Female or juvenile male. Nonbreeding male is similar.

Hooded Merganser (17")

Hooded Mergansers live in wooded lakes and ponds near the coast from Oregon to British Columbia. Some migrate to California for the winter but seldom to the southern half of the state. Good places to see flocks of Hooded Mergansers from mid-fall to early spring are on lakes from the Klamath region to Tahoe and along slow-moving rivers in the north. A small number appear in the south, usually on ponds, lakes, and reservoirs and along the Colorado River and its tributaries.

The hairdos of both males and females have been copied by humans for millennia.

Voice: Usually silent. The female can croak and bark.

Below: Pair in their usual plumage (September to June). In July and August, the adult males look like females. Immature males do too.

Loons

Loons are large duck-like birds with long, dagger-like bills. They are expert fishers that dive and swim underwater for their supper or stalk fish on the surface with their necks stretched out in front of them.

We have three species of loons in California and all are fairly common.

A loon's legs are placed well back on their bodies, which is great for underwater propulsion but makes walking difficult and awkward. To get airborne, both Common Loons and Pacific Loons need a long runway. Their pattering across the water on large webbed feet while flapping their wings wildly is so laborious that you can't help but root for them to get airborne. Occasionally, one of these loons will land on a pond that is too small for a successful takeoff and becomes stranded. Red-throated Loons are much lighter and don't require a running start, or not much of one.

Breeding plumage is usually only seen in the north and during migration. In nonbreeding plumage, as they change, the species can be difficult to tell from one another—especially the juveniles.

Male and female loons look alike.

Common Loon (32")

Common Loons breed on inland lakes, mostly in Canada, and winter as far south as central Mexico. In California, they usually remain on the ocean close to shore but also visit reservoirs and lakes, especially during migration. Some nonbreeding birds stay in California all year.

In the southern half of California, Common Loons are almost always in their nonbreeding plumage. Their colorful breeding plumage lasts from March to October and is usually seen only in the north.

Voice: On the breeding grounds they sound like screaming lunatics. Crazy as a loon. They can also sound similar to a howling wolf.

Top: Adult in breeding plumage. **Middle:** Nonbreeding or immature. **Bottom:** Transitioning. **Photo on the previous page** is of a juvenile.

John Dykstra

Jack and Petra Clayton

Jeff Bleam

Pacific Loon (26")

Pacific Loons are Arctic breeders that winter along the coast down to the tip of Baja California. Spring and fall migrations can be spectacular from points along the coast—large flocks can seem endless. Monterey Peninsula is a great place for Pacific Loons in the fall. Pigeon Point, Point Reyes, Patrick's Point, and other northern headlands are just as good for watching huge flocks pass by during the spring migration.

In California, Pacific Loons are usually seen in shallow coastal waters, often in bays, coves, and estuaries. They are rarely found inland.

Nonbreeding birds can be distinguished from Common and Red-throated Loons by their **shorter bill**.

Voice variations are similar to the squealing of a coyote pup, the wailing of a mating tomcat, and the croaking of a frog. They can also squeak, often at the end of a long wail. But they are usually silent in California.

Top: Breeding plumage. (March to October) **Bottom:** Nonbreeding.

Red-Throated Loon (25")

Red-throated Loons are Arctic breeders that winter along the coast as far south as the southern tip of the Baja Peninsula. Fall arrival begins in September; they also leave early. Their preferred habitat in California is on the ocean and in bays and estuaries. They are not found inland.

Red-throated Loons **point their bills higher than other loons**. Also, the bill, although long, is not as massive as the Common Loon's.

Voice: Usually quiet in California. Voices include a guttural growl, a wailing at different pitches, and a quack as if through a kazoo.

Top: Breeding plumage (April to November) and typical loon's nest. **Bottom:** A nonbreeding bird. Breeding plumage is seldom seen south of the Central Coast.

Shorebirds

A shorebird is any bird that frequents the shore of any body of water, and we have already looked at many. This section focuses on another large grouping of such birds. All feed on animal life found on the coast and in other wet habitats, and all have their particular foraging place, which becomes evident at a pond or lagoon and to a lesser degree on the coast. Some prefer the water's edge, some prefer very shallow water, some prefer to be in a little deeper, and some stay back from the water's edge altogether.

Likewise, each species has a particular foraging method. Some poke around on the surface of the water, others probe into the mud or sand. Some sweep their bills back and forth, and some bob up and down like a sewing machine.

Below: In this photo, taken on March 20 at Oceano Dunes, are Sanderlings, Whimbrels, a Long-billed Curlew, and others.

Roger Zachary

Plovers

With one notable exception, plovers are short-billed shorebirds. Four of the five common species found in California forage on beaches and mudflats. The sexes of plovers look alike or similar.

Killdeer (10.5″)

Killdeer are year-round residents throughout the state in open habitats where the vegetation is short or lacking. Although they often forage close to water but away from the water's edge, they are just as likely to be far from water. Killdeer are typically seen in small groups searching for insects, worms, and the like, both during the day and at night.

When flushed, Killdeer sound an alarm, which spooks all the other birds in the area. When only slightly unsettled, they run away instead of fly. When nervous, they frequently bob up and down.

Voice is a high-pitched kill-deer, *sometimes stuttering. When alarmed—and they are easily alarmed—their call turns into screaming that, if kept up, makes you want to say, "Give it a rest, dude. It's not that bad!"*

Above: Adult in ice plant.
Right: Courtship display.

Semipalmated Plover (7.25")

An Arctic breeder, the Semipalmated Plover is common along the California coast from fall to spring. It is found on beaches, on mudflats, and in wetlands. Some birds travel as far south as South America for the winter and during migration can be seen in open, wet, sparsely vegetated fields just about anywhere in California.

A smaller version of the Killdeer, the Semipalmated Plover has a collar but not a breast band like the Killdeer. Semipalmated refers to their partially webbed feet. *Note the yellow legs and full collar.*

Voice is a sharp, high-pitched, thu-weet *or* chee-up, *often repeated.*

Top: Breeding plumage (May to September). **Bottom:** Nonbreeding.

Black-Bellied Plover (11.5")

Black-bellied Plovers are high Arctic breeders that winter all along our coast. A few birds, usually immatures, are not ready to make the trip north in the spring and remain here through the summer.

Black-bellies forage alone yet together. They often space themselves evenly along our beaches, in the mudflats, and in open, wet fields.

A similar-looking bird, but much less common, is the **Pacific Golden Plover**, which has golden highlights that are sometimes faint when in nonbreeding plumage.

Voice: Calls are high squeaking whistles reminiscent of a boatswain's whistle. Typically the calls are one or three syllables.

Top: Nonbreeding adult. **Bottom, left to right:** Juvenile in pickleweed; adult breeding plumage (April to August).

Snowy Plover (6")

The tiny Snowy Plover is a year-round resident on sandy beaches where the human population does not dominate. They are also found on river bars and at the edges of alkali lakes, salt evaporation ponds, and lagoons, where vegetation is minimal. Their nests are simply depressions in the sand lined with grasses. In more out-of-the-way areas (e.g., Owens Lake, east of the Sierras, and Harper Dry Lake, in the Mojave), Snowy Plovers nest in colonies. They are not common and camouflage so well that a nesting bird is frequently almost stepped on before it is seen.

Voices include a whistled orrr-wheet *or* orrr-wee-it; *a buzzy, sputtering* quirr; *and buzzy chits and churps. Sometimes all together.*

Top: A nonbreeding bird posed with sea rocket flowers. **Bottom:** A breeding bird (February to August). The photo was taken in February; the forehead and **partial collar** will be darker in a month. Note the **gray legs**. The Semipalmated Plover has a full collar and yellow legs.

Melissa Kung

Jeff Bleam

Mountain Plover (9")

Mountain Plovers are neither of the mountains nor do they resemble other plovers in their way of life. They are insect-eating grassland dwellers, and unlike other plovers, they favor dry areas to wet ones, so they are not shorebirds either. But Mountain Plovers belong nowhere else taxonomically, so they are listed here.

These birds breed on the short-grass plains just east of the Rockies, and a small number winter in California in our grassland valleys. Mountain Plovers are **easy to overlook**, first, because they camouflage well in dry grassy fields, and second, because unlike most birds, they stand motionless waiting for their prey to come to them. In rocky fields, they can look just like rocks until they move.

Look for Mountain Plovers where the soil is poor and the grass is thin and short. From November to February, Panoche Valley, east of Pinnacles National Park, is a good place to find them in the north. In the south, they arrive in the San Jacinto Valley in October and are more numerous then. The grassland adjacent to the San Jacinto Wildlife Area, east of Perris, is one place to look. They are usually in flocks, so if you see one, look around. (The story of a similar case is on page 469.)

Voice: A buzzy, scolding krip; krip *without the buzz; a buzz followed by* dweet, *rapidly repeated; and a sweet, compressed* poit. *If disturbed, scolding chatter.*

Below: A winter bird. Breeding birds (March to August) are brighter overall, have a black frontal cap, and the line between the bill and eye is black.

Black Oystercatcher (17")

Black Oystercatchers inhabit rocky shores where tide pools are present. They do not migrate and are more common in the north. A similar species, the **American Oystercatcher**, has a white breast and belly and is found on the East and Gulf coasts and along the west coast of Mexico, but they rarely come north into California.

The best time to see these tide pool experts at work is at low tide, especially at dawn or dusk. Oystercatchers eat small fish, crabs, shellfish, and other tide pool fare and are often seen in pairs or small groups.

Their nest is a simple depression in the ground lined with gravel.

Voice is a piercing wheet, *often repeated with slight variations.*

The above bird was at Point Lobos State Park, south of Carmel, where Black Oystercatchers are almost always present.

Peter Pearsall / USFWS

Waders

A wader is any wading bird. The next two don't fit elsewhere so are here.

American Avocet (18"

Avocets are common year-round residents of shallow freshwater and saltwater ponds in the Central Valley and near the coast from Mendocino to San Diego. They are also found on mudflats, in flooded pastures and fields, and even in alkali marshes around Mono Lake.

These wading birds sweep their bills back and forth like brooms to strain out small aquatic organisms from the surface of the water or wet mud. They can also turn bottoms up and feed like a dabbling duck and can swim, but they typically don't do either.

Avocets stay together in (usually small) flocks and are often seen with Black-necked Stilts. Avocets hide their nests in plain sight on the ground.

Voice: When disturbed, avocets utter a high-pitched kleet, kleet, kleet! *And they can keep it up for a while. (Dad got really ticked at me when he saw me photographing Mom with the kids on the next page.)*

Below: Breeding plumage (March to August). The female's bill has a deeper curve (left).

Right: Adult in nonbreeding plumage.

Below left: Early June chick.

Below right: Three weeks later, juvenal feathers are coming in. This young one will look like the bird above it by September.

Black-Necked Stilt (14")

Stilts are saltwater or freshwater marsh dwellers that work the shallow water. They live year-round in the Delta and wetter areas of the Central Valley and in coastal marshes from the San Francisco Bay to San Diego. Some also breed along the eastern border of the state, from the Klamath Basin in the north down to the Owens Valley in the south. During the rainy season, Black-necked Stilts can also be found in flooded fields and pastures. They are primarily carnivores and eat just about any form of animal life that they can swallow whole.

Stilts are almost always in close flocks. They are often seen with Avocets, with which they get along well—except if they have chicks. Both will viciously drive off any chick that is not their own.

Although stilts are large birds, they are great tight-formation fliers and can make lightning-quick avoidance maneuvers. I know this from experience. On one occasion, a flock of about 50, flying fast and low, suddenly came up over a bank right at me. When they saw me, the flock split in half, carving out just enough space for me to stand there in awe. They could not have missed me by more than a foot or two.

Voice is a peeping reminiscent of a small dog's yapping. When alarmed, they use the same notes but with a raspy voice.

Below: Male in breeding plumage; nonbreeding is slightly duller.

Bottom row: Juvenile; adult female (brown back).

Sandpipers and Sandpiper-like Birds

Sandpiper is a catch-all term for shorebirds with long, slender bills. They forage mostly by probing into the mud or sand and are found in a wide variety of wet habitats. Most of the sandpipers we see in California breed in Alaska, Canada, or even in the high Arctic. Flocks of several species begin showing up in California marshes and along the coast in mid-summer; others come later. Flocks prefer more remote areas where they won't be disturbed. In sheltered areas, such as bays and estuaries, they may stay for the season. The shore around San Francisco Bay is an excellent place to find many of these birds.

Unless otherwise noted, all the species listed in this section are at least fairly common in season where they occur. In the late spring, when most of these birds fly north, there are always some stragglers left behind. These birds are typically too young or too weak to make the trip.

Male and female sandpipers look alike or similar. Plumage for some species changes seasonally; others look essentially the same all year.

Below: Godwits, Willets, and others. **Next page:** Western Sandpipers.

Jerry Ting

Large Sandpipers

Long-Billed Curlew (22–24")

These beauties breed in the Sierra Valley and to the north and east as far as the Dakotas. They winter in the Delta, in the San Joaquin and Imperial Valleys, and along our coast, especially in the south.

Curlews require a wetter habitat for foraging than do their cousins, the Whimbrels. On the mudflats and in the Delta, Curlews probe deep for worms, crabs, and crayfish; in flooded fields, they usually pick insects off the surface.

The breakneck speed at which curlews and some other birds occasionally plunge their long bills into the mud leaves the observer in a state of awe. I have never seen one with a broken bill, so they obviously have built-in sensors to warn them if a rock is below the surface.

The shape of the Long-billed Curlew is similar to that of a Whimbrel, but the curlew's bill is longer.

Voices include a rising, gull-like, two-note scream and a stuttering of three high-pitched notes.

Below: Smaller birds with shorter bills are males or juveniles. I don't know for sure which the top bird is. Plumage is fairly consistent all year.

Jack and Petra Clayton

Whimbrel (17.5")

Whimbrels breed in Alaska and are common in coastal California from fall to spring. They are found on beaches and mudflats, in flooded fields where the vegetation is short, and on well-watered lawns where open space is plentiful.

During migration and when feeding in grassy areas, Whimbrels typically remain in tight flocks. In winter, on the beach, they tend to spread out somewhat evenly and are often interspersed with Godwits and Willets. Whimbrels are fairly fast runners and often prefer running to flying.

Despite the long bill, Whimbrels prefer to pick their food off the surface and seldom plunge deep into wet soil. They will, however, plunge freely into the wet sand at the beach.

Note that the bill is shorter than that of the curlew.

Voice is a loud, high-pitched, stuttering peeping. They have three or four variations.

Below: Like the curlew on the previous page, the Whimbrel's plumage is quite consistent through the seasons.

Marbled Godwit (18")

Marbled Godwits breed in the wetlands of the short-grass prairie in the Dakotas and the Canadian provinces north of them; they winter along our coast from Eureka to San Diego and in the Delta.

Godwits are often seen along our beaches interspersed with Whimbrels and Willets. Their upturned bill makes them easy to identify.

Voice is a crazy-sounding squawking of one or two notes, often repeated.

Below, top: Marbled Godwit, left; Willet, right. **Bottom:** Both species.

Jeff Bleam

Willet (15–16")

Willets breed in the meadows of the Great Basin and are seen from fall to spring all along our coast, especially in the southern half of the state. They are regular breeders in the Sierra Valley, northwest of Reno.

Hungry flocks arrive in coastal areas in the late summer and early fall and at that time can often be seen marching across our tidal marshlands while gorging themselves on worms. In the spring, all but a few stragglers have left for the breeding grounds by May.

When a flock of Willets takes off, it is a spectacle of black and white—a surprise that is hidden under their wings when they are on the ground. (See photo on the previous page.)

Voice: When flushed, kleep! *When alarmed, a high-pitched, squeaky, quavering* Oh, you really scared me, *that starts off slow and builds. It is repeated until the bird runs out of gas. Several other hard-to-describe calls.*

Top: A nonbreeding bird in the surf grass; photo was taken January 2. **Bottom:** Breeding plumage (April to August); photo was taken April 13. See the previous page for photos of Willets with Godwits.

Greater Yellowlegs (14")

Greater Yellowlegs are common birds that breed in northern Canada and southeastern Alaska. They spend the rest of the year in temperate areas, including much of California. Yellowlegs are found in wet habitats, including estuaries, ponds, marshes, mudflats, and flooded agricultural fields. They begin arriving by late July and leave by mid-May.

Yellowlegs typically feed on invertebrates and minnows in shallow water. They are often more solitary and wade in deeper water than other sandpipers.

Voice: Call is a loud, ringing, three-note descending whistle, perhaps tu-tu-tu. *Just as often it may sound like* chew-chew-chew. *When alarmed, the tempo goes up, the call becomes piercing, and it is sure to flush all the other birds in the vicinity.*

Below: A juvenile. Nonbreeding and winter adults are similar. **Next page:** Greater and Lesser Yellowlegs in breeding plumage.

Lesser Yellowlegs (10.5")

Like their Greater brethren, Lesser Yellowlegs breed in Alaska and northern Canada. A relatively small number of Lessers winter in a variety of wet habitats around San Francisco Bay, in the Central Valley, and along our southern coast.

Lesser Yellowlegs are distinguished from Greater Yellowlegs by their considerably smaller size. Their bill is also slimmer and not as long in proportion to their head. **Bill length** is about equal to that of the head measured in the same direction. The bill of the Greater Yellowlegs is noticeably longer than its head.

During migration, Lesser and Greater Yellowlegs are frequently seen together.

Voice is a high-pitched whistle of tu *or* tu tu *that is mellow compared to the Greater Yellowlegs. When alarmed, they may repeat it several times.*

Below: "Lesser, Greater, and Least" (a Least Sandpiper is at right.) Both yellowlegs below are in breeding plumage (March to September). Nonbreeding plumage is like that of the Greater on the previous page.

Midsized Sandpipers

Long-Billed and Short-Billed Dowitchers (11")

In 1957 the American Ornithologists' Union divided the dowitchers into two species. Since that time, countless words have been used to try to explain their visual differences. When taken into the field, if you are not observing a large flock close up, all the explanations end up being as clear as the mud the birds feed in. The bill length varies for both dowitchers, so without a fairly large sampling that trait is not very helpful. In winter, the birds look identical. In breeding plumage, some say that the color palette of the birds is different. But considering the wide range of changes the birds go through in a season, I have not found that information the least bit helpful. So I won't try to explain what others have struggled with. Often, the only way to make a certain distinction is to hear their voice.

Long-billed Dowitchers breed in northern Alaska and Siberia and are seen in the fall and spring in marshes, estuaries, lagoons, and bays all along the West Coast. Many spend the winter months in **inland** Southern California or in Mexico. They begin arriving by mid-August and leave again for the breeding grounds by May. Ponded meadows on the east side of the Cascades and Sierras are common migration stops.

Short-billed Dowitchers breed in northwestern British Columbia and southeastern Alaska and winter from southern California to South America. They are seen in California at nearly the same time as the Long-billed but are found in **coastal** areas, especially estuaries. Most of the dowitchers we see are just passing through.

The mannerisms of the two species are identical. On the water, dowitchers bob up and down like a sewing machine when feeding. On the mudflats, they poke around somewhat randomly in the manner of many other species. Dowitchers are virtually always in flocks. Like most shorebirds, they can swim but usually don't.

Voice: The two dowitchers have distinct calls:

The Short-billed's call is a high-pitched, sweet, rapid, tu tu, tu-tu-tu. *Less frequently,* zweet *or* zooweet; *sometimes the latter is compressed.*

The Long-billed's is also sweet and high-pitched, but more like peet *or* peet-up, *often repeated as a trill that sounds like a sputtering tea kettle.*

Next page, top: Short-billed in alkali weed, photo taken January 20. **Middle, left:** Short or Long-billed in breeding plumage (April to August), April 10. **Middle, right:** Likely Short-billed, mostly transitioned to nonbreeding plumage, August 26. **Bottom:** Juvenile, October 2. The colors look similar to the transitioning plumage of an adult.

Sandpipers

Jerry Ting

Fredrick F. Petersen

Keith Carlson

Red Knot (10")

Red Knots breed in the high Arctic and winter along the Pacific coast as far south as Tierra del Fuego—the tip of South America. For those that take the long flight, that's a 9,200-mile journey, one way, fueled by worms, snails, and crustaceans. Many Red Knots do not take the long flight but stay, for a short or extended time, in bays, lagoons, mudflats, and estuaries along the way. In Northern California, preferred stops are at Humboldt and San Francisco Bays. In the south, a very few stop at Bolsa Chica, in Huntington Beach, and at the lower San Diego Bay. They typically don't stay very long.

Although uncommon in California, individual birds may appear at any time between August and May or small flocks in April and May and from July to September. They are usually in their nonbreeding plumage when seen here, but in the spring some are at least partially in breeding plumage. Individuals often hang out with dowitchers and may have migrated with them.

Voice is seldom heard in California. Occasionally when flushed or in flight, a soft nasal knutt *or* du-weet.

Below: Red Knot and dowitchers in winter plumage. The photo was taken on January 3 at Bolsa Chica. Note the shorter bill and dark wingtips of the Red Knot at right.

Next page: All photos were taken around the southern part of San Francisco Bay. **Top:** Breeding plumage; photo was taken April 14. **Middle:** January 31. **Bottom:** Full breeding plumage; photo was taken May 2. By early September the birds have turned dull again.

Sandpipers

Wilson's Snipe (formerly called **Common Snipe**) (10")

Wilson's Snipes commonly breed in the northeast corner of California and are winter birds in temperate areas throughout the state. Less commonly, they also breed east of the Sierras as far south as the Owens Valley. During migration and in the winter, snipes can be plentiful in the Central Valley, perhaps especially at the wildlife refuges, but they are secretive and may not be easy to find.

The snipes inhabit freshwater marshes and flooded fields, and are occasionally found in saltwater habitats. Although they usually remain hidden, during the breeding season the males throw off all inhibition and put on a display similar to that of a hummingbird and produce a similar loud sound at the end of their dive (see page 271). Snipes migrate at night, which explains how they suddenly appear. They can sometimes be spotted near a flock of dowitchers.

Snipes are easy to identify by their behavior. They bob their tails rapidly when nervous, and when flushed fly erratically. They also crouch low when alarmed, giving them a squatty look and making them easy to distinguish from a dowitcher. A snipe's legs are also shorter than a dowitcher's.

Voice: Call is a hard, sharp jick, *often repeated louder and louder, then trailing off. When flushed, a similar but louder and quavering* jick *is repeated. You would think they were being stabbed to death.*

Below: Plumage is quite consistent through the seasons. Juveniles look like adults.

Jeff Bleam

Wandering Tattler (11")

Wandering Tattlers breed in Alaska and spend the rest of the year along the Pacific coast as far south as South America.

Outside of their breeding grounds, tattlers are uncommon and are usually seen alone. They forage in rocky areas of the coast and are constantly bobbing their tails. They are regulars at Santa Cruz from mid-April through May and from late July to mid-September. The timing is typical along our coast; they are seldom seen at other times.

Voice: Call is kleep. *Like other birds of the coast, their voice can be heard despite the loud sound of the surf—a marvelous lesson in acoustic physics and design.*

Top: Bird in breeding plumage (April to September) on sea lettuce. **Bottom:** Nonbreeding plumage.

Surfbird (10")

Surfbirds breed in Alaska and travel up and down the coast the rest of the year. They may go as far south as the southern tip of South America or may turn around earlier. Along the California coast, Surfbirds are usually seen between late March and May and in August and September. They are typically found on rocky or stony shores in small flocks of about a dozen birds. An exception to the small flocks is the fall gatherings at Bodega Bay, which are usually in September and may include hundreds of birds.

The Surfbird's diet consists of aquatic invertebrates and insects. They also pull barnacles and small mussels loose from the rocks and swallow them whole; their gizzard grinds up the shells. Since they forage for the same foods, migrating Surfbirds are often seen with turnstones. (See pages 153 and 154.)

Voice: Usually quiet in California. When heard, voice is short squeaky or scratchy calls; at times, longer and buzzy like a tern.

Below: The second bird from the left is in breeding plumage (March to August); the two birds on the right are juveniles; the bird at the far left is transitioning and is likely a subadult. Nonbreeding adults look like juveniles but are gray. The photo was taken April 25.

Marlin Harms

Rock Sandpiper (9")

Rock Sandpipers are high Arctic breeders that are occasionally seen in *winter* on rocky shores along the West Coast as far south as Marin.

This uncommon bird looks similar to the much more common Surfbird but is smaller, has a longer bill that curves down, has a different voice, and is here at a different season. Although rarely seen in California, they are worth mentioning because when they show up, they are often with turnstones and could be mistaken for Surfbirds. All these birds make their living on the sea rocks. A good place to be on the lookout for Rock Sandpipers in winter is at Point St. George, near the Oregon border.

Voice: Usually silent in California. When heard, a chattering of five or six syllables of the same mid-range note.

Top: Nonbreeding adult (gray) in red algae. A breeding bird (rare in California) has a black belly and some orange on the back and wing. **Bottom:** Juvenile (brown) in sea lettuce.

Small Sandpipers

Solitary Sandpiper (8.5")

Solitary Sandpipers breed in Canada in bogs and around freshwater lakes and streams. They winter in southern Mexico, Central America, and South America.

These birds are seldom seen in California, partly because the great majority migrate east of the Rockies and partly because they are solitary except during the breeding season. The best time to see them is during the fall migration—mid-September in the north, a week or so later in the south. They don't stay but do make brief stops at freshwater ponds, marshes, and flooded fields. Then they are off again.

Solitary Sandpipers can be mistaken for the much more common yellowlegs; however, the former are easy to identify by the bolder white eye-ring, greenish legs, different spotting pattern, and a black patch on the wing that is not always visible.

Voice is a rapid, sharp, high-pitched kleep-kleep, *often repeated, and sometimes with other high-pitched, excited phrases added.*

Below: Full breeding plumage (May to September). Nonbreeding birds are lighter and don't have the black wing patch.

Pectoral Sandpiper (8.5")

The Pectoral Sandpiper is so named because the spotting on the breast terminates in an abrupt line at the bird's white belly.

These birds breed in the high Arctic and winter in South America. Most Pectoral Sandpipers migrate east of the Rockies, but a small number come through California in the early fall. They are usually seen in September in flooded grasslands in the Central Valley or in marshes, and are pretty regular at Hayward Regional Shoreline in Alameda County. They typically don't stay for more than a few days—just long enough to rest a little and be replenished so they can make it to the next stop.

Voice: Pectoral Sandpipers are usually silent when in California but when flushed, a trilled chirk.

Below: Likely nonbreeding plumage (photo taken September 14). Breeding plumage can be darker. Juveniles may have a reddish tinge on the back. Breast to belly line is consistent.

Dunlin (8.5″)

The squatty Dunlin is easy to identify by its size and by its thicker, drooping bill. They are Arctic breeders that winter all along our coast on sandy beaches, on mudflats, and in wet areas of the Central Valley. Dunlin flocks arrive later than most shorebirds, usually in October. They are much more common in the north. In season, they are numerous around San Francisco Bay and abundant at Arcata Bay.

Voice is an electronic-sounding, raspy, buzzy krreee *of three major variations that differ mostly in pitch.*

Top: A nonbreeding Dunlin with Least Sandpipers. The pose is typical—they commonly wade almost belly-deep. **Bottom:** Breeding plumage (April to August). Some are brighter than this one.

Ethan Winning

Jeff Bleam

A winter flock of Dunlins

Sanderlings (8")

The definitions of both cute and fascinating, Sanderlings are the little guys that everyone loves to watch at the beach, as tight groups run in unison toward, then away from, the waves on the wet sand. Their little black legs motor faster than the eye can see or the mind can comprehend.

Sanderlings breed in the high Arctic, but some start changing into their breeding plumage before they leave California in the spring. They often move to the mudflats to feed on fat-rich worms before heading north.

Voices are a squeaky twittering and a single, high-pitched squeaky note.

Below: Nonbreeding spring plumage (photo taken April 2).

Next page, from the top: Breeding plumage (April 26); partial breeding plumage (July 10); nonbreeding fall plumage (September 5).

Jeff Bleam

Sandpipers

Jeff Bleam

Jeff Bleam

Spotted Sandpiper (7.5")

Spotted Sandpipers breed from Northern California to Alaska and spend the cooler months scattered around the rest of our state and southward into Mexico.

The foraging method of the Spotted Sandpiper is unique. They walk along the edges of streams, lakes, and ponds looking for insects, all the while bobbing their tails. Some birds also have what appears to be a nervous twitch. Spotted Sandpipers are also found on the coast but not as commonly. During the nonbreeding season, they are usually seen alone.

Spotted Sandpipers fly low, using two or three fast wingbeats followed by brief glides.

Voice is one or two loud, high-pitched whistles: weet! *or* tu-weet! *and is usually heard when the bird is flushed. At times, many repeats.*

Top: Breeding plumage (April to August). **Bottom:** Nonbreeding adult. Juveniles look similar. Note the yellowish legs.

Peeps: The Smallest Sandpipers

Our smallest sandpipers are commonly called "peeps." The Least and Western Sandpipers, discussed next, are about the size of a sparrow. Both are abundant in California from fall to early spring.

Least Sandpiper (6")

Least Sandpipers breed in Alaska and northern Canada and winter in California's muddy areas. They are very common on the mudflats, in estuaries, sloughs and marshes, and in flooded fields of short grass. They are less commonly seen on the coast, except at river mouths. While here, they are nomadic and fly from one location to another in tight flocks, both large and small.

These little bundles of energy begin arriving in mid-summer and leave by mid-spring. Some are in their breeding plumage before they leave in the spring.

Note the *light legs*, which distinguish the nonbreeding bird from the similar-looking Western Sandpiper.

Voice is sweet high-pitched peeping. They're not called peeps for nothing.

Top row, left to right: Photo dates are September 19 and April 15, breeding plumage. **Bottom row:** July 27 and April 24, a juvenile.

Western Sandpiper (6.5")

Flocks of Western Sandpipers start arriving in California in mid-summer from their breeding grounds in northwestern Alaska.

Like other peeps, Western Sandpipers are mudflat specialists, foraging when the tide is out and resting in tight flocks on higher ground when it is in. Less commonly, they are found on sandy beaches and in wet agricultural fields. Before they leave in the spring, Western Sandpipers form huge flocks around San Francisco Bay and put on spectacular air shows. The swirling clouds of birds that we see flying in zigzag fashion, flashing white, then brown as they make a turn, are usually Western's and are murmurations or the result of a falcon attack.

Breeding plumage is from March to August. Note the **black legs**, which distinguish the nonbreeding bird from a Least Sandpiper.

Voice: High-pitched peeping that may be sweet, harsh, buzzy or twittering.

Below: Right turn; murmuration. **Next page, top to bottom:** Photos taken April 14, (breeding plumage), August 26, and January 31.

Jeff Bleam

Jerry Ting

Black Turnstone (9.25")

Black Turnstones breed along the far northwest coast of Alaska and spend the rest of the year along the Pacific coast as far south as the tip of Baja. They are common on California's rocky shores in season.

Turnstones are well named because they use their bills to turn over stones to find fish eggs, crabs, worms, snails, and other delicious fare. They also hunt by the tide pools for crustaceans, barnacles, limpets, and the like. Black Turnstones are usually seen on rocky shores, but they also forage on sandy beaches, picking flies from washed-up seaweed. They are usually seen in small groups.

Voice is a squeaky buzz, often as chatter and at times stuttered. Pitch varies from high to mid-range. Landing voice differs but fits description.

Top: Breeding adult. **Bottom:** Juvenile. **Next page:** Nonbreeding adult.

Ruddy Turnstone (9.5")

Ruddy Turnstones breed in the high Arctic and winter along the Pacific coast as far south as South America. They are typically found in sheltered areas on rocky beaches and on jetties and breakwaters but will visit sandy beaches if debris is plentiful. Ruddys are not nearly as common as Black Turnstones and are usually in small groups. They are often seen at Hayward Regional Shoreline, in the north, and much less frequently at Bolsa Chica, in the south, from July to early May.

Voice, in California, consists of several calls, including a single metallic note, swallow-like raspy or gurgling chatter, and a hawk-like keer.

Top: Black and Ruddy Turnstones in January. **Bottom:** Ruddy, mostly in breeding plumage, in August. Full breeding colors are brighter from May to July, but I thought he or she was cute, so I chose this photo.

Phalaropes

Phalaropes are long-legged water birds that frequently spin in a circle on the water to stir up aquatic organisms. This brings them to the surface where the phalaropes capture them with darting pecks. Another foraging method, just as unique, is their darting about in a smooth yet helter-skelter way on the surface of the water.

The sexes differ in appearance; the females are much more colorful in breeding plumage than the males. How's that for a switch!

Wilson's Phalarope (9")

The Wilson's Phalarope breeds in the northern Great Plains and winters at ponds in the grasslands of Argentina as well as on saline lakes in the Andes. In California, they are not commonly seen in the spring because their northern migration route is mainly through the Great Plains. During their migration south, small flocks stop at lagoons, marshes, lakes, and flooded grain fields across our state. They prefer super-salty lakes and may stay at a stop for a few days or they may not.

Good places to see hundreds of Wilson's Phalaropes from July to mid-September are Mono and Owens Lakes and the Salton Sea. Smaller numbers often appear in southern coastal marshes in July and August.

Voice is a nasal barking/quacking. It can be low and guttural or mid-range.

Below: Nonbreeding birds in Water Pennywort (photo taken July 22).

Next page, from top: Breeding female; transitioning female; breeding male. Breeding season is April to July. The birds are most colorful in May.

Red-Necked Phalarope (7.75")

Unlike the Wilson's, the Red-necked and Red Phalaropes migrate primarily offshore. Both are Arctic breeders that migrate to South America for the winter and travel over the ocean in flocks commonly numbering in the thousands. Of the two, the Red-necked is more frequently seen from land, usually in coastal waters and estuaries and usually in small numbers.

During the fall migration, flocks of hundreds of Red-necked Phalaropes are also found inland on saline lakes, especially at Mono Lake and the Salton Sea from early July to September. From May through September, a relatively small number of Red-necked and even more Wilson's Phalaropes can be seen at Harper Dry Lake, near Barstow. If any breed there I don't know, but that time span includes their breeding season. Small groups of both species can also be found in inland marshes and coastal lagoons, usually from late July through August.

The sexes differ in appearance during breeding season (April to July), with females the more colorful. Identifying nonbreeding phalaropes can be difficult, but if one is on a marsh pond and wearing thick eyeliner, it must be a Red-neck.

Voice is a squeaky chittering; also, a single high-pitched squeaky note.

Below: Note the spinning action of these two nonbreeding birds. The bird on the right is a juvenile. Photo was taken August 28.

Next page, top: Pair in breeding plumage. **Bottom:** Breeding plumage; April 26.

Phalaropes

Red Phalarope (8.5")

Red Phalaropes are high Arctic breeders that winter off our coast. Like the Red-necked, they travel in huge flocks and most continue farther south. Some stay in California waters for the winter, usually 10 to 50 miles out. During winter storms, individuals or small groups occasionally appear in bays, coves, and coastal lagoons.

Voicings include a whistled squeal, a staccato peeping, and a raspy zhee!

Top: Breeding female (April to September). **Bottom:** Breeding male.

Next page: Nonbreeding bird and part of a large offshore flock.

Coots, Gallinules, and Rails

American Coot (15.5")

Coots are year-round California residents that are abundant in the south during the cooler months and in the north, where they breed, during the warmer months. They are called Mud Hens by the old-timers and can be found on ponds and lakes up to about 8,000 feet.

On the water, American Coots peck at insects and other aquatic life. They can can also dive for their dinner. On land, they forage for tender shoots, which denudes many park lawns.

Voice is raspy squawking; also, a sweet Minnie Mouse-like squeaking.

Below: Because their feet are only partially webbed, coots need a long runway.

Common Gallinule (aka Common Moorhen) (14")

Common Gallinules live in freshwater and saltwater marshes and along lazy rivers. They look and behave like a cross between a duck and a rail (next page). Gallinules are fairly common year-round residents of the Delta and other wet parts of the Central Valley and also of the Colorado River Valley. They are less commonly seen around San Francisco Bay and in coastal marshes in the south.

Gallinules are shy and prefer to stay hidden in the vegetation around the ponds and along the rivers where they live.

Voice: Clucks, cackles, and squawks like a chicken but with nasal overtones.

Top: Adult. **Bottom:** Subadult. Males and females look similar.

Ridgway's Rail (14.5")

Ridgway's Rail is a year-round resident of the marshes along the Colorado River, its tributaries, and in the freshwater and saltwater marshes of Orange and San Diego Counties. A relative few are found in marshes and around ponds in the San Francisco Bay Area.

Until 2014, the Ridgway's was considered a subspecies of the **Clapper Rail**, which is common along the East and Gulf Coasts.

Rails live in dense vegetation, are shy, and are usually seen at dawn and dusk. They forage by slowly stalking their prey and will eat just about anything. Rails swallow their prey whole and later regurgitate pellets made up of bones, shell fragments, fish scales, and other indigestible matter. Rails can fly but rarely do.

Voice is a barking clack, clack, clack, *or* chuck, chuck, chuck, *sometimes as a rant. All the notes are at the same pitch. The bird in the photo would not shut up. I don't know what the offense was, but it sure wanted everyone to know about it.*

Below: Adult in Saltwort. Male and female rails look alike or similar. **Inset:** All rail chicks are black.

Virginia Rail (9.5")

Some Virginia Rails are year-round residents of temperate areas throughout the state; others breed in the Klamath Basin and in the Cascades and Sierras and migrate to warmer areas in winter. They live in freshwater and saltwater marshes among the cattails and rushes.

Virginia Rails are fairly common but are shy and usually remain hidden. They are heard more often than seen and are easier to find at dawn and dusk. They are often seen walking on floating mats of vegetation while foraging for anything that moves.

Voice is a metallic kick *or* kik-it, *sometimes strung together like the clatter of a teletype machine. Also, a loud, nasal quack/grunt or squeal, which may be repeated.*

Howard Patterson

Above: Adult
Right: Juvenile

Sora (8.5")

A fairly common bird in California, but not commonly seen, the Sora is a year-round resident of the wetlands of the Sacramento Valley and the Delta. Many more Soras breed in the Great Basin and across Canada and are cool-weather residents of our coastal marshes; others migrate to the Colorado River Valley or as far south as South America. During migration, Soras can be found in flooded fields, pastures, and irrigation ditches throughout the state. They migrate at night and seem to suddenly appear, then disappear a day or two later.

Soras eat mostly seeds, grain, and insects but don't turn down snails, worms, and the like.

Voice is a descending whinny, like that of a horse but higher. It starts out high-pitched, then descends to lower notes and slows until it fades out. It is surprisingly loud for such a small bird.

Below: Soras typically remain hidden in dense vegetation, however, juveniles can be stupidly fearless, walking out in plain sight in the middle of the day. Apparently, it takes some youngsters a while to learn about hawks, herons, coyotes, and others that would like to make a meal of them.

Jeff Bleam

The Heron Family: Herons, Egrets, and Bitterns

This family is composed of larger, long-legged, long-necked, spear-billed marsh dwellers that live on fish, frogs, gophers, mice, and anything else that moves. They swallow their prey whole and later cough up balls of bones, fish scales, hair, and other inedible animal parts. Herons can stand with neck erect or sunk back into their shoulders, and all can strike their prey with astonishing speed. In flight, many fold their necks back like a Brown Pelican. Some are colony dwellers; others live alone or in pairs. Most are year-round residents where they occur.

Unless otherwise noted in this section, the sexes look alike or similar.

Green Heron (17–18")

Green Herons are small, colorful herons that live in marshes and along reed-lined lakes and streams at lower elevations. They are fairly common year-round residents of both the Sacramento-San Joaquin Delta and areas south of it.

Like most herons, Green Herons will eat any and all aquatic animal life that they can swallow whole. When alarmed, they raise an otherwise hidden black comb on top of their heads.

Voice: Most commonly, an explosive, low, muffled, raspy, sneeze-like a-chow!; *a high, scratchy* skee-ow!; *and a nasal* kuck *repeated sporadically.*

Below: An adult. Juveniles are duller with more streaking on the breast and neck. Young juveniles are spotted on the back.

Great Blue Heron (45–47")

The Great Blue Heron is our largest heron and is as adaptable as any bird. They will eat just about anything and are as happy stalking and catching gophers in a field or lizards on a path as they are foraging for crayfish in a marsh or fishing from kelp beds on the ocean.

That brings up something worth pondering: the soil is rocky in some places where these birds forage and they strike their prey with astonishing speed, yet I have never seen one with an injured bill. When the engineering behind that is considered, it leaves one in a state of wonder.

Voice is a deep croaking and is often uttered as an expression of displeasure upon being flushed.

Below: Adult with a carp. The tassel-like plumes at the back of the head are only present on a breeding bird.

Next Page: Great Blue Herons mature in four years and go though many sets of feathers during the process; the youngest bird is at the top.

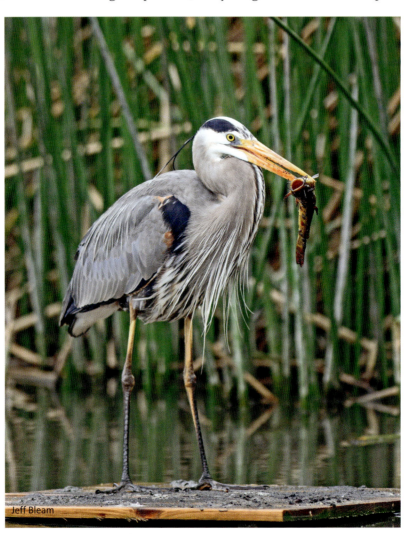

Little Blue Heron (24")

A rarity in California but fairly common in the Gulf states, the Little Blue Heron is a study in color changes. The juvenile's plumage is entirely white (**bottom left**), making it look similar to a Snowy Egret. However, the Snowy is thinner and has black legs and bill (**bottom right, at right**). As the heron matures, dark blue-purple feathers come in and mingle with the white, giving it a blotchy appearance (**bottom right, at left**). At maturity (**top**), the bird's plumage turns grayer, and the head and neck become reddish brown, making it look somewhat like a Reddish Egret.

Although rare in California, some breed in marshes along the Colorado River and winter in coastal lagoons near San Diego.

Voice is a nasal, hoarse croak or squawk. They are seldom heard.

Tri-Colored Heron (26″)

The Tri-colored Heron is a relative rarity in California. In the fall and winter, they are sometimes seen in coastal saltwater marshes south of Point Conception. Tri-colored Herons also inhabit freshwater marshes and swamps but rarely in California. They are much more common on the Gulf Coast, where they are year-round residents.

Note the **white belly** and **white stripe** down the neck.

Voice is the drawn-out, nasal croak of a perturbed bird, which is usually the only time you will hear them.

Top: Adult. **Bottom:** Juvenile in pickleweed, probably at Bolsa Chica, in Huntington Beach, where I see them occasionally.

Black-Crowned Night Heron (25")

Black-crowned Night Herons live in colonies in freshwater and saltwater marshes. They are fairly common year-round residents of the coastal half of California, of the far north, and of the Colorado River Valley. Night Herons can often be seen early in the morning, evenly spaced and sunning themselves at the edge of a pond. In the evening, they often roost in trees near a pond's edge.

The Night Heron's neck is shorter than that of other herons and is usually withdrawn, making the bird look hunchbacked. However, their neck is plenty long enough to be effective when striking prey.

An immature bird can be mistaken for an American Bittern (page 177), but its bill is not as long or as pointed, its legs are shorter, and its back is spotted, not mottled like the bittern's. Breeding Night Herons have two long, white tassels on their heads that lie most of the way down their back.

Voice is the typical croak of a heron.

Left: Adult. **Right:** Juvenile in pickleweed.

Egrets

Cattle Egret (20")

This African species is a recent newcomer to North America, probably arriving in the early 1950s. They have spread quickly and are now found in wetter cattle-grazing areas and in freshwater marshes throughout the United States. Cattle Egrets are common year-round residents of the Central and Imperial Valleys, and populations are increasing in southern coastal areas.

Cattle Egrets make a living following cattle and eating the bugs and grubs unearthed by their footsteps. They are one of several birds sometimes seen riding on the backs of water buffalo and other cattle in Asia and Africa.

Voice is raspy clucking. Maybe rick rack *with soft guttural sounds mixed in. They sound fussy.*

Below: Cattle Egrets are colony dwellers. The ones sporting orange are transitioning into breeding plumage, during which the orange is a little brighter. As with all egrets, the sexes look alike.

Great Egret (38")

The tall, stately Great Egrets are common, well-adapted birds that inhabit marshes, fields, and other wet areas all over California. They are year-round residents of the Central Valley and are also frequently seen standing in kelp beds in coastal waters. A small number are late summer visitors at Lake Tahoe and other mountain lakes.

Great Egrets are colony dwellers. Their preferred food is fish, but they will eat anything that moves. Breeding birds have lace-like feathers.

Voice is a low, hoarse croak.

Below, top: Note the black feet and yellow bill. I don't know what the additional tail plume is but have seen it a few times.

Marlin Harms

Snowy Egret (24")

Snowy Egrets are year-round residents of coastal marshes and of wet areas in the Central Valley. Some breed in the Great Basin and winter along the coast, which greatly increases the coastal population.

During breeding season (February to July), the egret's plumage becomes lace-like, an endowment that brought them to the brink of extinction in the early 1900s, when embellishing ladies' hats with their feathers was the latest fashion. Thankfully, the fad died out before the birds did, and now they are common once again.

Snowys are colony dwellers and are highly social. They are often seen with Great Egrets and Double-crested Cormorants, with which they frequently cooperate on fishing expeditions. The cormorants scare the fish toward the shoreline, where the egrets are waiting for them, and the egrets scare the fish back into the open water, where the cormorants are also waiting for them. Not a good position to be in if you're a fish.

In marshes, one can often observe a Snowy using one foot as a stir stick to find crayfish for supper.

Voice is a low, nasal, raspy craw *that is expressed in many ways; all sound like they're dying.*

Below: Somebody's excited. Note the **yellow feet and black bill.**

Reddish Egret (30")

The Reddish Egret lives in saltwater marshes along the south coast. It is a rare bird in California and is more often seen along the coast of Mexico and on the Gulf Coast. For years, there have been at least two birds at Bolsa Chica, in Huntington Beach, and others at lagoons and marshes near San Diego.

The Reddish Egret also has a white morph that can easily be mistaken for a Great Egret. However, the Reddish Egret is smaller and its bill is not yellow like that of a Great Egret. The neck feathers of the two birds are also quite different. Because it is so scarce, the white morph is unlikely to show up in California.

Voice is a nasal grunt.

Below: Adult.

Next page: The "dance" of the Reddish Egret is unforgettable. The jumping and gyrations of a similar bird are, no doubt, the inspiration for some of the dances of the Watusi in Africa. Actually, the bird is simply stirring up the muck to uncover mudbugs and startle fish.

American Bittern (28")

An uncommon bird of marshes, lakes, and ponds, American Bitterns live among the reeds, camouflage well, and are easy to overlook. They are year-round residents of the Central Valley and the north coast. Some breed in the inland far north and winter in temperate areas throughout the state. About one in four winters I'll see an American Bittern at Bolsa Chica or San Joaquin Marsh in Orange County. Sometimes they stay for a while, sometimes not. The preserves in the Central Valley are a much better place to find them.

The slow, almost imperceptible, movements of the American Bittern qualify it to be called the sloth of the bird kingdom. But don't let that fool you—they can strike as quickly as any heron.

Voice is a deep resonating sound like the echo of large drops of water striking the water in a deep well. It consists of one or two syllables and is sometimes repeated. Bitterns are heard far more frequently than seen.

Below: Adult in pickleweed. The pose is typical. They often stand still in that position for some time and if they are in the reeds or rushes can be nearly invisible.

Least Bittern (12–13")

The Least Bittern is an uncommon, secretive bird of lower-elevation marshes and reedy ponds. In California, it is a year-round resident along the Colorado River and in the extreme south. Some birds breed in the Central Valley and migrate to Baja California for the winter.

The pose in the photo is typical. The bird easily makes its way through dense bulrushes and cattails by grasping vertical reeds as if it were walking on stilts.

Least Bitterns are usually seen at dawn or dusk and, like American Bitterns, are heard far more frequently than seen. I've seen a total of one—the one below.

Voice: Calls include a nasal, chicken-like clucking of about four syllables. There are at least two varieties, one higher than the other. Spring males also coo *like a pigeon and often put the two calls together.*

Below: Adult male in bulrushes. The male has a black back; the female and immature birds have a rusty-brown back.

Other Birds of the Wetlands

White-Faced Ibis (23")

These birds are found in freshwater and saltwater marshes, in flooded fields, and on wet lawns throughout California. They are common all year in the Central and Imperial Valleys and breed in the Klamath Basin. In southern coastal areas, they are common in winter, less common during fall and spring.

The White-faced Ibis looks identical to the Glossy Ibis of the eastern states when not sporting its white mask during the breeding season, which is from **March to August**. The iridescence of these birds is spectacular. When backlit, they appear black.

Voice: Soft grunts sound like a duck quacking through a kazoo.

Top: Breeding birds. **Bottom:** Juvenile or nonbreeding adult in Water Pennywort.

Next page, middle: Breeding adult flying over spike rushes; **bottom:** nonbreeding birds. Males and females look alike.

Sandhill Crane (36–48")

These majestic birds of wet fields and grassland are fairly common in the Central and Imperial Valleys during the winter and in the Klamath Basin during the summer breeding season. Most Sandhill Cranes breed north of California, so our winter population is much larger.

Flocks of Sandhill Cranes help themselves to waste grain and in winter are usually found in grain fields with flocks of other birds such as Snow Geese, Cattle Egrets, and Red-winged Blackbirds.

Voice in flight is like an ah-ooo-gah *horn on an antique car but staticky. When a flock flies over, they will certainly get your full attention.*

Below: Nonbreeding plumage. Breeding plumage (May to August) is rusty; transitioning has rusty patches. The sexes look alike. Juveniles are pale rusty and lack the red cap.

Rick Derevan

Deborah L. Stanley

Belted Kingfisher (13")

Kingfishers are unique birds that look like a cross between a Steller's Jay and a tern. They are expert fishers that hover over their prey until an opportunity to strike is presented, then dive with the forcefulness of a tern.

These birds live near rivers, lakes, bays, and inlets throughout the state and burrow deep into dirt banks to nest. In the north, many are year-round residents; others head south for the winter, which is when they are usually seen in Southern California.

Voice: In flight, they utter a loud, high-pitched staccato that lasts up to a second.

Top: Female. **Bottom:** Male.

Hawks and Hawk-Like Birds

Hawks are classified in three main groups: falcons; accipiters, or bird hawks; and buteos, or stocky soaring hawks.

It takes a few years for some hawks to reach maturity, and during those years their plumage goes through many phases. Some species also have light, intermediate, and dark morphs (see p. 510), and some have regional variations. Often, one must observe factors such as the bird's shape, voice, behavior, or flight to make a positive identification.

White spots on the backs of hawks may be fluffed or molting feathers and may not be helpful for identification purposes.

Female hawks are larger than the males, so two dimensions are given with their names. The sexes look alike unless otherwise noted.

Until the Endangered Species Preservation Act of 1966, the populations of many species of raptors had declined dangerously because of sport shooting. Also, the use of DDT made their eggshells thin and many did not hatch. Since the banning of these practices, many raptors —including our national bird, the Bald Eagle—have recovered very well.

Falcons

Falcons are slender hawks with pointed wings and long tails. They are exceptionally fast and agile fliers and are found in open areas.

Prairie Falcon (16–19"; males are smaller)

Prairie Falcons are relatively uncommon in California. They prefer vast, open, arid habitats like the drier grasslands of interior valleys and desert-like areas with both scrub brush and grass.

Ground squirrels and other rodents, as well as meadowlarks and other birds, are the preferred diet of Prairie Falcons. Many don't migrate but simply follow the food supply, which in winter means to the cattle feed lots, where starlings and blackbirds are plentiful. During the rest of the year, they avoid places where people are present.

Good places to find Prairie Falcons are the Carrizo Plain, west of Bakersfield; Henry Coe State Park, near San Jose; and, in the summer, along Bodie Road on the way to Bodie State Park in Mono County.

Voice: Alarm is a yelping kackkackkack *or* kreekreekree *that continues. Call is a nasal squeaky scream, at times interspersed with other squeaks.*

Next page, top left: Adult. **Right:** Juvenile. Note the heavier streaking on the underparts. Colors for both can be lighter or darker than shown.

Peregrine Falcon (16–20")

Once endangered, Peregrine Falcons have made a tremendous comeback since DDT was banned in the 1960s. They are year-round residents of all our coastal areas, some winter in the inland valleys and deserts, and they may now be encountered even in the high mountains in the summer. Small hollows in cliff faces are their preferred nesting sites.

Peregrines are known for their strafing flights. They seem to come out of nowhere and fly low and fast over a flock of ducks or shorebirds, terrorizing and scattering them. After the falcon makes a few passes, the prey birds are weakened, and the falcon can make another pass and easily pick one off. Any attacking bird risks injury, so if the prey is weakened before the attack, the attacker is less likely to be injured.

All that being the case, many bird-watchers have also seen Peregrines strafing flocks of birds seemingly for the fun of it. Sometimes, after strafing a flock repeatedly, they do not return to grab a meal but instead go to sleep on their perch or take off for somewhere else.

Voice is a drawn-out rheeek, rheeek, rheeek *that is all business. Also, a nasal* kak-kak-kak *that is scratchier than that of a Cooper's Hawk.*

Below: Daddy, get us food. NOW!

Next page, top left: Juvenile. Note the thick *vertical* streaking on the breast and belly. **Top right and middle:** Adults. Adults may be gray, brown, or a combination of the two. Note the fine *horizontal* streaking on the underparts. **Bottom:** Strength.

Gary Weller

Mark Schulist

Stephanie Lee Smith

American Kestrel (formerly called Sparrow Hawk) (9.5–10.5")

American Kestrels are year-round residents in most of California. They are found in a wide variety of habitats and move around during the course of the year following the food supply. Many more from farther north join the locals in winter.

Kestrels are both the most common and the smallest falcon in the state. But don't let the size fool you. They are one tough bird. Although kestrels usually eat grasshoppers and beetles and an occasional mouse or small bird, they are not afraid to attack much larger prey. I once saw a kestrel attack a flicker that was enjoying a large trove of bugs on a lawn. The flicker is much larger and has a sharp sword on the front of its face, but the little kestrel didn't care. The flicker stood his ground, however, and after a while the kestrel gave up.

Voice: Most commonly, a high-pitched, rapid klee-klee-klee-klee.

Below: Pair; juvenile. **Next page, top two**: Males. **Bottom**: Females.

Jerry Ting

Jerry Ting

Merlin (11–12")

Fall to early spring residents or migrants, Merlins are not nearly as common in California as the smaller kestrels. Most breed in Canada, and some winter as far south as South America. They are widespread in California during the nonbreeding season and are usually seen alone.

Merlins are bird hawks and typically catch their prey in midair using surprise tactics. The clouds of swirling sandpiper flocks during migration are often the result of an intruding Merlin or Peregrine Falcon, which can sometimes be spotted in their midst.

Although Merlins naturally prefer habitats with open space, they are now often seen in spacious suburban areas.

Voice is a shrill trill (see definition, p. 510) that lasts a second or more. It starts slowly and gains momentum, and is much faster, softer, and higher-pitched than a kestrel's. Alternate voicing is similar but slowed (slower than a kestrel).

Photos: Sex can be difficult to determine, as in two of the photos here, but males are grayish; females, brown. Juveniles look like females.

Rob English

Falcons

Rob English

Ken Shults

Donna Pomeroy

Accipiters or Bird Hawks

Accipiters are similar to falcons but are adapted to make a living among the trees, not in open areas. Their wings are shorter and their wingtips are rounded, not pointed like those of a falcon. Accipiters are also identified by their long tails, which are like those of falcons and much longer than those of buteos. They prey mostly on other birds.

Accipiters seldom soar, like a buteo; instead they are known for their glide. All have a similar flight pattern: a few short, stiff, rapid wing flaps followed by a short glide.

Northern Goshawk (21–26")

The size of a Red-tailed Hawk, Northern Goshawks live in dense old-growth forests in the far north of the state. They also live in the Sierras but seldom south of Yosemite. During cold winters, mountain birds may move lower, and northern birds may go farther south.

Goshawks are secretive and need much more space than Cooper's or Sharp-shinned Hawks. Goshawks are scarce in California and, other than in winter, are usually seen within the forest or at the forest edge.

In an old-growth forest in the far north, if you come across a pile of mixed feathers, look up. You may be under a goshawk's plucking perch.

Voice: Alarm is ki-ki-ki, *usually lasting about two seconds. Also screams.*

Below: Juvenile on a Quaking Aspen. Note the white eyebrow and vertical streaking on the breast.

Rob English

Adult Northern Goshawk on a Western Hemlock.

Cooper's Hawk (14–20")

Although Cooper's Hawks are year-round residents in most of California, their numbers increase significantly in the fall with the arrival of migrating birds. They move from place to place to follow their food—other birds. Small birds are usually too quick for them and don't provide much nourishment, but starlings, robins, doves, and quail are just right.

Cooper's Hawks inhabit forests and woodlands and are also at home in the suburbs, especially around your bird feeder. They are masters of stealth and of understanding trajectory. They come out of nowhere, grab a meal on the fly, and are gone—all in less than two seconds.

Once, while on a walk with my wife, a Cooper's Hawk shot right past our heads and into the middle of a leafy tree after a Mourning Dove. He missed the dove but left us in a state of amazement. I still cannot understand how he did that without risking crashing into a tree branch and sustaining serious injury.

Cooper's are similar in appearance to the smaller Sharp-shinned Hawk. See photos at the bottom of the next page and Sharp-shinned on p. 195.

Voice is a loud, nasal kik-kik-kik-kik-kik-kik *that is monkey-like in cadence and often continues for nearly two seconds; also a soft* kik.

Below: Juvenile in a California Live Oak.

Top: Male and chicks in a Cottonwood. **Middle:** Juvenile; adult female.

Below left: Cooper's Hawk. **Right:** Sharp-shinned Hawk. Note the rounded tail and tail feathers of the Cooper's, the squared of the Sharpie. Also note the rounded wingtips. A falcon's wingtips are pointed.

Sharp-Shinned Hawk (10–14")

Sharpies are a smaller version of a Cooper's Hawk and can be difficult to identify with certainty because a small (male) Cooper's is the size of a large (female) Sharp-shinned. The Sharpie's tail and tail feathers are squared instead of rounded like a Cooper's (p. 194). Its head is also rounder than a Cooper's, but voice may be the best identifier. Behavior is like Cooper's.

Some Sharpies are year-round residents east of the Sierras and Cascades and also in the mountain forests of the north coast. Migrating birds from as far away as Alaska begin arriving in California in late September. Most stay for a short time and then move farther south; a few stay until they head north again in the spring. Sharpies are not nearly as common as Cooper's Hawks in most of California.

Voicings are similar to a Cooper's Hawk but much higher and squeakier.

Below left: Adult. **Right:** Juvenile.

Note: White spots on the backs of accipiters may be fluffed feathers and are not helpful for identification.

Juvenile Sharp-shinned Hawk chasing a Steller's Jay.
Note the vertically streaked breast.

Northern Harrier (18–21")

A small number of Northern Harriers, formerly called **Marsh Hawks**, are seen year-round in the Central Valley, in the Klamath region, and along the coast, but California's winter population is much larger due to migrants from Canada. The migrants arrive with the ducks beginning in October and leave with them in the spring.

Like the Cooper's and Sharp-shinned Hawks, the harrier's white rump shows in flight, but the harrier's wings are longer and more slender, which makes identification easier. The owl-like circle of feathers around the face directs sound to their ears.

I don't know why, but wherever I have seen harriers, the females are usually far more numerous than the males. Perhaps partly because of this, the male is nicknamed "the Gray Ghost."

The harrier's diet is mostly birds, small mammals, and ducks, and their foraging resembles a crop duster. They glide low over the ground, then swoop up sharply, make a hard banked turn, and take another pass. Apparently they are looking for a weak duck or bird that will not put up much of a fight, reducing the harrier's risk of injury. The Peregrine Falcon's method is similar. Harriers also hover.

Voice: The harriers' voicings include a high-pitched scream, a whistle-like squeal, and a rapidly repeated kek or kep of a few varieties.

Photos: The males are gray; the females are brown.

Ken Shults

Jeff Bleam

Jeff Bleam

Jeff Bleam

Buteos, or Stocky Soaring Hawks

Red-Tailed Hawk (19–22")

The Red-tailed is by far our most common buteo, or stocky-shaped hawk. They are well known for their intimidating, long scream, *keeeeeaar*, that starts out piercing and fades into hoarse static.

There is a lot of variation in the species. Red-tails acquire adult plumage in four years and make several changes along the way—before they get their red tails. Additionally, some birds are dark; others are light. And there are regional differences. The sexes look alike to us, so that part is easy. The rest isn't, so **the next three pages deal with Red-tails**.

Next page, middle row: Rufous adult; light morph. **Bottom:** Juveniles.

Below: A cutie with a story.

***

I was out birding one spring day in a remote place and was walking along the edge of a field when I became aware I was being watched. After looking around a while, I saw this little guy peeking at me through the willow leaves. He was fascinated by me, but his momma had told him he was supposed to stay hidden. Eventually, his curiosity got the best of him; he raised up in the nest, and I got a good look at him. I took a few photos and left, knowing that that was better for both of us.

***

Deborah L. Stanley

Top: Adults or subadults. **Middle and bottom:** Juveniles

Top: Crows mobbing a Red-tail—a common sight. **Middle:** Adult.
Bottom: Red-tail with large snake; dark morph. **Add'l photo:** P. 502.

Red-Shouldered Hawk (16–20")

The Red-shouldered Hawk is a common year-round resident mostly in the western half of the state. They are relatively comfortable around people and often live in parks that provide stands of tall trees for perching and cover, and a free lunch in the form of squirrels and birds.

When not in suburban parks, Red-shouldered Hawks prefer oak and riparian woodlands. They do not migrate but do travel short distances following the food supply. Red-shoulders are noisy, so easy to find.

Voice is a piercing kear *or* kear-ah, *usually repeated three or more times.*

Below: Adults—in the willows and flying over grassland.

Next page: Adult with prey; soaring juvenile; juvenile perched in a Black Willow.

Jeff Bleam

Lack Lindahl

Swainson's Hawk (19–21")

The uncommon Swainson's Hawk is a hawk of the grasslands. In California, they are primarily found in or near the Central Valley, where a relative few are year-round residents. Most winter in the pampas, or grasslands, of Argentina.

During the spring migration, large flocks of Swainson's Hawks can be seen at funnel points on the coastal side of the southern mountains. Typically in mid- to late March, hundreds will pass just east of the city of Riverside. Although some are stragglers, most pass through within a few days. A good place to see them in early spring may be at the San Jacinto Wildlife Area, outside of Perris. In late September or early October, wind currents usually take them to the inland side of the mountains, out near Blythe. Sometimes several dozen can be seen riding a thermal column at or near these locations. (See page 36.)

The Swainson's Hawk eats any animal life found in the grass including rodents, lizards, snakes, birds, grasshoppers, and other large insects.

According to the California Department of Fish and Wildlife, California probably has fewer than 1,000 breeding pairs, maybe only half that many.

Voice is a scream similar to that of a Red-tailed Hawk but clearer and not static-like at the end. Also a softer, peeping pick, *usually repeated.*

Below, left to right: Juvenile; dark morph adult; intermediate adult.

Next page: Some different looks. Note the white on the face and the dark bib on three of these birds. **Additional photo:** Page 508.

Rob English

Rob English

Stephanie Lee Smith

Jeff Bleam

Jeff Bleam

Rough-Legged Hawk (21–22")

Small numbers of these Arctic breeders come to California for the winter, mostly east of the Cascades and at the edges of the Central Valley. In these areas, in season, you are likely to see many Red-tails before seeing a Rough-legged Hawk. They are considerably more common in the states to the north and east of California.

Rough-legged Hawks live primarily on rodents. They are often seen in wide open grassland, hovering as they face the wind or perched on utility poles or fence posts. Winter populations are irregular, but a good place to find them is at Tule Lake from mid-October through March.

Rough-legs are the size and shape of a Red-tail, but note the **dark patches at the wrist, white tail base, and dark band near the tip of the tail** of the soaring Rough-legged Hawks. Feathers extend to the feet.

Voice is a quavering scream like that of a highly annoyed cat.

Photos show some of the major plumages of a Rough-legged. They have many, including a morph as dark as the dark Swainson's on page 205.

Rob English

Rob English

Ferruginous Hawk (23–24")

Another uncommon species, the large rust-colored Ferruginous Hawk, breeds primarily in the Great Basin, in the Rockies, and as far east as central Nebraska. A relative few winter over a large area of California.

Look for Ferruginous Hawks both perched on the ground and soaring above expansive grasslands in remote areas and in areas of mixed sage and grass east of the Sierras. The prime time to see them in California is from late October to March. Although outnumbered by Red-tails, Ferruginous Hawks are often present in season on the Carrizo Plain, west of Bakersfield; in the Sierra Valley, northwest of Reno; and in the Owens Valley, off Highway 395.

As with the other buteos, there is a lot of variation in the species, but there are similarities too. Comparing the photos shown here with the photos of the other buteos will make identification in the field easier. Like the Rough-legged Hawk, the leg feathers extend to the feet.

Voice is an eerie cry similar to that of a Rough-legged Hawk.

Below: Light adult.

Next page, from the top: Light juvenile, dark adult, light juvenile. Dark morph adults and juveniles can be nearly as dark as the dark Swainson's Hawk on page 205.

Sam McMillan

Jerry Ting

Jerry Ting

Jeff Bleam

Osprey (23–24.5")

Ospreys are commonly seen throughout California over just about any body of water where fish are present. Many ospreys breed or live year-round in the northern quarter of the state and their numbers decline, as the water does, as you go farther south.

Formerly called Fish Eagles, Ospreys are the most streamlined California raptor. Their wings are proportionally long and slender for soaring, and their wingbeats appear to be labored.

Ospreys hover and dive for fish, talons first. I once watched a frustrated osprey gliding haltingly over a pond he was accustomed to fishing in. The pond had been mostly drained, which forced the fish into tight quarters. White pelicans, cormorants, grebes, and egrets were having a field day, but my poor osprey friend must have thought it too crowded to join the party. It looked to me like he was working the angles but couldn't find a safe approach. I suppose he wasn't all that hungry.

Voice is a variety of whistled, sparrow-like chups, cheeps, and chirps that can be loud, soft, or warbled. Also, a rising cheer-ear-ear-ear-ear-ear *that gains momentum then fades. The Osprey's voice is much higher in pitch than what you would expect from such a large bird.*

Photos are of adults. Young juveniles have a buff wash on the breast and head and pale scaling on the back.

Jeff Bleam

Jerry Ting

White-Tailed Kite (16")

White-tailed Kites are year-round residents of open grasslands and marshes all along the coastal side of California. They do not migrate per se but do travel widely, following the food supply. Although kites show up every year at many locations, their number and how long they stay vary greatly. Sometimes they can be seen roosting in flocks of 20 or more birds, usually in winter in the evening.

Kites live mostly on field mice and other small rodents, but if these are in short supply, they will take lizards, birds, and large insects.

Perhaps there is no bird more fascinating to watch ply their trade than a White-tailed Kite. They glide over a field watching the ground intently and then stop to hover, always facing the wind. Sometimes they hover as high as 70 feet but usually much lower. They are patient, make constant adjustments, and wait for the right time to dive down on their prey. They often hit the ground hard, and I suppose the need to take those kinds of blows every day teaches them to be efficient. But I do marvel that they do not get all broken up by the impact, and I assume they have been given the ability to avoid rocks.

Voices: A sweet cheep, chup, and chew; *at times* chup, chup, chup, chup.

Photos are of adults; juveniles are rusty on the breast.

Jerry Ting

Eagles and Vultures

Golden Eagle (30–40")

The majestic Golden Eagle is a bird of the open country. They need space—a lot of space—so they avoid developed areas other than to occasionally fly high over the edges of them.

If you see a bird gliding very high, fast, and straight across the sky, it's an eagle. No other bird covers distance as effortlessly as an eagle.

Golden Eagles dine mostly on small mammals—rabbits, ground squirrels, and marmots are some of their favorite foods.

Although not common, Golden Eagles can be found year-round in California in just about any mountainous area with abundant open space. They seldom perch out in the open unless it is on the ground. With a long history of being shot at, Golden Eagles usually stay away from anything having to do with people.

Voice: Golden Eagles are usually silent. When they talk, the sound falls between a gull's squawk and a bark and is higher than expected.

Photos: Adults and juveniles look similar. ***The golden feathers on the neck and head*** easily separate the Golden from the Bald Eagle.

George Gentry / USFWS

Bald Eagle (31–37")

Our national bird, the Bald Eagle, was named for the white head of the adult. They fish for a living, so are almost always near bodies of water. When fish are in short supply, they eat ducks, small mammals, or just about anything else, including carrion.

Until laws with stiff penalties were passed banning the practice, raptors of all kinds were commonly shot by sportsmen and hunters. If that was not damaging enough, the insecticide DDT came into use after World War II, which softened the shell of the birds' eggs, causing many to break. By the early 1960s, the Bald Eagle was headed toward extinction in the lower 48 states. Fortunately, they recovered and are now somewhat common at many lakes and reservoirs around the state. Bald Eagles are far more common in the far north of the state, where they are year-round residents.

Bald Eagles take four or five years to mature. **The white head does not appear until the fourth year**, and by that time the underside of the wings has turned as dark as the top side. (**See photos**.) The sexes look alike.

Voice consists of soft, high-pitched, scratchy piping notes—not at all what you would expect from such a large bird. They also scream but like a timid gull and not with authority like a Red-tailed Hawk.

Next page, top: Youngsters in a nest high in a redwood tree. **Bottom:** A juvenile. Note the heavily worn tail feathers.

John Dykstra

Rob English

Turkey Vulture (26–27")

The Wright brothers studied these masters of soaring intently, and, because they are large and move slowly, much of what we know about flight was learned from them.

Turkey Vultures live in colonies, are abundant throughout the state, and serve as the cleanup crew at landfills and wherever carrion is found.

Voice is a pneumatic fuss, but they, and condors, are almost always silent.

Top: Adult on a Blue Gum Eucalyptus warming up its feathers for lighter soaring. **Bottom:** Note the under-wing pattern.

Rick Derevan

California Condor (46–47″)

With a nine-foot wingspan and a face that only a mother could love, the California Condor was almost extinct before the decision was made in the 1980s to capture and breed the remaining population. They are still with us, all sporting numbers on their wings.

Many condors have now been released at a few remote locations from Ventura County to Monterey County. The easiest place to find them is above the highest peaks at Pinnacles National Park. If you go there and don't see them, wait. They've gone to the coast and will be back by the end of the day, because that is where they are fed. Getting them to fend for themselves is not so easy, and much of the current population knows little about how to do that.

Photo: Compare the under-wing pattern with the Turkey Vulture's.

Gary Weller

Donna Pomeroy

Owls

Twelve species of owls are regularly found in California. The smallest are the size of a sparrow; the largest, bigger than our largest hawks. Not all are nocturnal and some are rarely seen.

Smaller owls usually eat insects; larger owls usually prefer small mammals. Most owls will eat just about anything that moves, including songbirds. For that reason, songbirds often mob an owl, which gives away the owl's location.

The face of an owl is shaped like a satellite dish and was designed long before for the same purpose—to enable the owl to locate prey. Most owls hunt from a perch and listen and watch for dinner.

Owls are silent in flight. They surprise their prey, capture it with their powerful talons, and paralyze it with a hard bite at the back of the neck.

Tree cavities are the owls' preferred nesting sites. When these are in short supply, they often use nooks and crannies of man-made structures. In recent times, many owls have been using owl boxes set out by farmers who appreciate their help in controlling mice, rats, and other rodents. In this endeavor, it is often said that ten cats are not as effective as one owl.

Larger owls, when not feeding chicks, often swallow their prey whole. The indigestible parts of their meals, including bones, fur, and feathers, are later coughed up in the form of pellets. By finding the pellets, we can often locate a roosting owl, and by examining them, we can tell exactly what the owl has been eating (**see photo below**).

Male and female owls look alike or similar; males are smaller.

Great Gray Owl (26–28"; males are smaller)

Dressed in banker's gray with a white bow tie, our largest owl, the Great Gray, inhabits the edges of coniferous forests in the Cascades and northern Sierras. Uncommon in California, the Great Gray forages in mountain meadows most of the year but in winter may head downhill into the oaks on the west side of the mountains.

Voles, moles, gophers, mice, and chipmunks make up most of the Great Gray's diet. They hunt from low perches and, although night creatures, will often hunt during the day, especially in winter.

There are two major groupings of Great Gray Owls in California: one is mostly in and around Yosemite National Park, the other resides between Mount Shasta and Crater Lake, Oregon.

Voice is a low whoo-oo *that rises at the second syllable.*

Below: An adult at the edge of the willows.

Ken Shults

Great Horned Owl (20–22")

Our most commonly seen owl, the Great Horned, is a year-round resident throughout California wherever tall trees adjoin open space.

Although they eat a wide variety of mammals, reptiles, birds, and other fare, the Great Horned Owl is a rat and mouse specialist and as such is a welcome neighbor anywhere.

Great Horned Owls do their work at night but are often seen in the late afternoon and early evening, perched and waiting for nightfall.

Since tree cavities are in short supply, Great Horned Owls usually use abandoned hawk or raven nests high in mature trees. Sometimes they add a lining to the nest, sometimes not. They often occupy the nest all year and even from year to year.

The owl's "horns" are neither horns nor ears but feathers. There are many theories about their function, but that's all they are—theories.

Voice is the deep classical owl's whoo, *which is slightly deeper and of a different cadence than the similar-sounding Mourning Dove's, usually* whoo, h-whoo, whoo, whoo. *They also whistle, hiss, bark, shriek, and cry.*

Below: Adult.

Next page: Subadult in a California Fan Palm; bambino in a pine.

Long-Eared Owl (15")

The lanky-looking Long-eared Owls are much less common than the Great-horned. They are year-round residents in isolated pockets along the coastal side of the state from the Bay Area to Baja California and along our eastern border as far south as Death Valley. In the winter, migrating birds from farther north or from the Great Basin can appear all over the state, especially in the Central and Colorado River Valleys.

Long-ears forage for small rodents mostly in grasslands, scrublands, and open wooded areas, and they hunt in crop duster fashion. They roost in dense coniferous or deciduous trees, usually at the edge of a clearing.

Although an uncommon owl, the Long-eared is a colony dweller during the nonbreeding season, so if you see one roosting during the winter months, look around—you may find more. In winter, in desert oases, they often roost together in fan palms; in the Mono Basin, in willow thickets. Long-ears are regular winter visitors at Mercy Hot Springs in the Little Panoche Valley near Pinnacles National Park.

Voices include a hollow, deep whoo *and a higher yelping of* yup, yup.

Below: Note the vertical stripes on the breast; the Great Horned Owl has horizontal stripes. The ear tufts are not ears but feathers (see page 223). Sometimes the tufts are down, as in the photo on the right.

Jack Lindahl

Jeff Bleam

Short-Eared Owl (15")

Short-eared Owls are birds of **open grasslands**, marshes, and meadows. They are year-round residents in those habitats in Northern California and are occasional winter migrants in the rest of the state.

Short-ears build their nests of grasses on the ground and often roost on the ground. Seeing them on the ground is quite another thing because they blend in well with their surroundings. Look for them at dusk when they forage for small mammals by flying low over the ground.

Short-eared Owls are uncommon in California. The highest concentration of sightings in the state from fall to spring is recorded in and around Grizzly Island Wildlife Area south of Fairfield. In the south, a good place to look for them from November to March is on the Carrizo Plain, west of Bakersfield.

Voice: Short-ears are usually silent but can fuss like a cat, bark, and scream a scratchy chew, *like the second syllable of a sneeze. Males* hoot *repeatedly.*

Below: Adult on a Quaking Aspen. The "ear" tufts are usually not visible and are much shorter than those of their long-eared cousins on the previous page.

Barred Owl (20–21")

A year-round resident of the coastal far north and of the Klamath National Forest, the ghostly Barred Owl lives in **thick mature forests, almost always near water**.

Barred Owls are common in the East and have spread west and into California in the last century. They interbreed with Spotted Owls.

Like most owls, Barred Owls hunt from a perch and swoop down upon their prey, which are mostly small mammals. When their preferred food is scarce, they will take birds, fish, crayfish, reptiles, amphibians, and insects.

Barred Owls are cavity dwellers and occasionally use owl boxes. They do not migrate and are uncommon in California.

Voice is a loud, nasal, squeaky, hooting of about four hoots that speed up and end with a whinny. Once heard, never forgotten.

Below: Adult on a Western Red Cedar.

Spotted Owl (17–18")

The **Northern subspecies** of the Spotted Owl in the photo below is a year-round resident of mature coniferous forests in the far northwestern corner of the state. The **California subspecies**, which is lighter in color, is more widespread, and inhabits mature oak woodlands and coniferous forests throughout the state.

Logging greatly reduced Northern Spotted Owl numbers in previous generations. Now, competition with the newcomers—the Barred Owl, with which they interbreed—has further diminished their remaining numbers.

Spotted Owls become active at dusk and are usually seen at that time. Look and listen for them at the edge of forests in the Sierras in the summer and among the oaks in the Sierra foothills in the winter.

Voice: Commonly, a squeaky, nasal, hollow hoot *or* whoo, *sometimes repeated increasingly fast, as if the bird is winding up. At other times, the whoos are deeper and drop at the end. Also, a short, rising scream that ends abruptly and dog-like yapping.*

Christopher Lindsey

Barn Owl (14-16")

The Barn Owl's face is, in effect a satellite dish, receiving sounds and transmitting the data so accurately that they can locate and capture prey by sound alone. Imagine how the scientists who conducted those experiments must have marveled!

Barn Owls are well-named birds. By nature, they are cavity dwellers but now commonly nest in barns and other buildings. Barn Owls are common year-round residents across California (and the lower 48) in a wide variety of habitats but can almost always be found around barnyards and in unkept windrows of tall trees. They need open space but will live in suburbs where mature trees and open space are adequate.

Farmers and those of us who live near open fields are thankful for the Barn Owls because they are experts at catching rats and mice. Mice may make up to 90 percent of their diet.

When caught in the headlights of a car, they appear brilliant white. **Note that Barn Owls are smaller** than the owls previously discussed.

Voice is a raspy, static-like screech you would expect to hear from a Screech Owl but don't. They also hiss at intruders and often make a tinkling or clicking sound while flying.

Below: Adult in a willow tree.

Jeff Bleam

Western Screech Owl (8.5")

The little Western Screech Owl's natural habitat is thickly wooded areas at lower elevations. However, some don't mind being around people and live in suburbs where mature trees are plentiful. They are cavity dwellers and in a housing crunch will inhabit owl boxes.

Screech Owls will eat anything from bats and mice to worms and snails. They are often mobbed by songbirds, and for good reason—they eat them too. Screech Owls also frequently attack prey such as quail and squirrels that are larger than they are.

Voice: Western Screech Owls don't screech. My theory is that the Barn Owls stole their voice, but I can't prove it. The Screech Owl's voice is a repeated, whistled whoo—*slower for the first three notes, up-tempo for the last four or five. Cadence is like a bouncing ball and similar to a Wrentit's, but the owl's voice is muffled and much lower. When agitated, a squeaky, squirrel-like bark.*

Below: Adult in a cottonwood. Overall color can be brown or gray.

Stephanie Lee Smith

Northern Saw-Whet Owl (8")

The cat-faced Northern Saw-whet Owls are forest dwellers. They live year-round mostly in the far north of the state, in the Sierras, and along the coast as far south as Big Sur. They are less common in the high mountains in the south. Some also winter in the rest of the state, usually in heavily wooded areas.

Northern Saw-whet Owls are mousers that hunt for their prey from low perches. They will take other mammals, small birds, and insects when their primary food is scarce.

Although fairly common in their habitat, Northern Saw-whet Owls are seldom seen because they are cavity dwellers and highly nocturnal. Perhaps the best way to find them is by their unmistakable voice.

*Voice: The Northern Saw-whet Owl's name is derived from one of their calls, which sounds like a saw blade being sharpened against a whetstone. Another call **sounds like a truck backing up**. It is a high-pitched piping toot, toot, toot, toot, at about two notes per second. They also have several other calls including a squirrel-like squeal; a raspy, drawn-out screech; and a cat-like wail. When approached, they may snap their bill, which sounds like a sharp hand clap. Other owls do the same.*

Below: Adult on a Red Alder. **Inset:** Juvenile on an Alligator Juniper.

Northern Pygmy Owl (7")

The tiny Northern Pygmy Owl lives year-round in coniferous and mixed forests along the coast and in the high mountains. The mountain birds follow the food supply to lower elevations in winter.

These cute, little harmless-looking guys are bird-watchers—for a living. They are very aggressive and will take birds much larger than they are. If birds are scarce, they eat small mammals or insects.

Northern Pygmy Owls usually hunt by day when birds are active and often perch somewhat in the open, so they are seen more frequently than most of our other small owls. They are often mobbed by the same birds they prey upon, and the ensuing ruckus can reveal their location to bird-watchers.

The flight pattern of Pygmy Owls is similar to that of woodpeckers—rapid wingbeats followed by long glides. They appear to bounce through the air.

Although they are widespread around the state, a couple of good places to find Northern Pygmy Owls are at Sanborn County Park, near San Jose, and at Calaveras Big Trees State Park off Highway 4.

Voice is composed of hollow-sounding high piping hoots, often about two per second followed by a short pause, then repeated. At other times, much slower—about one hoot every two seconds.

Photos: Northern Pygmy Owls were given "false eyes" on the back of their head that likely serve to ward off predators. Note the long tail, which is proportionally longer than the tails of our other small owls.

Flammulated Owl (6–7")

The sparrow-sized, inconspicuous Flammulated Owl was thought to be rare until people started studying it. Now they are known to be common, but that does not make them any easier to find.

These little guys breed in the dry pine forests of the far north, the Sierras, and the high southern mountains. They winter in southern Mexico and Central America. On the trip north, they travel through the lowlands; on the trip south, they travel through the mountains, following the supply of crickets, beetles, and moths that constitute almost all of their diet. They are usually seen in California between May and August.

Flammulated Owls hunt at night by gleaning insects off vegetation or by occasionally flying out a short distance to capture them in the air. Since they prefer the treetops, are not active during the day, and usually hunt by sitting still and waiting for their prey to come to them, locating one is challenging, to say the least.

Voice is a low-pitched hollow hoot *that sounds like it should be from a larger owl. They also have a hollow, muffled scream that sounds like a crazy person. Both voicings are difficult to trace, so the Flammulated Owl remains, for the most part, unseen.*

Photos: The name refers to the flame-shaped markings on the plumage, which are hard to see at night. The ear tufts are rarely up as at left.

Michael Woodruff

Christopher Lindsey

Burrowing Owl (9.5")

These little darlings are year-round residents in open habitats in the southern half of the state. Burrowing Owls are not afraid to be around human development but avoid areas with many trees. They often live on the banks of drainage ditches in agricultural areas and are common in the Imperial Valley.

Diet is primarily insects, especially grasshoppers, crickets, beetles, and moths, supplemented with lizards, mice, toads, and ground squirrels.

It is ironic that ground squirrels are on the menu because Burrowing Owls do not burrow—they let others, including ground squirrels, do the work.

Voice: Although commonly seen during the day, Burrowing Owls are usually heard at night. Typical voice is a high-pitched, two-syllable cooing that falls between that of a Mourning Dove and a quail. They also chatter like a monkey, scream, and make a noise like radio static.

Below: Burrowing Owls are often seen standing next to their burrows in the middle of the day as this one is. They are colony dwellers and, unlike most owls, are quite active during the day.

Jack and Petra Clayton

Nighthawks and Poorwills

Nighthawks are not hawks at all but are similar to swifts. These streamlined acrobatic flyers are usually inactive during the day and are most commonly seen at dusk. They forage like a swallow or swift, gliding and maneuvering through the air with their extraordinarily wide mouths open, capturing flying insects. The camouflage of nighthawks and poorwills is second to none, and when perched, they sit lengthwise on a branch, probably because their tiny feet cannot grab a branch the way most birds do. Males and females look alike.

Lesser Nighthawk (8.5–9")

A bird of the arid Southwest, the Lesser Nighthawk winters in southern Mexico and Central America and comes to California to breed. Between mid-March and September, they breed and raise their young in deserts, grasslands, and at the edges of agricultural fields throughout Southern California. Lesser Nighthawks are common in the Colorado River and Imperial Valleys, less common in the San Joaquin Valley.

One way of finding them is to go out at dusk, find a vantage point with the sunset at your back, and watch an agricultural field. Take your dinner with you—you may be in for quite a show. And after it's dark, watch the parking lot lights at nearby business establishments.

Voice: When on the ground during breeding season, a long, eerie, hollow, low, toad-like trill that lasts 7-12 seconds. In flight, a hoarse, nasal bark or bleating. All are strange sounds.

Next Page: Lesser Nighthawks.

***

One summer afternoon I took my daughter on one of my favorite hikes in the Santa Ana Mountains. It was so pleasant that we stayed late and didn't get back to the truck until it was almost dark. From the trailhead, there are seven miles of a rough dirt road before you come to a paved one. The road must be taken slowly, and by the time we had driven halfway down, it was completely dark. Suddenly, out of nowhere, more than a dozen birds began swarming in the glow of our headlights. They were feeding on insects that were attracted to the light, and they were having a feast. As we drove on, they came alongside us from behind, flew up to catch their prey—sometimes just in front of the windshield—then peeled off to the side. I had read that nighthawks forage in groups but had not seen it before. The habitat was more that of poorwills, however (page 238). I've gone back to the same location to try to find them again but never have.

***

Tom Edell

Mark Schulist

Common Nighthawk (9.5")

Common Nighthawks are not so common in California, where the Lesser Nighthawk usually represents the family. Common Nighthawks winter in southern South America and breed east of the Sierras and in the far north of the state. They are much more common to the east and north of California.

A good place to see Common Nighthawks in the summer is at Mono Lake. In early August, flocks start gathering there for the trip south, and at dusk the birds can be seen flying erratically as they forage at the edge of the lake. They are gone by the end of the month.

The two nighthawks are easily distinguished by their voices.

Voice, while flying, is a buzzy, nasal beer, *often repeated.*

Photos: Both nighthawks have flashy white patches on their wings, but the Lesser's are closer to the wing tips. (Compare with page 236.)

Greg Lavaty

Greg Lavaty

Common Poorwill (7.5")

Common Poorwills are night birds that live in arid areas and avoid moist, thickly vegetated ones. They live year-round in the southern deserts and in the canyons inland from the south coast. During the breeding season, from May to August, they are widespread around the state, usually in dry woodlands or in steep rocky regions of chaparral.

During cold weather, poorwills can go into a hibernation-like state, called torpor, in which their metabolic rate slows greatly. Unlike hibernation, however, torpor may last for just a few days or for much longer periods, probably depending upon the weather. The Hopi Indians called the bird Holchoko, "the sleeping one."

Poorwills typically forage by sitting on the ground or on a low perch and making short upward flights to catch their prey. Look for poorwills at night along roadsides in the deserts where they forage for insects that are attracted to the headlights of cars. You may see the orange reflections of their eyes first.

Voice: A loud, high, popping poor-willup *or* poor-willa. *Barks if disturbed.*

Below: Plumage colors vary as in the photos. The lack of white stripes on the wings easily differentiates a flying poorwill from a nighthawk.

Game Birds

Doves and Pigeons

The terms *dove* and *pigeon* lack precise definitions. What one person calls a pigeon, another may call a dove. In scientific nomenclature, they are the same. In common usage, a dove is usually smaller.

All these birds have proportionally small heads and short bills. They are primarily seed eaters, swallowing them whole along with some coarse sand to aid the gizzard in grinding them up.

Doves and pigeons live up to 20 years—much longer than most birds their size. When not nesting, they will be in flocks.

All California doves and pigeons make a rattling or whistling noise with their wings when they take off, and each species can be identified by that noise.

The sexes look similar or alike.

Mourning Dove (10-12")

The Mourning Dove, our most common dove, gets its name from its mournful cooing. They are seen in open country all over the state, except in the high mountains, and are abundant in many areas. Northern birds often fly south for the winter and travel in flocks.

Mourning Doves are delightful, peaceable birds that don't mind being watched. Their flight is fairly straight and can reach speeds of about 45 miles per hour (I've clocked them as they have flown along side my car). They forage on the ground for seeds.

If conditions are right, Mourning Doves may raise as many as six broods in a year—more than any other native bird. For protection from crows and other nest robbers, they often make their nests close to humans. My wife's mother had one return year after year to nest in a hanging basket on her porch near the front door. I found out later that Daisy's behavior was not unusual.

When flushed, Mourning Doves take off at a steep trajectory, maybe as sharp as 45 degrees. They usually do not fly far but make a circuitous flight and often end up fewer than 20 yards from where they took off. When gliding, Mourning Doves can sometimes be mistaken for a falcon.

Voice: Ooo WEE-ooo, woo, woo, woo. *The* WEE *is higher and louder. The last part sounds like an owl. The wings make a squeaking noise on takeoff.*

Above: Juveniles have a scaly appearance that is faint on adults.
Below: Some adults are colorful, as here; others are basically brown.

White-Winged Dove (12")

The well-named White-winged Dove is a fairly common resident of the Sonoran Desert. Most White-wings that we see in California winter in Mexico, come here to breed in April, and leave in September. Some remain year-round, but they are the exception.

White-winged Doves are often seen alone or in pairs and are found in a wide variety of desert habitats, from agricultural land to desert washes, deserts full of thorn bushes and cacti to suburban areas, and oases to streamside wooded areas. In California, they are not as common as Mourning Doves in their range.

Like other doves, White-wings are mostly seed eaters that also ingest grains of sand to help pulverize the seeds in their gizzards. Unlike Mourning Doves, they also eat berries and fruits, especially cactus fruits. White-winged Doves follow the crops—including some planted by humans—and settle where food is sufficient. Their foraging behavior is different from a Mourning Dove's—they peck slowly rather than quickly.

Voice is scratchy, hollow, hooting coos, often expressed as Who cooks for you? *On takeoff, their wings make a whopping sound.*

Below: Adult. Some, like this one, are more colorful than others.

Mick Thompson

Common Ground Dove (6.5")

The sparrow-sized, short-tailed Common Ground Dove is not common in California. Some are year-round residents of the Imperial Valley and the Colorado River Valley, where they are often seen in residential neighborhoods and farm yards. The population declines noticeably in winter, which likely means that many migrate south. Also, from late April to September they are found in San Timoteo Canyon just south of Redlands. Less often, in winter and early spring, they occasionally appear in orchards and washes in other areas of western Riverside County and eastern Orange County. Like other doves, they are usually in small flocks.

Common Ground Doves favor fallow fields with minimal brush, desert washes, and other arid habitats. They glean small seeds from grasses and weeds and, unlike most of our other doves, also eat insects and berries. Common Ground Doves build their nests on the ground or in low shrubs or trees.

When flushed, their wings flash rusty red and make a whistling sound.

Voice is nasal cooing, repeated several times or maybe for a long time. Sometimes the sound is hollow, at other times, more like who-up.

Below: A male. Note the red at the base of the bill. Females are duller and have a pink bill base. The degree of scaling varies with individual birds.

Inca Dove (8.5")

The scaly-looking, long-tailed Inca Doves are year-round residents of the Colorado River Valley. They are comfortable living with humans, generally favor suburban residential neighborhoods, and will be happy to come to your feeder.

Like Mourning Doves, they usually do not fly far if startled but settle down somewhere close by.

Voice: Call is a loud, mournful cooing that sounds like no hope*. A variation sounds like the same call mixed with the stammering clucking of a chicken. On takeoff, their wings make a dry rattling sound.*

Below: A male. Females are duller; juveniles are brownish and duller yet.

Eurasian Collared-Dove (12.5")

The Eurasian Collared-Dove is a native of Asia that has occupied much of Europe, and, since 1978, has spread across the United States. We first saw them in the open areas surrounding our neighborhood in Orange County around 2008. Since then they have displaced a significant part of the smaller Mourning Dove's population.

Eurasian Collared Doves have found a niche here in California: They stay at the fringes of human activity and avoid developed areas where Rock Pigeons are dominant. They also shun the wilder, hilly territory of the native Band-tailed Pigeons. Farm country has historically been the territory of the Mourning Dove, but that is now being challenged by the newcomers.

Like other doves, Eurasian Collared-Doves are usually in small flocks. They are basically year-round residents in semi-open areas with a few trees and often congregate in fields where weeds or tall grass has recently been mowed.

Voice: Their coo *is like a Mourning Dove that can't get it quite right; also a louder, raspy* hwaah, hwaah. *Their wing noise during takeoff is like that of a pigeon.*

Below: Adult in filaree.

Band-Tailed Pigeon (15")

A huge native pigeon the size of a crow, the Band-tailed Pigeon is found in flocks all over California in the lower elevations of mountainous areas, especially in the oaks. Northern birds migrate south in cold weather, some to Mexico.

Band-tails breed from the damp forests of the northwest to the dryer southern mountains and foothills and are usually seen roosting in the treetops. Flocks often gather at water seeps in the mountain areas.

Their diet is mostly acorns, which they swallow whole. When the acorns fail, Band-tails become nomadic and search out seeds, berries, and other wild fruits in season. Favorite berries include toyon, madrone, and elderberries. In drought years, these foods also may be in short supply and the birds resort to grain fields and vineyards.

Voice is a slow, deep, owl-like cooing that gets off to a stuttered start. Also, a raspy version of the same and a low, raspy, pig-like grunt. Wings make a loud slapping noise on takeoff.

Below: Adult. Juveniles are paler.

Rock Pigeon (aka **Rock Dove**) (12.5")

Originally natives of Europe and North Africa, Rock Pigeons, or Rock Doves, are abundant in cities all over the world. In California, they can be found anywhere near people except in the most extreme environments.

These pigeons were domesticated long ago and have been bred for color, size, and racing. The birds have excellent homing instincts and, if taken far away, will readily find their way home.

During the Great Depression, one of my uncles raised pigeons for racing and for food for the family. Better to be fast, I suppose.

The beauty of Rock Pigeons is offset by the fact that they are notorious disease carriers. At one time, these birds made their homes in cliffs; now most settle down in, on, or close to human dwellings. That can be problematic because inhaling the dust of their droppings can cause respiratory illness.

I should also note that it is almost impossible to remove the odor of pigeon droppings in or on a building where they have been allowed to roost.

Voice is a throaty cooing that is sometimes rapid like a chicken's voice and sometimes drawn out as if struggling to dislodge something from deep in the throat.

Quail

We have three species of quail in California. All are year-round residents, and there is some overlap in their ranges.

Quail live in groups, or coveys, commonly of 10 to 40 birds, and prefer walking or running to flying. If they do fly, it is for a very short distance.

All our quail live in thickets, but some forage in the open at times.

California Quail (10")

Our beautiful state bird, the California Quail, is abundant in the coastal half of the state and in the far north. They inhabit brush and grassland areas, especially near the oaks. They do not migrate but do follow the food supply.

California Quail are mainly seed eaters but also eat mites, beetles, caterpillars, and the like. They dance a cute little jig to uncover seeds and stir up dust mites, which they peck at with earnest.

Although they spend most of their lives in the underbrush, in the early morning and late afternoon, California Quail often forage in the open and post sentries to warn the covey of danger. In cooler weather, they commonly blow up big enough to look like a billiard ball (below).

Voice is a loud, monkey-like chi-CA-go, *often repeated a few times. At times, just the* CA. *Call is a soft* pik or pik-pik-pik. *Also, fussing noises.*

Below: Adult pair. Some are much brighter than others.

Above: Male and female on a Coast Live Oak.
Below: Female in the blackberries. Juveniles look like pale females.

Gambel's Quail (10.5")

The Gambel's Quail takes the place of the California Quail in the southern deserts. They inhabit the washes or arroyos and, like other quail, usually stay in or close to the brush. In agricultural areas, they are frequently seen near irrigation ditches.

Their diet is mostly plant material—tender leaves, seeds, and berries. Away from agricultural areas, they favor mesquite seeds.

Gambel's Quail are common, but like all desert creatures they stay in the shade during the heat of the day.

Voice is similar to the California Quail's but higher and clearer. The Gambel's pik *call is also similar to the California's but is definitely different. If you are familiar with California Quail and are in the desert, and you hear one that doesn't sound quite right, it's a Gambel's.*

Below: Adult pair.

Mountain Quail (11")

Year-round residents of mountain areas throughout the state, Mountain Quail migrate—on foot—to lower elevations during the winter. In the summer, they inhabit open coniferous forests and mixed woods with a thick understory up to about 9,000 feet. In the winter, they live in chaparral and scrubland. Unlike California Quail, they are rarely seen in grassland.

Although somewhat common and widespread, Mountain Quail prefer remote areas and usually stay under cover, so they are not seen as frequently as our other quail.

Through the seasons, Mountain Quail eat leaf buds, insects, berries, and acorns. Unlike our other quail, the sexes look similar.

Voice is unlike the California and Gambel's Quails. Call is a squeaky, chicken-like chirk *or* quirk *that is often interspersed with drawn-out squeaks that drop in pitch. The calls may also be buzzed or quavering. The spring males call a loud, squeaky* que-ar! *Calling males are hard to find.*

Below: Adult. Females are slightly duller; juveniles, mottled brown. The head plume sticks up when the bird is alerted, lies down when relaxed. The photo was taken at Oak Glen in the San Bernardino Mountains.

Grouse

Greater Sage-Grouse (male, 27"; female, 22")

A well-named bird of the Great Basin, the Greater Sage-Grouse is found in California on the east side of the Sierras and Cascades. They do not migrate but may go to lower elevations in winter. Sage-grouse are uncommon and highly localized in remote areas of flat sagebrush habitat that are not too far from water. They are frequently seen in and around Bodie State Park, north of Crowley Lake, and west of Bridgeport, all of which are in Mono County.

The early morning displays of the males in the spring are showy, to say the least. Several males come to an open arena (lek), puff up their chests, fan their tails like a turkey, and, using both voice and mechanical means, all but shout, "Hey, baby, look at me!" Sometimes they inflate two large, yellow balloon-like air sacs on their chests. The females observe from under cover, then come out to choose a mate, and the species continues.

The adults' diet is primarily sage leaves. Young birds eat mostly insects.

Voice, when flushed, is a chicken-like cackling. On the lek, stranger noises cannot be heard anywhere and include a hollow sound like a conga drum or like water dripping into a deep well complemented with assorted pops and whistles—all performed musically.

Below: In the foreground is an adult female; the other may be a juvenile.
Next page: Males, one displaying, the other just before or after; a lek.

Sooty Grouse (20")

Formerly classified with the Dusky and called a **Blue Grouse**, the Sooty is a year-round resident of high mountain coniferous forests in the far north, in the Sierras and Cascades, and at scattered localities in coastal forests as far south as Sonoma County. The Sooty's diet is primarily the needles of firs, supplemented in season with insects, flowers, and berries.

I was hiking in Mineral King once, on a trail that was carved into a steep slope. I stopped to rest, took off my pack, and looked out, and there, 15 feet in front of me, downslope of the trail, was a chicken sitting in a fir tree and staring at me. It was a female Sooty. She stayed put as we admired each other. Or, at least, as I admired her.

Sootys usually stay hidden but come out to open areas in the early morning and late afternoon. Good places to see them are in remote, often steep, areas of the Tahoe Basin and Sequoia National Park between 5,000 and 8,000 feet. They will be lower in winter, higher in summer. Listen for them in the spring.

Voice: In the spring, the male repeats a loud, deep, hollow thook, *often from high in a tree. The sound is like that made by blowing over the top of a bottle. The sound is hard to trace; if you hear him but can't find him, look up. The female has a nasal* kuk-kuk-kuk. *Sootys also bark, whinny, and scream.*

Top: Adult female. **Bottom:** Male display; female with tail fanned.

Ruffed Grouse (17")

In California, the Ruffed Grouse is found only in the humid forests of the far north. They will be in the ferns or close to them. Although forest dwellers, Ruffed Grouse need open space and favor areas of new growth, such as recently logged or burned areas. They are year-round residents where they occur. Their diet is mostly vegetable matter and includes fruits, buds, and leaves. Chicks, like all grouse chicks, eat insects.

A good place to look for Ruffed Grouse is in Redwood National Park, but they are not common there or anywhere else in the state. You have a decent chance of seeing them there in the early mornings or early evenings in the habitat described above. It may be helpful to check the local birding reports first; otherwise, find a sheltered place at the edge of a clearing on high ground that overlooks an open area and wait in the shadows. If Ruffed Grouse don't show up, other birds will and the time won't be wasted.

Voice: Ruffed Grouse are usually silent. However, the female will cluck like a hen and squeak or squeal on occasion. In the spring, the male beats his wings to make a very low, muffled drumming that can be felt as much as heard, like the bass turned up on a stereo. It starts slow and accelerates.

Below: Outstanding camouflage! Ruffed Grouse can be rusty colored, as in the photo, or gray but are usually rusty in California. Juveniles are brown.

The male's courtship display is similar to the Sooty's and consists of fanning his tail and ruffling his neck and shoulder feathers.

Wild Turkey (female, 37"; male, up to 46")

Wild Turkeys were introduced in California by the Fish and Game Department beginning in about 1900. At first, they were released in mountainous areas, including in Yosemite and Sequoia National Parks, and in the San Bernardino Mountains. These introductions were unsuccessful, and the birds died out. Later, they were introduced in the foothills around the Central Valley, and there they have done very well. Now they can be found in oak woodlands all over the state.

Turkeys are usually seen in tall grass or under oak trees scratching for grubs and acorns. What effect the introduction of wild turkeys has had on other species of birds and animals that live on acorns is largely unknown.

Some people who live where the turkeys do say that during the hunting seasons (basically April and November), these large birds vanish. The birds know when the season is over, however, and reappear in spacious residential neighborhoods again, foraging on lawns and under oaks as if nothing had happened.

Voice: The male makes the rapid-fire gobble, gobble *sound. Both sexes cackle when flying down from a roost. Alarm call is* pit! *Also a fussing* pit!

Below: Females are much smaller and less colorful, as at left. They also don't strut around with their tails fanned like the males do.

Ring-Necked Pheasant (female, 21" ; male, up to 33")

Beautiful imports from Asia, Ring-necked Pheasants were released as game birds in California in the late 1800s. They have adapted well here in grassy areas where grain is grown, especially in the Sacramento Valley and in the Klamath Basin. Ring-necked Pheasants are common all year at the Sacramento Wildlife Refuge near Willows and are seen less commonly at the Palo Alto Baylands. As with most birds, the best time to see them is in the early morning and late afternoon.

Voice sounds like a short version of a sick rooster crowing. Also, a sharp, two-syllable, static-like call.

Below: Male and female.

Cuckoos and Roadrunners

Yellow-Billed Cuckoo (12")

Although fairly common in some parts of the southeastern United States during the breeding season, Yellow-billed Cuckoos are scarce in California. They have been sighted irregularly in many places all over the state, always near water, and usually in the cottonwoods. A small number regularly breed along the Colorado River in dense groves of cottonwoods and willows. They winter in South America.

Cuckoos are as shy as they are beautiful and prefer to sit motionless in the middle of the tree so you can't see them. And for such a big bird they do a good job of it. Actually, they are waiting for a caterpillar, their preferred food, to move and give away its location.

Good places to look for Yellow-billed Cuckoos in California between May and July are at the Palo Verde Ecological Reserve, which is along the Colorado River near Blythe, and at the Kern River Preserve, east of Bakersfield.

Voice is expressed in a wide array of unique hollow wooden or nasal sounds. Yellow-bills chatter like a squirrel, cackle like a hen, and coo like a pigeon but all with hollow, wooden or nasal overtones. The male's song is a knocking/clucking that starts slow and becomes slower— something like ka, ka, ka, ka, kow kow kow, kalup. Parts of this sequence also serve as calls. The bottom line: if you're in the cottonwoods in season and hear strange noises, investigate.

Greg Lavaty

Greater Roadrunner (23")

Roadrunners inhabit the dry scrubland and deserts of Southern California and, less commonly, the dry, short-grass areas around the Central Valley.

The diet of the roadrunner consists of mice, lizards, bugs, and snakes, including rattlesnakes, which they swallow whole. Like other birds that swallow their prey whole, roadrunners will often smack their catch on the ground repeatedly to make it more pliable and easier to swallow.

Roadrunners are well named—they can run fast when in the open. They fly but only for short distances. When alarmed, their crest is raised, and if really excited or threatened, a red patch shows in back of the blue patch behind the eye.

Voice: The male's cooing is similar to that of a Mourning Dove but lower in pitch and without the wheezing introduction. The females sound like a bad human imitation of a baboon. Both make clacking sounds.

Below: I think all of us who have watched a roadrunner for some time would agree that their expressions and gestures made them quite deserving of a cartoon.

Additional photo is on page 496.

Crows, Jays, and Allies

Unless otherwise noted, the sexes of these birds look alike.

American Crow (17.5")

Crows are highly social. They place their nests in trees near other nesting crows, and the older offspring help raise the new young ones. In colder weather, crows form large flocks—sometimes numbering several hundred or more—and fly together to a common roosting site for warmth. On the way, they first stop somewhere nearby to talk about the day. In the morning, they commute to work much the way we do. In suburban areas, the crows' commute is often to the local landfill.

Other than in extreme habitats, crows are found all over the state. They are mobile and follow the food supply—usually grain, grubs and garbage.

Crows are nest robbers and eat the eggs and young of songbirds. When the crow population grows, the songbird population declines. In our neighborhood, we had no crows until about 1985; then they came, their population exploded, and the songbirds almost disappeared. The West Nile virus outbreak, in about 2002, affected crows as well as people and thinned the crow population significantly. As a consequence, the songbird population recovered. This is one of many examples I have seen of the fluid nature of bird populations.

Crows do not like Red-tailed Hawks (or any other birds for that matter) and will drive the Red-tails out of their area by tag-teaming them and preventing them from landing. (See page 202.)

Voice, most commonly, is a raspy caw! caw! *at varying pitches. Crows also utter a wide variety of other calls and sounds, including clicking noises, a call that sounds like snoring, and irritated, fussing noises.*

Common Raven (24")

Ravens look like crows but are much larger, thicker billed, and have a lion-like mane. They are usually seen alone, in pairs, or in small groups.

A highly intelligent bird, the Common Raven is a scavenger and predator and can survive almost anywhere. They are seen all over the state where open space is adequate and are easily identified by their voice and by the loud whoosh of their wingbeats.

Since a large crow can be the size of a small raven, the two can be difficult to tell apart at a distance. However, if you watch them in flight, you'll notice the raven is more powerful and acrobatic and often soars like a hawk. Also, a raven's tail is wedge-shaped in flight; a crow's, softly curved.

Ravens and crows don't get along very well. Both are thieves and robbers and don't want the other working their territory. In that regard, they are interesting to watch. When the crows are gone, or when there are few of them, the ravens are at home in our neighborhood. When a large number of crows arrive, they drive the ravens out. Interestingly, the crows allow the ravens the strips of land where the electrical transmission lines are and also the stretch of land along the railroad tracks.

Voice is usually a baritone croaking of kraaaw *at one of two pitches. Other calls include sounds like a hollow knocking, clicking, popping, and snoring. The snoring is lower in pitch than that of a crow. Young ravens, like young crows, are higher pitched.*

Yellow-Billed Magpie (17")

Strictly a California bird, the beautiful Yellow-billed Magpie lives in the oak savannah areas in the center of the state, from just inland of Santa Barbara in the south to Redding in the north.

Yellow-billed Magpies are colony dwellers and nest in groves of tall trees. The nest is placed high in a tree, usually an oak, and usually on top of a clump of mistletoe. It is constructed of sticks and fine plant materials, sometimes cemented with mud, and is nearly as large as any birds' nest.

Magpies will eat *anything* but dine mostly on insects, acorns, grain, and fruits in their seasons. They will forage in the open but stay close to trees and flee for cover in them if they are made uneasy. Like the other members of the corvid family, which includes jays and crows, given the opportunity, they steal food from other birds and animals.

Corvids were susceptible to the West Nile Virus that hit California in the early 2000s, and like the crows, the Yellow-billed Magpies took a big hit. Before that time they were much more common. Scrub jays were not affected very much and have increased in the Yellow-bills' habitat.

Voice is loud, scratchy squawking that includes at least two versions of shek-shek-shek. *Also,* whek!, *a whistle, and other cartoon-like noises.*

Below: These birds are a lesson in iridescence. They look black and white when in the shadows, but their colors come to life in the sunlight.

Jerry Ting

Black-Billed Magpie (19")

A common bird of the Great Basin, the Black-billed Magpie is nearly identical to its yellow-billed cousin and its habits are similar. Diet is also similar to the Yellow-billed Magpie's, but wild fruits and berries take the place of the Yellow-billed's grains and acorns.

In California, Black-billed Magpies live year-round in the sagebrush and grassland east of the Sierras and Cascades. They nest in trees along streams. Although they require a lot of space, magpies are not fearful of humans and human development as long as they see an easy opportunity to get food. They are not afraid of mobbing any predator and stealing its kill.

Voice includes scratchy squawking like that of the Yellow-billed Magpie and an up-slurred, nasal wock? weck? *and* weer? Also, whispering sounds.

Below: The sexes of magpies look alike; juveniles look like adults.

Jeff Bleam

Jeff Bleam

Jays

Steller's Jay (11.5")

A common bird in our coniferous forests, the Steller's Jay is seldom found elsewhere.

Steller's Jays own all the picnic tables in the forested areas of California and are not shy about demanding use tax. They can swoop down from a tree quietly and with great speed, and if you are not watchful, you will lose that little bag of Cheetos or bunch of grapes.

When not stealing your lunch, Steller's Jays feed on insects and acorns and bury the latter for retrieval during the winter. They are aware of their surroundings and have excellent memories for finding acorns they have stashed. Steller's Jays also raid the caches of other birds and animals and round out their diet with the eggs and young of other birds.

Steller's Jays are social among their own kind but don't think much of their cousins, the scrub jays, and will run them off if they come into their territory.

Voice is expressed in loud, nonmusical, usually scratchy, nasal tones— commonly a scolding sheck, *a chatter of* shack-shack-shack-shack, *and a faster, higher, smoother* shook-shook-shook. *Also, a variety of other calls, some guttural, some soft, and some mimic other birds or noises.*

California Scrub Jay (aka **Western Scrub Jay**) (11.25")

The well-named California Scrub Jays like to stay in scrub habitat and in widely spaced oaks. They venture right to the edge of the pine forests but don't go in very far, so there is little overlap in habitat with the Steller's Jay.

Scrub jay's and Steller's Jays have nearly identical habits and diet, but scrub jays are bolder in advising all other birds that they are trespassing. Both are abundant in their habitat throughout the state.

Voices include a raspy greeet, *often repeated with pauses; a similar but less-raspy* cheer, cheer, cheer *with shorter pauses; and* sheck, *similar to a Steller's Jay. Sometimes, softer, starling-like chatter. Scrub jays also make a loud whooshing sound with their wings on strafing flights when they approach from behind and fly close to anyone they think has infringed on their personal space.*

Below: Adult on a juniper tree. Note the berries, which are highly resinous and a staple food of many birds in the fall.

Pinyon Jay (11")

A bird of the Great Basin, the Pinyon Jay is found along the eastern border of California, in the Mojave Desert, and, to a lesser degree, in the San Jacinto and San Bernardino Mountains.

Pinyon Jays are nomadic and travel in noisy flocks. They prefer pinyon-juniper forests, where they feast on pinyon nuts and juniper berries. When those foods are scarce, Pinyon Jays venture into open ponderosa pine forests, oak scrub, and desert chaparral and sagebrush. Like other jays, they store seeds and easily retrieve them later. In late winter and early spring, they feed on yucca blossoms in the deserts.

Pinyon Jays can usually be found at Black Rock Canyon in Joshua Tree National Park in the late winter and in the forested areas southeast of Mono Lake in the summer. They are noisy, so if present are easy to find.

Voice: Common calls are higher, nasal versions of a crow's, caw, caw, caw. Another is a rapid, three-syllable nasal squeaking that goes down, then halfway back up in pitch. Also, quavering chatter and chucking sounds.

Top: Winter birds are mostly gray, like this one on a Joshua tree. **Bottom:** Summer birds are blue, like this one on a pinyon pine.

Gray Jay (aka **Canada Jay**) (11.5")

Gray Jays can be found in the far north of the state, which is the southern limit of their range. They are not common in California but are seen with some regularity year-round along the coast and, from May to October, inland in the Lower Klamath area near the Oregon border. Gray Jays are usually found where spruce trees are abundant and seldom found where they are not present. Like other jays, they are not shy in the least.

These birds travel in small groups and are often seen in picnic areas where they can be rather bold. Their diet is largely insects, berries, and seeds, but they will eat just about anything, including fungi, carrion, and junk food.

Although Gray Jays are mobile folk, you have a reasonable chance of seeing them at Van Damme State Park, near Mendocino, and at state parks along the coast from Patrick's Point to the Oregon border.

Voice: Gray Jays are often surprisingly quiet, even when in small groups, and frequently sing in a squeaky whisper. They have a large number of louder calls, including clear whistles and harsh chatter and an odd squeaking that changes pitch, perhaps weeoo *and* weeoo-ah. *Gray Jays also mimic the voices of many birds, including those of the hawks and owls that prey on them.*

Below: Adult. Juveniles are gray all over, like they've been dipped in soot.

Clark's Nutcracker (12")

Clark's Nutcrackers inhabit the dry pine forests of the high mountains up to the tree line from Sequoia National Park and northward. Some are also found in the high mountains in the south. In the winter, they may go down to slightly lower elevations.

Nutcrackers typically forage in pairs or in small groups and are often found by their calling to one another. Their presence is also announced by their distinctive loud wingbeats, which are similar to a raven's but higher in pitch.

A good place to find Clark's Nutcrackers is at Tioga Pass or at many other passes over the Sierras for that matter. Although much less common in the southern mountain ranges, I have seen them on Mount Pinos and heard them near Big Bear Lake in the fall and winter.

Voice: A common call sounds like a high-pitched crow with a narrow nasal passage. Another call is the same note but scratchy. They also make clicking noises similar to a crow's but higher in pitch.

Below: The Clark's Nutcracker's menacing large bill is for tearing pine cones open to extract pine nuts, which they store in surprising quantity in a pouch under their tongue. Nutcrackers bury a large number of pine nuts for the winter and, in the process, plant innumerable trees. When the cone crop fails, they will eat just about anything.

Jerry Ting

Great-Tailed Grackle (male 18"; female 15")

A nomadic resident of the southern two-thirds of the state, the Great-tailed Grackle travels in flocks, struts like a rooster, and sounds like the introduction to a kiddie cartoon show.

Grackles follow wherever people go and like fast food, so they frequent the corresponding food courts and parking lots. In more natural settings, they prefer to be near water and are often found in marshes and flooded fields. In summer, grackles are primarily meat eaters and will eat anything that moves. In winter, they often join blackbirds and cowbirds to feed on grain at feedlots, dairies, and grain fields.

Great-tailed Grackles were rarely seen in California before the 1960s. They are now common and their range is expanding northward.

Voice is like none other and consists of a wide variety of often scolding and cartoon-like whistles, clucks, clacks, peeps, squeaks, pipings, and rusty-gate-hinge noises that are often strung together into what, with some imagination, could be called a song. Their whistles can be piercingly loud. Once heard, never forgotten.

Left: Male. **Right:** Female on bulrushes.

Hummingbirds

Hummingbirds have been called jewels of the air for millennia and rightly so. The play of light on the feathers, especially on the male's head and gorget—the vividly colored throat patch—is quite complex and has been explained in many ways. The more you study this mystery, the more it defies explanation. As with everything else in the creation, for the serious student, every mystery that seems to be solved eventually proves to be even more mysterious.

***

One winter day, I was out walking at first light, long before sunrise, and spotted a hummingbird perched on a short, leafless tree in front of me. I was facing east, and the dawn was just beginning to break behind the bird, making a nice silhouette. I took out my pocket camera, snapped a picture (the shutter closing very slowly), and put it back in my pocket. The bird then turned around and saw me, and his gorget glowed full and bright. The sun was not to rise for another half hour or more, and he was facing away from the dim morning light. I have searched this out carefully but have not found an explanation for how he glowed like that in such limited light. (My photo of that bird is on page 498.)

***

The hummingbird's diet consists of insects and nectar from flowers. They pick aphids off plants and often catch gnats and other insects in midair.

Male hummingbirds are highly territorial and protect their flower sources with ferocity. They often perch in a tree to watch over their flowers.

Female hummingbirds lack the bright gorget of the males, and some are difficult to identify in the field if not seen from the front or side.

Jeff Bleam

This wonderfully camouflaged nest is an engineering marvel. It is constructed of willow down for warmth and comfort, and of spider webs to allow it to expand for the growing chicks. The chicks are fed insects while in the nest and for a few more weeks after they fledge. Later, they learn to sip nectar from flowers. This nest was located only 10 feet from a heavily used path, but almost no one saw it.

Anna's Hummingbird (4")

Anna's Hummingbirds are abundant throughout California except in the Death Valley area. Some are year-round residents where they are found, but those found in harsher environments move to more hospitable ones seasonally.

The male Anna's has a spectacular way of showing off his stuff to attract a female. He calls to her, then flies high, hovers, and descends toward her at breakneck speed. He then flips his tail feathers to stop the dive and produce a loud pop, and levels off into a tight arc right in front of her. He then goes up to repeat the maneuver in precisely the same air space and may continue the show for several passes.

Voice is often a squeaky buzzing, part of which sounds like tuning in an old radio but at high speed. They also utter sharp chip *notes, sometimes stringing them together like Morse code.*

Below: Females. Note the throat patch varies. The Anna's back is usually green but can be golden or turquoise. Two birds are on Cleveland Sage.

Next page, top two rows: Males. **Middle, right:** Juvenile male.

Special Interest Note:
The mechanics involved in a hummingbird's ability to fly backwards out of a flower are an aeronautical engineer's dream. Watch the sequence of tail and wing angle adjustments closely, and marvel.

Below: An Allen's Hummingbird backing out of a flower.

Allen's Hummingbird (3.75")

The Allen's Hummingbird breeds in a narrow strip along the coast as far north as the Oregon border but not much farther. Most winter in central Mexico and during migration can be seen across the western half of the state. They arrive in February and almost all are gone by late August, at which time some migrate through the mountains.

Allen's Hummingbirds are the most common hummingbird along the coast in season and are usually indistinguishable from a Rufous in the field.

The male's display is similar to that of an Anna's Hummingbird, but before ascending to make his dive, the Allen's flies a series of shallow arcs in front of the female as if swinging from a pendulum. He then makes his ascent and descent similar to an Anna's. Unlike the Anna's, the Allen's typically does not repeat the performance.

Voice: Call is a sharp chip! *Also, a buzzy* zeeee-chuppity-chuppity *and* chorpel-chorpel. *During his courtship display, the male makes many noises with his wing and tail feathers, including a buzzing noise that sounds like a horsefly. While making his descent, the male makes a low wound-out motor-like noise, followed by* rat-a-tat-tat *machine gun-like bursts and a grating scream, caused by the tail feathers, at the bottom of his dive.*

Below: Female or immature male on Mulefat.

Above: Males with lights on, lights off.

Rufous Hummingbird (3.75")

Rufous Hummingbirds look just like Allen's, but the life cycles of the two species are different. The Rufous breeds from Oregon to Alaska and winters in southwestern Mexico. They are seen mostly along the coast during the spring migration, which peaks in March, about a month after Allen's. In the late summer, most travel south through the mountains.

Voicings are similar to Allen's. Calls are chup! *and a short buzzy warble like Allen's. During courtship display, the male's sounds produced by the feathers are also similar to Allen's: a buzz like a horsefly, a high-pitched jackhammer-like sound, and a high-pitched grating squeal.*

Below: Although all but indistinguishable from the Allen's, these photos were taken far from the Allen's range, so they are Rufous Hummingbirds. The top bird's **back is redder and browner** than an Allen's, but most appear no different. The bird at lower left is a female.

Rob English

Rob English

Jeff Bleam

Costa's Hummingbird (3.5")

Costa's Hummingbirds prefer an arid environment and are common in and around Palm Springs all year. They are also found in the Coachella and Colorado River Valleys, the Mojave, and less commonly in canyon areas a little inland from the coast, mostly south of Point Conception. Many that we see during breeding season spend the winter in Mexico.

The purple throat patch (gorget) of the male that extends to the sides like a long mustache is the main identifier of the male Costa's Hummingbird. The female looks similar to an Anna's but is smaller and much whiter in front.

Voice: Calls are tic *and* tic-it, *at times repeated like Morse code. Also, a similar twittering buzz. During courtship display, males make a soft, very high-pitched, buzzing whistle with their feathers as they fly by.*

Below: Female on a creosote bush, male on a penstemon.

Mick Thompson

Black-Chinned Hummingbird (3.75")

Black-chinned Hummingbirds prefer semi-arid habitat. They breed in ravines and canyons west of the Central Valley and in the southern coastal ranges, especially in oak and sycamore woodlands. In the Owens Valley they breed in the willows. Black-chins winter along the west coast of Mexico and during spring migration can be seen briefly in the deserts. They are in California from late March to late September and are not nearly as common as Anna's or Allen's Hummingbirds.

To identify a male Black-chinned, **look for black, purple, white**: a black chin under the eye and bill; below that, a narrow purple patch (that often looks black); and below that, a white collar. A male Anna's may have a black chin, but the gorget shape is different. A female Anna's can look similar to an immature male Black-chin; the Anna's has a purple throat patch, the Black-chin, purple spots. The Black-chin's bill is longer.

Voice: Call is chip. *Also, somewhat musical chipping and chirping. The male's display is accompanied by a rhythmic, pump-like buzzing noise made by the wing and tail feathers.*

Top, and bottom left: Males. **Bottom right:** Female.

Calliope Hummingbird (3.25")

Our smallest hummer, the Calliope, is a bird of the mountains. It breeds in the far north of the state and in the Cascades and Sierras and winters in southwestern Mexico. They can be seen briefly in the lowlands and foothills during the spring migration, typically in April. The males leave in July, the females with the young by early September. Both gather into large flocks before leaving. Look for them in aspen groves, meadow edges, and ravines between 5,000 and 9,000 feet. A good place to find them from May to early July is in Lundy Canyon, near Mono Lake.

The purple or deep-pink gorget of the male Calliope is streamered with white and unlike that of any of our other hummingbirds. Female and juvenile male Calliopes can be confused with a juvenile Anna's, but the Calliope has a peachy wash across the front.

Voice: Calls are tisp, chik, *and buzzy, squeaky chittering. During displays, males make a high-pitched zinging sound, which is accompanied by a bumblebee-like sound. Both sounds are made by their wing feathers.*

Below: Male on Pride of Madeira, a hummingbird favorite; female.

Woodpeckers and Sapsuckers

Woodpeckers

Woodpeckers excavate their homes in tree trunks or branches using their tail as a brace as they chisel away at the wood. Most woodpeckers hollow out a new home every year and abandon last year's model, and that habit provides housing for other cavity dwellers.

Other than the Acorn Woodpecker, all California species are primarily insect eaters. And except for some Lewis's, all our woodpeckers are year-round residents where they occur, although some travel short distances to lower elevations during cold weather.

Woodpeckers can be identified by the sound of their hammering on a tree because each species has a unique pattern. Sometimes, when we hear a woodpecker hammering, the sound resonates more than usual. In that case, they are likely "drumming" to communicate with other woodpeckers. For this purpose, they often select a loose piece of wood to amplify the sound. If you listen, you will often hear another bird answering.

Acorn Woodpecker (9")

The clown-faced Acorn Woodpeckers are found wherever oaks are abundant. Their diet is largely acorns, which they store in granary trees, as in the **top photo** on the next page. If the acorn crop fails—and in drought years it may—the birds eat insects, which they often catch on the wing, flycatcher-style. In years when acorns are scarce, the Acorn Woodpeckers may not reproduce. This life-preserving reaction to food or water scarcity is common for both plants and animals.

Unlike our other woodpeckers, Acorn Woodpeckers are colony dwellers with several adult birds often sharing the same dwelling and child-rearing responsibilities. While photographing the birds in the **middle photo**, I saw no less than four adults fly into the tree hole.

The female's red hat is separated from her white forehead by a black band. The males lack the black band. ***Juveniles look like adults*** but are smaller.

The hammering of an Acorn Woodpecker is purposeful and often with many stops and starts. For example, after placing an acorn in a hole at the granary tree, securing it in place is delicate work. Their flight pattern is also interesting. It often consists of one or two very rapid, strong wingbeats followed by a long torpedo-like glide (**bottom photo**).

Voice is commonly a cartoon-like squawking of weka-weka-weka *(or* jeka) *that increases in tempo. Another voice is a raspy* kazoonta, *often repeated with short pauses. When a few get going, the symphony can be quite humorous. Additionally, they utter a smooth but loud* ear *or* eh.

Downy Woodpecker (6.5")

The common, sparrow-sized Downy Woodpecker lives year-round north of Point Conception in the lower elevations where trees are plentiful and adjoin open space. A relative few live farther south, mostly close to the coast. Downys are generally replaced by Nuttall's Woodpeckers in the south and by Hairy Woodpeckers in the Sierras, Cascades, and high southern mountains.

Downys forage for insect larvae this way: tap, tap; listen. No movement heard? Try close by. If movement is heard, drill like crazy and get 'em.

Voice is a sharp, **squeaky** *tweek, sometimes followed by a nine-syllable descending whinny that is slower than the Nuttall's (page 283).*

Drumming is rapid but countable; it is about nine hammers per phrase and noticeably slower than the larger, similar-looking Hairy Woodpecker's.

Below, left: Adult male. **Right:** Female. Coastal females, like this one, usually have a buff wash on the breast and belly; ***inland birds are whiter***. All Downys have a **white patch on the back**. Juveniles are grayish. A juvenile male's red cap is forward, in back of the bill.

Hairy Woodpecker (9")

The Hairy Woodpecker is a large version of a Downy with a longer bill and a different voice. They are forest and woodland dwellers and are common in the mountains throughout the state. The name refers to the white hair-like feathers on the bird's back.

I watched the mother **in the photo below** for about 20 minutes while she was teaching her youngster how to forage. The mother was pecking around and finding food (probably insect larvae or eggs). The youngster was pecking around too, but obviously had no idea what she was doing and was not finding anything. So Mom would turn around and feed her something every few minutes—an incredibly tender scene.

Voice is a sharp, high-pitched tweek *with pauses or as a staccato.*

Drumming is too fast to count and is longer than the Downy's.

Below: Inland females. Coastal females have a buff wash on the breast and belly like the Downy on page 281. **Inset:** Juvenile male. The adult male's red cap is like that of the Downy on the previous page.

Jerry Ting

Nuttall's Woodpecker (7.5")

Nearly endemic to California, and one of our most common woodpeckers, Nuttall's are birds of the oak woodlands. They are also common in areas of alder and willow and are at home in our parks and residential neighborhoods with mature trees. Nuttall's are all but absent along the far north coast and are uncommon in the Sierras above 6,000 feet.

Typical voice is two high-pitched, **sharp** *chip notes; a pause; then three more identical notes followed by a staccato; all are at the same pitch. The staccato is faster than the Downy's. At times, a segment of these.*

Drumming is steady and noticeably faster and longer than the Downy's.

Top: Male. **Bottom:** Female. Note the horizontal stripes on the back.

Ladder-Backed Woodpecker (7.25")

The well-named Ladder-backed Woodpecker takes the place of the Nuttall's in the deserts. The two species look almost identical but the Ladder-backed's bill appears longer, and the red cap of the adult male extends to the eye. The juvenile male's cap is centered on top of the head for both species. Some males and females of both species have a buff wash on their breast and belly.

Ladder-backs inhabit the riparian wooded areas in the deserts as well as arid brushland. Desert areas with yucca, agave, and Joshua trees usually host Ladder-backs as well.

Voice differs from Nuttall's. Call is cheep, *often followed by an 8- to 10-note high-pitched staccato that fades at the end. The* cheep *call and staccato are* **squeaky**, *not sharp like the Nuttall's, and the staccato is slower.*

Drumming is very rapid and shorter than the Nuttall's.

Left: Male on a willow tree. **Right:** Female on a cottonwood.

Gila Woodpecker (9.25")

A desert species, Gila Woodpeckers drill their nest holes in Saguaro cacti in the deserts of Arizona and Mexico. In California, they inhabit only the southeastern corner of the state, where they are somewhat uncommon but are found in riparian woodlands and in the towns of Imperial County. The pair below was at Cattle Call Park in Brawley.

Voice is a high-pitched, quavering, squeaky staccato of about five syllables, often repeated. Also a squeaky, gull-like barking, usually of five barks.

Drumming is an evenly spaced rolling of about seven strikes that lasts about a second and is followed by a slightly delayed strike.

Below: Pair. The female lacks the red cap.

Lewis's Woodpecker (10.5")

A more showy bird you may never see in California. The iridescent colors of a Lewis's Woodpecker sparkling in the sunlight are dazzling.

Lewis's Woodpeckers are highly mobile folk that inhabit sparse, dry pine-oak woodlands with abundant grassland, as well as burned or logged areas, but are not found in the same locations every year. Some live all year in northeastern California and in the Sierras, others move down into valley orchards or towns or into the southern part of the state for the winter. Most are short-distance migrants. They are not as common as most of our other woodpeckers. **The bird below** was at Lake Hemet in March.

The habits of Lewis's Woodpeckers are as different from those of other woodpeckers' as is their appearance. They seldom probe for insects like other woodpeckers but instead catch flying insects in midair like a flycatcher. When they do probe, they do so very slowly. Lewis's chop up acorns and store the pieces, as well as pine nuts, in tree-bark crevices. Flight is direct, like a crow's, not undulating.

Voice: Unlike most woodpeckers, Lewis's are usually quiet. Call is a sparrow-like chur *or* chip. *They also have a squeaky chatter and a buzzed, high-pitched alarm scream reminiscent of a Red-tailed Hawk.*

Drumming: First, a single soft strike, as if setting a nail, then an evenly spaced rolling that is softer and more like that of a sapsucker.

Below: Adult; the sexes look alike. Juvenile is muddy and lacks the colors.

White-Headed Woodpecker (9.25")

White-headed Woodpeckers are year-round residents of the mixed forests of the Cascades, Sierras, Trinity Alps, and the high mountains of Southern California. They are fairly common where oaks mingle with pines in these areas.

Like several other woodpecker species, when selecting a new homesite, a White-headed often chooses a place where a branch has broken off and decay has softened the wood. Easier work.

Voice: Three very rapid, squeaky, high-pitched notes at close to the same pitch, perhaps pee-ta-tic. *The call is often repeated and is occasionally followed by a long roll at the same pitch. Also, squeaky, monkey-like chatter.*

Drumming is like a jackhammer in bursts of nearly two seconds.

Below: Adult male. The female lacks the red skullcap. **Juveniles** of both sexes have a red cap like the adult male, but it is centered on the head much like that of the Hairy Woodpecker shown on page 282.

Pileated Woodpecker (17")

The size of a crow, the Pileated Woodpecker is by far the largest woodpecker in California. It is a forest dweller—from the coastal redwoods to the Sierras and Cascades—and specializes in carpenter ants. These large, black ants require rotting wood, so this uncommon woodpecker is usually found where the forest has not been groomed.

Pileated Woodpeckers drill holes in (usually dead) trees for their homes, but theirs are oval or rectangular, not round like those of our other woodpeckers.

These magnificent birds are widespread throughout the state and are often heard before they are seen. Calaveras Big Trees State Park, off Highway 4, is a good place to find them, as is McArthur Burney-Falls State Park, northeast of Redding. Less commonly, they can be found in the less crowded and ungroomed areas of Yosemite National Park, between 4,000 and 8,000 feet. I have seen them in Wawona Meadow and others have at Bridal Veil Campground in recent years.

Voice is loud, nasal barking that varies and often lasts a second or more. Perhaps hank-hank-hank, kek-kek-kek, *and* wuk-wuk-wuk. *Rhythm and inflection also vary. Overall, similar to a flicker but lower.*

Drumming is deeper, a little longer and slower, and unmistakable, as only a large bird could make that sound.

Below: A female with her boys. The red crop of the male extends to the bill; the female's stops behind the eye. The photo was taken at Los Gatos.

Black-Backed Woodpecker (9.5")

These woodpeckers are found in coniferous forests from the central Sierras to the Oregon Border, usually above 6,000 feet. They prefer burn areas—the more recent the better—where they aggressively strip bark from trees for their preferred meal, the larvae of wood-boring beetles. As a forest heals over several years, the beetles become scarcer, and the Black-backed Woodpeckers move on. If burn areas are scarce, they go to places of beetle infestation, which are easy to locate because a lot of trees are dead or dying.

Black-backed Woodpeckers are uncommon but are not that difficult to find if you follow the above.

Voice is a sharp, squeaky chirt, chet, *or* kik, *at times as chatter or as a short, descending whinny.*

Drumming is like a jackhammer, lasts nearly two seconds, and is similar to a White-headed's. Like other woodpeckers, they also peck slowly.

Below: Adult male. Female lacks the yellow cap; juvenile's bill is short.

Tom Benson

Special Interest Note:

In the introduction to woodpeckers I mentioned that woodpeckers can be identified by the sound of their hammering. Here is a case in point. I heard the staccato hammering of what I thought was a woodpecker, but it didn't sound right so I went over to investigate. Eventually I found this **Oak Titmouse** that was hammering on an acorn trying to crack the shell. Steller's Jays do the same thing.

Sapsuckers

Like humans who collect maple sap, sapsuckers drill holes in tree trunks that serve as sap wells and return later to feed on the sap that collects in the wells. Sapsuckers drill holes either singly or in horizontal rows, making use of many species of trees. I have seen sapsucker holes in alder, birch, pine, fir, spruce, oak, sycamore, cottonwood, willows, apple, and eucalyptus trees. The sap of some individual trees is preferred over that of others.

Sapsuckers are often located by the sound of their softer tapping on a tree, which is unlike the usual hammering of our woodpeckers.

Top left: This sycamore at Big Sur was drilled from top to bottom, but the sycamores next to it were untouched. The holes toward the bottom of the tree (shown) are mostly healed over but the scars remain. **Top right:** A lodgepole pine at Bluff Lake. **Bottom:** An acacia at Santa Cruz.

Red-Breasted Sapsucker (8.5")

California's most common sapsucker, the Red-breasted, breeds in coniferous and mixed forests throughout California. Many birds that breed in the Cascades and Sierras spend the winter at lower elevations in riparian woodlands, city and county parks, and in orchards. These winter birds are usually nomadic. Along the north coast and in the southern mountains, some are year-round residents.

The long white shoulder patch on the wing, which can be entirely or partly covered, is an identifying feature of California sapsuckers.

Voice: Red-breasted Sapsuckers are seldom heard. Their voice is a one-syllable cry, perhaps waah. *Also, a high-pitched, gull-like squawking.*

Drumming consists of soft, short, rapid, uneven bursts.

Top: Adults. **Bottom:** A juvenile and an adult in Arroyo Willows.

Jerry Ting

Red-Naped Sapsucker (8.5")

Red-naped Sapsuckers breed in the Great Basin and in the Rockies and usually winter in Mexico. They are relatively uncommon in California but many breed east of the Cascades and some as far south as Death Valley. A relative few winter in California, especially along the Colorado River. From fall to spring, Red-naped Sapsuckers are scarce but regular visitors in a wide variety of habitats south and east of Los Angeles.

These beautiful birds inhabit ponderosa pine forests, aspen groves, and riparian woodlands. They are usually seen singly or in pairs.

The Red-naped and Red-breasted were formerly considered subspecies of the **Yellow-bellied Sapsucker**. Hybrids of Red-breasted and Red-naped are not uncommon. The one **pictured below is a hybrid.**

Voice is seldom heard but similar to a Red-breasted Sapsucker's.

Drumming is also like the Red-breasted's.

Below: A hybrid.

A female. Note the white patch under her chin. Males lack the white patch. Juveniles are duller overall.

Williamson's Sapsucker (9")

The uncommon Williamson's Sapsuckers nest in the lodgepole pine forests of the Sierras, Cascades, and San Bernardino Mountains. Elevation will be about 6,000 to 8000 feet. In the winter, they move down to the lower pine forests. They are summer residents at Bluff Lake, in the south, and at Donner Lake, in the north.

The Williamson's foraging pattern is similar to that of a creeper: they start low in a tree and work up, then fly to the next tree and do the same.

Unlike our other woodpeckers and sapsuckers, the male and female Williamson's Sapsuckers are very different in appearance.

Voice is a scratchy, hawk-like scream, cry-ah. *They are not often heard.*

Drumming often differs considerably from a woodpecker's. It can consist of short, extremely rapid strikes. At times, a pause, then shorter bursts with accents. At other times, more like a woodpecker.

Left: Adult male. Young males lack the red patch under the bill. **Right:** Female. Both sexes can have a yellow or white belly.

Jeff Bleam

Jeff Bleam

Northern Flicker, Red-Shafted Subspecies (12.5")

Flickers are common throughout California wherever mature trees are plentiful and adjoin open space. They are so named because they use their long, pointed bills to pry bark loose and flick it aside to find insects, larvae, and eggs. They also feed on the ground.

The bright orange on the wings is hidden most of the time, but if you see a large orange bird fly through a forested area, it's a flicker.

Voice: Flickers have a large vocabulary. A common call is a high-pitched keer! *that drops. It is similar to a Red-tailed Hawk's but is not as harsh. Also common is a nasal, rapid rant of* wek-wek-wek-wek *that is reminiscent of a Steller's Jay. Also, squeaky chatter that can vary greatly.*

Drumming is surprisingly rapid for such a large bird, is evenly spaced, and lasts about a second.

Top: A male. Females lack the red lipstick; juveniles look pale.

Jack and Petra Clayton

Jeff Bleam

Swallows and Swifts

Swallows

The great majority of swallows we see in California spend the winter in Central or South America and come here in the spring to breed. Most live in colonies.

Spring migration for some species is spectacular, with hundreds or thousands arriving at the same time. Fall migration is different, with fewer numbers spread out over a longer time period.

The most graceful of fliers, swallows forage for flying insects above bodies of water or open wet areas. At times, they are at the surface; at other times, they can be a hundred feet or more overhead. They catch their prey on the wing and seem to be—but are not—tireless fliers.

Swallows often pass food to their fledglings in the air. They typically perch on bare branches, not on leafy ones.

The sexes look different for some species but are similar for others.

Tree Swallow (5.75")

Some Tree Swallows are found all year in the western half of the state between Point Reyes and Santa Monica but most winter in Mexico and come to California, or north of the state, to breed. Like all swallows, they are always near water.

In Orange County, a few are seen in late January; the rest arrive en masse by late February (**middle photo**). Pairs that are able to claim a homesite immediately begin nest building; the others stay a day or two, then head farther north. If tree cavities are not available for nesting, they readily use bird boxes. Tree Swallows are colony dwellers and stick close together. To stand in their midst while dozens fly around you as they energetically prepare for their little ones is a truly awesome experience.

Many migrating Tree Swallows that nest in the southern part of the state go farther north with their young ones by early May. By July, they begin heading south again, and a continuous stream from farther north passes through the state. Their numbers diminish by late August.

Voice is a mix of fast, liquid twitterings composed of chips, chits, and gurgles, some of which are sweet. Also, chatter similar to a House Sparrow's.

Next Page: The sexes can look alike but females are often duller. In addition, some females are brown. Juveniles are gray or brown. Brown Tree Swallows can be distinguished from other swallow species by the ***definite line between color and white on their faces.*** (See page 506.)

Greg Lavaty

Violet-Green Swallow (5")

Most Violet-green Swallows we see in California are winter residents of central Mexico or Central America that breed from California to Alaska. They cross the Colorado River into California beginning in February and return south by September. A small number stay year-round along the coast from the Bay Area to just south of Big Sur. In California, Violet-green Swallows are much more common in the north, as the habitat is wetter and therefore more suitable. In the south, they are seen mostly in the mountains and are common around Big Bear Lake.

Besides needing a plentiful water source, Violet-green Swallows usually prefer open woodlands and forests, especially those with standing dead trees with woodpecker holes. These swallows are cavity dwellers and, because of the shortage of appropriate tree cavities, will inhabit other cavities, including bird boxes. Colony size and density depend largely upon available housing. Violet-green Swallows are widely dispersed and are found from sea level to elevations above 10,000 feet. They are often seen flocking with other swallows.

Voice is a sweet chip *and* cheet, *with variations, and often strung together with sweet or squeaky chatter like that of a Lesser Goldfinch.*

Below: Adult male. Colors vary greatly due to iridescence. This one is on a tufa column at Mono Lake, a favorite nesting site.

Next page, top to bottom: Adult male in a Big Leaf Maple; fledglings; female in ryegrass.

Gary Weller

Cliff Swallow (5.5")

The Cliff Swallows winter in South America and arrive en masse in Southern California by late March. For a week or so, you see a few, then suddenly they're all here. Cliff Swallows breed from San Diego to Alaska in almost any habitat where there is water, mud, and flying insects. Northern breeders pass through California again by early October.

Cliff Swallows are colony dwellers and upon arrival immediately begin building their nests of mud, usually placing them under eaves or bridges. Old nests are frequently repaired and reused.

In Orange County, I have noticed that the Tree Swallow population thins considerably shortly after the Cliff Swallows arrive. By late June, most of the Cliff Swallows have also gone—I assume farther north or to higher elevations. Since they can raise two broods in a year, I have wondered, but have been unable to confirm, if at times they may raise another brood at a different geographic location in the same year. Incubation period is about 15 days, and the young fledge about 22 days after hatching, so it is certainly possible. I have seen Cliff Swallows building nests in mid-July at Big Bear Lake, elevation 6,500 feet.

Voice is a strange combination of mixed chatter. Calls include a nasal chur; *House Sparrow-like buzzy chips and chirps; a horrible-sounding grating squeak; and raspy, nasal squeaks. They are very noisy when nest building.*

Below: Gathering mud for building nests. The sexes look alike. Juveniles lack the bright colors; some look like they've been washed in mud.

Tom Benson

Barn Swallow (6.75")

Barn Swallows winter from southern Mexico to South America, begin to arrive in California in February, and are here en masse by April. By late August, as the young mature, the Barn Swallows start heading south. Migrating birds from as far north as northern British Columbia are still passing through California in October.

These beauties can be found all over the state where there is open land and water. Barn Swallows are frequently seen skimming gracefully over grassy agricultural fields, meadows, and large park lawns. Like other swallows, they also forage over bodies of water. In their season, they commonly nest and can be seen at most of the many wharves and piers along the coast.

The Barn Swallows' cup-shaped nests are made of mud and grass and are often attached to man-made structures, including barns in farm country, hence the name.

Voice is a squeaky twitter that consists of varying cheep *notes. Also, a more complex squeaky twitter/warble.*

Below: Adult pair. Adult males have a deeply forked tail. Females and juvenile males have a shorter tail and paler, or white, underparts. Adults can be much duller than those in the photos.

Next page, top: Fledglings on bulrushes. **Middle:** Juvenile (colors vary). **Bottom:** Adult male.

Jack and Petra Clayton

Jack and Petra Clayon

Jerry Ting

Northern Rough-Winged Swallow (5.5")

Northern Rough-winged Swallows are widespread across California from February to July but are not nearly as common as Tree, Cliff, and Barn Swallows. Some are year-round residents of the Imperial Valley and along the Colorado River. The others that we see breed throughout the rest of the state or are just migrating through to places farther north or east. They winter in southern Mexico and Central America.

Rough-wings build their nests inside burrows dug into dirt banks by other animals or in crevasses of man-made structures. Unlike most of our swallows, they are not colony dwellers.

Northern Rough-wings often migrate with other swallow species—commonly Tree Swallows.

Their name comes from the rough barbs on the leading edge of the male's primary flight feathers. The function of the barbs is unknown.

Voice: Call is a buzzy churt *that may be repeated a few times. At other times, it is drawn out and mixed with higher-pitched chirping and becomes a primitive song.*

Below: Adults. The sexes look alike and juveniles very similar.

Bank Swallow (5")

The well-named Bank Swallow is our smallest swallow and is relatively uncommon. They begin arriving in California from South America in April. Most are just passing through to places farther north and don't stay long. A small number breed primarily along the north coast, in the far north, east of the Sierras, and in the Sacramento Valley. All head south again by late summer.

Unlike Rough-wings, Bank Swallows live in colonies and excavate their own burrows for nesting in muddy stream banks. Foraging and other habits are like those of our other swallows. Their habitat is wet open areas with few trees.

Nesting Bank Swallows can readily be found from mid-April to late August at Año Nuevo State Park, north of Santa Cruz; at Bridgeport Reservoir, in Mono County; and in the dirt banks above the Fall River at Fall River Mills, east of Burney. Migrating flocks are often seen in the estuaries of Humboldt County.

Voice: Calls are a buzzy tsear *and* tsrt. *Also, buzzy chatter, at times like radio static.*

Below: The ***definite brown breast band*** of the Bank Swallow distinguishes it from the Rough-wing and the immature Tree Swallow. The sexes look alike and juveniles look like adults.

Purple Martin (8")

Our largest swallow, and scarce in California, the Purple Martin spends the winter in the Amazon Basin of South America and breeds along the West Coast, mostly from Monterey to southern Washington. Once much more common, these birds are now found only in isolated pockets, usually at the edges of mountain forests. An exception is downtown Sacramento, which hosts at least three small colonies under bridges, one under a freeway bridge just south of Cal State.

Purple Martins typically nest in cavities in large dead or dying trees near water. Such housing is limited, and the birds of different species that compete for it are many, so the martin population has declined. Western Purple Martins, including those that breed in California, do not live in large colonies and rarely use bird boxes, as do their counterparts in the eastern states. They do, however, make use of man-made cavities for nesting sites, as in the **photo below**, which was taken at a fish hatchery near Arcata where they are regulars from April to August.

Like other swallows, Purple Martins are insect eaters and catch their prey in flight. They are commonly seen foraging just above the water, but they also forage high overhead.

Voice: Call is usually chew *or* chee-chew. *Also, short warbles with creaky grinding sounds, sometimes strung together into a song. Their voices carry. I have followed their voices until it seemed like I was standing right on top of them, only to discover that they were very high above me.*

Below: Dad with the kids.

Male on the left, female on the right.
I don't know what he did, but he sure was getting an earful.

Swifts

Swifts look similar to swallows but are structurally different and their movements in flight are abrupt, not smooth and graceful like a swallow's. Like swallows, swifts are almost always close to water and forage for insects while flying with their short, wide bills open. The feet of swifts are so small that they cannot perch like swallows and most other birds. When not flying, they are typically in a nest or clinging to a vertical surface, in which position they sleep.

Some so-called experts say that the feet of swifts are underdeveloped—a strange thought, considering the perfection demonstrated in their every minute detail. Aeronautical engineers have patterned their aircraft after birds, including swifts, but have not come close to matching the wisdom displayed in the design of one of these creatures. And our pilots could never survive their darting, high-speed maneuvers.

Swifts spend most of their lives in the air. They eat, drink, gather nest materials, and often mate while flying. Swifts commonly fly higher than other birds and often feed so high up that from the ground they appear almost as dots. Even from such a distance they are easy to identify by their quick, darting flight.

The sexes look alike.

Below: Vaux's Swift fledglings.

White-Throated Swift (6.5")

California's most common swift, the White-throated, is a year-round resident along the coast as far north as Mendocino and inland, mostly south of Point Conception. Many also breed in the Cascades, in the Sierras, and east of the Sierras. Surprisingly, these birds nest from the lowest elevations in the state, in Death Valley, to above the tree line in the Sierras and Cascades.

White-throated Swifts nest in colonies, usually on rocky cliffs, although now they also frequently nest in sheltered parts of man-made structures, such as in nooks and crannies under bridges in wet areas. They build their nests of grasses, moss, and feathers and glue them together with saliva.

Unlike most smaller birds, White-throated Swifts may forage several miles from their nest site and even in dry mountain and canyon areas. They know where the water is, however, and are just following the bugs. Like swallows and other swifts, White-throated Swifts forage only in flight.

Voice is a rapid descending chatter made up of shrill, scraping notes mixed with sweet peeping. One would think they were half irritated. At times, single or double notes from the same collection.

Below: Adults. In the field, juveniles are distinguishable only by their behavior. They are fed by adults in flight.

Jerry Ting

Vaux's Swift (4.5")

The Vaux's Swift is much smaller and stockier than White-throated or Black Swifts. It is nearly identical to the **Chimney Swift** of the eastern states.

Vaux's Swifts begin arriving in California in April to breed in the Cascades and Sierras and along the coast north of Monterey. They winter in southern Mexico and Central America and can be spotted during migration just about anywhere in the state where there is water. Vaux's Swifts are most commonly seen foraging above forest streams and lakes in the late afternoon and early evening.

Historically, Vaux's Swifts roosted communally in hollow trees. Since the number of those trees has greatly diminished, the birds have adapted and now make use of unused chimney stacks for roosting sites. **The photo on the next page** was taken at McNear Brick in San Rafael, where several hundred migrating Vaux's Swifts arrive each September. They exit the chimney together in the morning, spend the day aloft in different areas, gather again in the evening to swarm around the chimney, and then descend into it, at times as if being poured through a funnel.

Voice is chits and chips, sometimes as very high-pitched, thin twittering.

Below: Note the pin-like spines at the tip of the tail feathers. These were designed as load-bearing structures that enable the bird to roost on vertical surfaces. (See introduction and photo on page 309.)

Robert Lockett

Gail West

Gail West

Black Swift (7")

Although uncommon in California, a small number of Black Swifts breed in a few isolated areas in the Sierras and Cascades. Many more breed north of the state, especially in western Canada. They winter in Brazil and are sometimes seen on our Central Coast during migration.

Black Swifts are typically seen around waterfalls, usually flying but also clinging to a vertical surface in back of the falls. (Look closely.) A good place to find them from May to early August is at McArthur-Burney Falls State Park; less commonly at Vernal Falls in Yosemite National Park; and much less commonly along the coastal cliffs at Santa Cruz.

Like other swifts, Black Swifts frequently feed high in the air—so high they appear to be little more than specks. But watch for a while, and their darting movements will reveal what they are.

Voice consists of rapid twittering chirps.

Top: At Burney Falls. **Bottom:** A typical nesting site.

Glen Tepke

Aaron Maizlish

Songbirds, I: Thick-Billed Birds

Sparrows

All sparrows forage and spend most of their lives close to, or on, the ground. In the spring breeding season, the males perch to sing, which they do both to bring us joy and to claim territory and attract a mate.

The sparrows' diet is primarily small seeds in winter, insects in summer, and fruit and berries in season.

Sparrows and other seed eaters often forage on the ground next to roads, especially in winter when food is scarce. The wind created by the cars whizzing by acts as a winnowing fan, exposing the seeds.

The sexes look alike for all but two of the species listed here, the House Sparrow and the Black-chinned. Some sparrows have significant regional or seasonal plumage variations.

Several California sparrow species look similar, so I put all the sparrows with heavily streaked breasts at the front of this section, beginning with the most common. Following them are the crowned sparrows, then the rest. Additional photos are included for species that are similar in appearance or have considerable variation within a species.

If you're looking for a sparrow-like bird, and it's not here or with the finches, see Palm Warbler, Pipit, and Red-wing BB (pp. 439, 464, 474).

Below: Brewer's and Black-throated Sparrows on a cholla cactus.

Song Sparrow (5.75–6.5")

These messengers of cheerfulness brighten the outlook of all who hear them. Song Sparrows are abundant year-round residents in most of the state and vary greatly in plumage color and voice, mostly by region. Many of the variants are considered subspecies.

Song Sparrows prefer to be near water in brushy areas with some trees and open space. Residential areas with these criteria are also acceptable.

Other than when the males perch to sing, Song Sparrows stay low and hop along the ground or flit among branches close to the ground. They are inquisitive birds and their demeanor is cherry like their song.

Flight is typically direct, low to the ground, and short—into cover or to another perch.

Voice: Call is a soft, sneeze-like tisp, *sometimes as a short staccato. Songs are rich and melodious and usually include a buzz or a trill. They commonly begin with four piping notes—the last lower and held longer, followed by a short buzz and then by a sweet warble. There is a lot of individual and regional variety.*

Photos are of some of the many variations of Song Sparrows in California; some are regional. Colors vary, but note the pattern of the markings and other features. **Below:** Coastal.

Next page, top row: Coastal and central. **Middle row:** Coastal; east of the Sierras. **Bottom row:** Young coastal birds. **Page 317, top:** More variations.

Sparrows

Song Sparrow, continued

Below, top row, left to right: Far north coast; Salton Sea area.
Second row: Far north. **Additional photos**: Pages 503, 519.

Lincoln's Sparrow (5.5")

Lincoln's Sparrows are similar to Song Sparrows but are smaller, thinner, more secretive, and not nearly as common. Some breed in the Sierras and Cascades, but most we see are migrants from farther north, some of which winter along our coast and in the Colorado River Valley.

Habitat for the Lincoln's Sparrow is damp scrubby areas and thickets. They are shy and usually stay under cover.

The Lincoln's Sparrow can be identified by its **buffy breast**, which **transitions to a white belly**. The streaking on the Lincoln's breast and flanks is sharper and finer than that of a Song Sparrow and the facial markings also differ. When in the open, a Lincoln's crest is usually raised at least a little, giving it a surprised look.

Voice: Song is wren-like and bubbly. If you hear a wren in a thicket that doesn't sound quite right, it just may be a Lincoln's Sparrow. Call is chip *and is softer than that of a Song Sparrow.*

Below: Lincoln's Sparrows. Top is a juvenile; the others are adults. The middle bird is in mallow; the bottom bird is in Mulefat.

Savannah Sparrow (5.5")

An abundant bird in California, the Savannah Sparrow is divided into an arguable number of subspecies. Some are year-round residents along the coast; others breed in the mountain meadows of the Great Basin and winter in our interior grasslands. As their name implies, they are birds of the grasslands, but flocks can be seen almost anywhere in the state in open country, from salt marshes and beaches to fields, meadows, and pastures. Savannahs have no need for trees. Nests are usually built of grasses on the ground.

Birds of this species can differ in appearance significantly. The **yellow eyebrow** is a sure indicator of a Savannah, as is a **slight yellow tint**, but many Savannahs have neither. The **Belding's subspecies** of the coastal salt marshes is much darker, but lighter Savannahs are also in the salt marshes. The various subspecies share these similarities: the **clear white** on the belly, the notched tail, and the white stripe through the crown. Although similar to a Song Sparrow, the facial pattern of a Savannah is different and its face is mostly brown, not gray like the Song Sparrow's. Most Savannahs are also more crisply streaked. Admittedly, if a bird lacks the yellow, it may take some study and experience to see the difference.

Voice: Song opens with a few tisp *notes with long pauses between, followed by a sweet note or short warble, and ends with an insect-like buzz. Sometimes the buzz is in the middle of the sequence. Call is* tisp.

Below: Adult in wild radish and mustard.

Next page, bottom row, left: Belding's in big saltbush. **Right:** Belding's in saltwort. **Photo of a juvenile** is on page 503.

Vesper Sparrow (6.25")

A bird of open fields and areas of short, sparse grass and scattered shrubs, the Vesper Sparrow breeds mostly in the Great Basin and winters in the Colorado River Valley and southward into Mexico. During the breeding season, look for them east of the Cascades and Sierras from our northern border to just south of Mono Lake. The Sierra Valley and the Mono and Crowley Lake areas are popular breeding sites. Vesper Sparrows are also uncommon winter residents of the Central Valley and migrating birds can appear briefly in their habitat in much of inland Southern California. They are virtually absent along the coast.

In California, Vesper Sparrows are not nearly as common or as widespread as the similar-looking Savannah Sparrows. Single birds are often seen with Savannahs during migration.

Although the Vesper is similar in appearance to the Savannah Sparrow, note the following features of a Vesper Sparrow: **complete white eye-ring**, not broken like the Savannah's; no white stripe in the crown; no yellow; and a **chestnut patch** on the shoulder (not always visible). In flight, chestnut patches under the wings at the shoulder are a sure identifier. When flushed, the white at the outside of the tail feathers flashes.

In addition to singing in the morning like other birds, the Vesper Sparrow often sings at twilight, hence the name.

Voice: Song is a whistled warble that often ends in a trill. Overall, it is not unlike the Song Sparrow's voice. Calls are a faint tink *and* tisp.

Below: Both photos are of spring birds that are in Big Sagebrush; the one on the right may be younger.

Steve Jones

Jeff Deam

Swamp Sparrow (5.75")

The well-named Swamp Sparrows breed in Canada and in the northeastern states and a small number winter along the West Coast. They are uncommon in California but winter visitors are seen, especially along the Central Coast from Point Reyes to San Luis Obispo County.

These birds are almost always in swampy areas. Most are alone, although individuals are sometimes found with flocks of Song Sparrows. The breast detail and reddish color pattern of Swamp Sparrows easily set them apart.

Voice: Call is a soft cheep. *Song is a sweet trill of nearly the same note.*

Top: Breeding plumage. Note the redder cap. Many are not as gray as this bird. **Bottom:** Nonbreeding plumage; possibly a first-winter bird.

Jeff Bleam

Christopher Lindsey

Fox Sparrow (7")

California's largest sparrow, the stocky Fox Sparrow, is divided into a few subspecies. The Thick-billed breeds in the mountains between 6,000 and 8,000 feet and winters in the foothills. The other varieties are migrants from as far north as Alaska and are widespread around the state through the winter. They are often found in flocks.

Fox Sparrows inhabit wooded areas near water and, other than when the males sing in the spring, usually remain hidden in the under- growth. Their foraging is towhee-like: they jump forward, then back with both feet to uncover bugs and seeds in the leaf litter.

Voice: Songs are cheerful whistles with an added buzz or trill. They are similar to the Green-tailed Towhee's. Calls: A soft sip *and louder* chuck.

Photos: Appearance varies more than the photos show. Some are chocolate brown. The Thick-billed (**inset**) has a gray head and mantle, but some others do too.

Rufous-Crowned Sparrow (5.5")

A secretive and relatively uncommon sparrow, the Rufous-crowned lives in dry, rocky, brushy, hilly areas that include some open grassland. It is a year-round resident where it occurs and is usually seen individually or in pairs. These sparrows can be found on the sunny slopes of the coastal ranges south of Willits, on the western slope of the Sierra foothills, and, more commonly, in the hilly areas of the southwestern part of the state.

Rufous-crowned Sparrows don't fly much but rather scamper around on the ground under cover. They are easily differentiated from juvenile White-crowned Sparrows (page 327) by their grayish (not yellow) bill, and shy behavior.

The adult Rufous-crowned Sparrow also looks somewhat like a Chipping Sparrow (next page) but, among other differences, has a larger bill, a bold white rye-ring and a red, not black, line in back of the eye.

Voice: Song is bubbly and similar to that of a House Wren. Common calls are a hawk-like peer *that ends abruptly and a squeaky trill of the same that they may keep up for a while. Both vary.*

Below: Adults. Juveniles are pale with subtle wing bars.

Jerry Ting

Chipping Sparrow (5.5")

The *long-tailed, small-billed* Chipping Sparrows breed in mountain areas throughout the state and prefer a dry, open-forested habitat of pines and oaks. Most winter in Mexico, but a relatively small number stay in California in the far south. They are fairly common all year in the San Gabriel, San Bernardino, and San Jacinto Mountains of Southern California but go to the lower elevations in winter.

The *dark eye line* is another identifying feature of a Chipping Sparrow. Breeding birds have a rufous cap; nonbreeding birds have a duller, browner cap, and the eye line is duller; juveniles have a streaked breast.

Voice: Song is a long, dry, insect-like trill. It can be sung at three different tempos, much like the settings on an old phonograph: 33, 45, and 78 rpm. Call is a faint, sharp tisp.

Top: Breeding plumage. **Bottom, from left:** First-year; nonbreeding.

White-Throated Sparrow (6.75")

White-throated Sparrows are an eastern bird that breeds in Canada, mostly east of the Rockies, but a few turn right on the way south and winter along the West Coast. They are uncommon in California but are seen regularly between October and April in the Central Valley and along the coast as far south as San Luis Obispo. These are usually individual birds traveling with flocks of White-crowned Sparrows. The two species look similar but the white throat is a sure identifier.

Besides the white throat, note the **yellow spot** between the bill and eye, the **grayish bill**, and the streaking on the breast. These field marks help distinguish the White-throated from the common White-crowned Sparrow.

Immature birds are heavily streaked on the breast.

Voice: A common call is a soft seep *that is all but identical to that of a White-crowned Sparrow. Song is a high-pitched, whistled, melancholy, slow series of four clear notes. Tune is* **"Here Comes the Bride,"** *the tempo is like taps (by a bugler). The song is rarely heard in California.*

Below: October and March adults. First-year bird is at bottom right.

White-Crowned Sparrow (7")

White-crowned Sparrows are found all year along the coast north of Point Conception. They also breed in the high mountains and are abundant winter guests throughout the rest of the state. Most of our winter birds come from breeding grounds in Alaska and northern Canada. The winter population of White-crowns in California is much larger than it is in the fall or spring, which is probably a reflection of how long the migration path is for many of the birds.

Winter White-crowns stay in large flocks and are comfortable in just about any habitat, including residential areas, where they are relatively tame. They love to sing and brighten any neighborhood.

Adult birds have a black-and-white crown; first-winter birds have a rusty-and-yellowish crown; juveniles have a rusty crown and a heavily streaked breast. Another identifying feature of the White-crowned Sparrow is its yellow-orange bill. A similar species, the White-throated Sparrow (page 326), has a grayish bill.

Voice: Song is a whistling somewhat like that of a meadowlark but is shorter, harsher, in a minor key, and ends with a buzz or trill. Varies. Calls include a soft pink, *often repeated, and* seep.

Below: Adult (at left) with a first-winter bird.

Next page, top: Adult. **Middle:** Molting adult and first-year bird. **Bottom:** Fledgling and juvenile. The definition of a juvenile songbird on page 509 is helpful.

Sparrows

Golden-Crowned Sparrow (6.5")

Fairly common fall-to-spring residents of the western half of the state, Golden-crowned Sparrows travel to British Columbia and as far north as Alaska to breed and spend the summer. They favor dense thickets of chaparral or broad-leafed evergreen shrubs and short trees.

Sometimes individual Golden-crowned Sparrows are seen in flocks of the much more common White-crowned Sparrows. Juveniles of the two species can look similar, but the Golden-crowned are **more uniformly brown** and have a **gray bill**.

Voice: Their most recognizable song is a minor-key whistling that descends, "I'm so-o tired" or "Oh, dear me." Calls are chip *and* tsee. *They also make Lesser Goldfinch-like sounds that may be made into a song.*

Top: Breeding plumage (March to August). **Bottom:** Nonbreeding adult on Laurel Sumac.

Next page, top and middle: Part of a flock of first-year birds. **Bottom:** Molting adult.

Sagebrush Sparrow (aka **Brush** or **Sage Sparrow**) (6")

The well-named Sagebrush Sparrow breeds in the Great Basin and winters in the southeastern deserts. Besides sagebrush, they are also commonly found in mesquite, creosote, and rabbit brush.

Other than when the males sing atop bushes in the spring and early summer, and occasional flocks foraging in grassy areas, Sagebrush Sparrows tend to stay under cover. They are typically in loose flocks, often mixed with other species. A good place to find them in the summer is along the road to Bodie State Park in Mono County.

Voice: Song is a medley of short warbles and buzzy trills. Call is a soft tink *similar to, but higher than, a California Towhee's. Although soft, the call carries, which is something I have never understood.*

Below: Adult on Desert Peach. Note the color transition from gray head to brown back.

Bell's Sparrow (5.5")

Although typically darker in appearance, the Bell's Sparrow is all but identical to the Sagebrush Sparrow. For more than a century, taxonomists have been trying to decide if they are one species or two. In 1910, they split the birds into two species. In 1957, another generation lumped them together again. In 2013, they were again considered two species. The birds and I don't care, but it makes the bird books confusing.

The Bells' Sparrow's differentiating field marks are the isolated black spot on its white breast and darker stripes on either side of its throat.

Bell's Sparrows live in the deserts and locally in the inner Coastal Ranges the length of the state. In the coastal region, they are darker and are usually found in coastal scrub and chaparral above 1,000 feet; in the deserts, they are as light as a Sagebrush Sparrow and are found in low scrub such as Big Sagebrush, saltbush, and creosote bush. Both populations are often year-round residents where they occur. Bell's Sparrows are widespread and not nearly as common as many of our other sparrows.

Good places to find Bell's Sparrows in the south are the Carrizo Plain, west of Bakersfield, and in the hills around Santa Clarita; in the north, they can be found in the Loma Prieta area of the Santa Cruz Mountains.

Voice: Call is identical to the Sagebrush Sparrow's. One song is like the Sagebrush Sparrow's; the other is similar but is mixed differently.

Below: Adult. Juveniles are similar but are pale with a streaked breast.

Black-Throated Sparrow (5.5")

A common year-round bird in the Sonoran Desert, the Black-throated Sparrow also breeds northward in the Mojave and in the Great Basin.

Black-throated Sparrows live in relatively barren areas and in washes containing sparse sagebrush, creosote, or mesquite. They forage on the ground and also catch insects in midair.

These sparrows perch out in the open and are not as shy as some other desert sparrows. A good place to see them in any season is at the Big Morongo Canyon Preserve near Yucca Valley.

Voice: Calls are high-pitched, metallic tink *and* chip *notes, at times as chatter. The tempo and spacing of the notes varies. Their typical song is sweet and consists of three high-pitched piping notes followed by any number of endings. Another song is two piping notes followed by a buzz.*

Below: Adult on a thornbush. **Inset:** Juvenile.

Black-Chinned Sparrow (5.5")

An uncommon, widespread, and highly localized sparrow of chaparral and brushland, the Black-chinned Sparrow breeds on dry rocky slopes. It is much more common in the south, somewhat inland from the coast. They arrive in early spring and return to Mexico in mid-summer.

Other than when the males come out to sing in the early spring, Black-chins typically stay hidden, a habit that makes them hard to find. One place they are seen year after year in April and May is on the Pacific Crest Trail near Kitchen Creek Road in eastern San Diego County.

Voice: Call is a faint chip, nearly identical to that of a California Towhee. Song begins with a few sweet whistled notes followed by the buzzy sound of a dropped ping-pong ball that gains speed until it stops. Cadence is similar to a Wrentit's song, but the sound is quite different.

Top: Adult female or nonbreeding male. Juveniles look similar but have a streaked breast. **Bottom:** A breeding male (April to August).

Lark Sparrow (6.5")

A sparrow of the open field and of sparse scrubland, the Lark Sparrow's unique facial features make it easy to identify.

Some Lark Sparrows are seen year-round in the western half of the state; many more arrive from the central states in the fall and spend the winter in the southern quarter of the state. These migrating birds arrive in flocks, which disband into small groups by late January. They are widespread, nomadic, not shy, and fairly common here until they leave in the early spring.

Voice: Songs are joyful, melodious, and reminiscent of a Song Sparrow but sweeter. Like the Song Sparrow, the Lark Sparrow has a rich variety of songs. Call is a soft tisk.

Below: Adult. Immature birds have the same facial markings but are less colorful.

Jerry Ting

Brewer's Sparrow (5.5")

A bird of the sagebrush and mixed grassland of the arid West, the Brewer's Sparrow is the *plainest looking of all our sparrows*. It breeds in the Great Basin on the eastern side of the Sierras and Cascades. Most Brewer's Sparrows winter in Mexico or in southern Arizona and New Mexico, but some stay in the California portion of the Sonoran Desert. In April, the males arrive on the breeding grounds before the females to claim territory by singing. In late August, they gather into large flocks before flying south. They are quite common in California in their range and habitat.

Voice: Call is tisp. *The male's territorial song is a cricket-like buzzing that slows and drops in pitch. Another song is a shrill piping that ends in a trill that changes pitch; another includes mockingbird-like phrases.*

Below: The birds in the Desert Deerbrush were part of a large flock near Bodie in late August. All were perched in the bushes facing the morning sun. They would soon be heading south.

Note the white eye-ring and small, short bill. Juveniles have streaked breasts. **Inset:** A spring bird on sagebrush. **Add'l photo:** page 314.

Grasshopper Sparrow (5")

Grasshopper Sparrows winter in Mexico and come to California grasslands to breed in the spring. They are stealthy in behavior, typically walk or run instead of fly, and camouflage well, so they are easy to overlook. When flushed, they fly only a short distance, then evaporate into the grass again.

Grasshopper Sparrows are widespread but uncommon. They range from Chico in the north to our southern border and prefer open, semi-arid, seldom-grazed or ungrazed land in the flats or low hills.

Our smallest sparrow eats mostly grasshoppers, while the sparrows in turn are a favorite meal of Loggerhead Shrikes. A good way to find Grasshopper Sparrows is to look around and listen wherever grasshoppers are abundant. Additionally, these sparrows can usually be found at the Santa Rosa Plateau Ecological Reserve near Murrieta between March and June.

Voice: Song consists of two or three tick *notes followed by an insect-like* tszeeeee, *and often ends with a buzzy warble. Sometimes, just the warble. Calls are soft and variations of* seet, *which can be a staccato or just one to three notes. Their voice may be the best way of locating them. It is unlike that of any other bird I am familiar with.*

Below: Grasshopper Sparrows are easily recognized by their small size and by their flat foreheads, which slope into their bills. Also note the relatively short tail and ***orange eyebrow***.

Jeff Bleam

American Tree Sparrow (6.25")

The American Tree Sparrow is a cold-weather bird that is rarely seen in California, but it does visit the northeastern tip of the state from November to February some years. They breed in northern Canada and Alaska, and are a common winter bird in the colder states of the north and east from late fall to early spring.

Despite its name, the American Tree Sparrow's preferred habitat is grassy and shrubby areas with few trees. In the winter, flocks wander from place to place wherever seeds are available. Snow and cold are a way of life for these birds, and as long as they can find food, they are happy in it. They are definitely not a typical California bird!

Although this book is not about rarities, the American Tree Sparrow is a good example of the hundreds of rarities that show up in the state irregularly. So, if you happen to be in Modoc or Lassen County in the winter and hear a different-sounding sparrow, take a look around.

Voice: Calls are a soft tisp *and a louder, sweet* tseet. *Tree sparrows begin singing in late winter. Their songs are sweet, complex, and vary considerably.*

Below: Adult eating Curly Dock seeds (see page 459).

Steve Jones

House Sparrow (aka English Sparrow) (6")

The House Sparrow was introduced into Brooklyn, New York, from Europe in 1851 and spread rapidly across the United States. They and two other European imports, the European Starling and the Rock Pigeon, have become three of our most abundant birds.

House Sparrows are as tame as any wild bird, and as their name implies, they favor living and nesting around and on our houses or other man-made structures. They are not as dependent upon people as a domestic dog or cat, but other than flocks in farm country where grain is grown, they are usually not found far from human dwellings.

Voice: Calls are cheech *and* cheech-up, *often together; a short trill; and a rattling chatter of eight to ten syllables of two adjacent notes. Song is a monotonous repetition of* cheech, cheech-up, *and* chillup.

Left: Breeding male (March to September). **Right:** Nonbreeding male. **Inset:** Fledgling taking a dust bath to remove mites, a nemesis of birds.

***

Once, while on my early morning walk, I heard the tremendous racket of dozens of House Sparrows coming from a clump of bushes. After a while, I slowly approached to try to find out what was going on. At a certain point someone gave the signal and instantly the cacophony became absolute silence. I never saw one bird.

***

Above: Female with a youngster in a California Walnut tree.
Below: These birds were part of a flock of like birds at Point Reyes in mid-September. Their plumage is that of fall and winter males from colder areas only. I assume they came from much farther north. Note the yellow bill.

Oregon Junco (6–6.5")

A subspecies of the **Dark-eyed Junco**, the Oregon Junco is one of California's most abundant birds. They live all year in the far north of the state, in the Sierras, and along the coast as far south as Big Sur. In winter, flocks from as far away as Alaska inhabit the rest of the state.

Juncos remain in flocks and are less secretive than most other sparrows. They are primarily open-forest dwellers but in winter can be found in just about any habitat.

Like other sparrows, juncos forage on the ground, but unlike our sparrows, they also forage from perches and have the ability to fly up and snag insects in midair. **White outer tail feathers flash when the birds are flushed.**

Voice: Juncos have a large assortment of calls and songs. A typical call is stip. *In the spring, they sing a sweet trill and warbling songs with many variations. Another common song is a rapid, melancholy* He didn't see me. *Songs can be sung low and slow or higher and faster. Some songs are goldfinch-like, some are buzzy, others, beautiful. Often just segments.*

Below: Male and female.

Below: Oregon Junco juveniles.

Slate-Colored Junco (6")
This is another subspecies of the Dark-eyed Junco. It breeds east of the Sierras and some winter in the desert. This is a male; female is brown.

Towhees

Sparrow-like but larger, towhees are long-tailed birds that forage for seeds and bugs by stirring up leaf litter with their feet. We have four species in California. Except for some of the Spotted, the sexes look alike.

Spotted Towhee (8")

A common species in California, Spotted Towhees are found throughout the state where there is a combination of some trees and thick undergrowth. They feed mostly on insects but also eat berries and seeds if insects are not available. In temperate areas they remain all year.

Voice: Calls include a soft tisp, *a sweet trill, a grating* rheeak!, *an insect-like buzz, and a drawn-out nasal fuss reminiscent of a cat that got its tail stepped on. Song is two or three short sweet notes followed by a sweet trill.*

Top: Male on a juniper. **Bottom left:** Fledgling. **Right:** A light female. Adult females in the Great Basin are light brown like this one; the others look like the male or just a little duller. **Additional photos:** P. 498.

California Towhee (9")

An abundant year-round resident of the western half of the state, and especially of the coastal slopes, the California Towhee is often described as a dull-looking bird. But it's not, if you look closely.

These quiet birds are comfortable around people and are common in sheltered areas like backyards. Their foraging is quite different—they lunge forward with both feet and then hop back with their feet still together to turn over the leaf litter.

Voice: Calls are a metallic chip *and* tink *and a soft* seep *or* seet. *The male's song (spring, summer) begins with slow, clear* tink *notes followed by a descending trill of the same and ends with* chup *notes. Timing varies.*

Below: The species has considerable plumage variation. Some birds are grayer, some have more orange, and others have a darker throat pattern, as in the **inset photo**. Streaking on the breast is more prominent on younger birds, as on the sparring youngsters in the **top photo**. The sexes look alike.

Notes: The bird at right has no black in front of its eye like the Abert's Towhee (next page).

The **Canyon Towhee** of Arizona is similar but has a whitish belly, a contrasting rufous crown, and a more distinct necklace.

Abert's Towhee (9.5")

A close cousin to the California Towhee, the Abert's Towhee lives year-round in the Colorado River Valley. The ranges of the two towhees do not overlap. Abert's are commonly found in areas of mesquite and, like other desert creatures, retire to shady areas during the heat of the day.

Abert's Towhees forage by vigorously motoring their feet in the dust, sand, or leaves to uncover small insects and seeds (**bottom photos**). They are easily identified by the black between the bill and the eyes and the black-streaked beard. Like the California Towhee, there is a lot of variation in the species. Some individuals of both species are much lighter or darker than others, and some are more colorful.

Voice is similar to the California Towhee's but is higher in pitch.

Top: Adult. **Bottom:** This bird's foraging action was hilarious. The bird was at Salton Sea National Wildlife Refuge, where they are common.

Green-Tailed Towhee (7.25")

Smaller than other towhees, Green-tailed Towhees breed in brushy scrub and semi-open pine forests in the Sierras and Cascades, in the far north, and in the southern mountains, usually above 6,000 feet. They winter in the Colorado River Valley and southward into Mexico.

Healed-over burn areas of thick scrub brush are also a favorite habitat of the Green-tailed Towhee. They can be found in the brush as high as the tree line in the summer and are fairly common in their range and habitat.

Voice: Song is a pleasant succession of chirp, sweet, sweet, *a buzz, and a sweet trill. It is similar to the Fox Sparrow's song and both species mix it up some. One call sounds like a cat meowing through a kazoo; another is a high, thin* tsip. *They also squeak and chatter.*

Top: Adult on Big Sagebrush. **Bottom:** Adult; juvenile.

Finches

The three finches described next—the House, Purple, and Cassin's—are similar but are typically found in different habitats. House Finches like our neighborhoods; Purple Finches like moist woodlands and forests; and Cassin's Finches prefer dryer forests in the higher mountains. All three eat mostly seeds, buds, and berries. *Fledglings look like pale females.*

House Finch (5.75–6.25")

The House Finch is one of the most abundant birds in California and, as their name implies, is commonly found in areas inhabited by humans. They prefer a mix of trees and open space with grasses, so our suburban neighborhoods and parks are perfect for them. House Finches avoid areas without any trees as well as heavily forested areas.

Breeding males are red—some much brighter than others. During the nonbreeding season, the red diminishes. Some females are more heavily streaked than others. Streaking is less distinct than the Cassin's.

It is easy to tell year-round residents from migrating birds in the fall. Although all stay in flocks, the migrating birds remain in much tighter flocks, are more fearful of humans, and their colors are typically paler. They begin arriving in August. The early migrating flocks stay for a while and fuel up on berries; the later ones only stay a few days, eat seeds (because the berries are gone), then head farther south.

Voice: The male's song is bright and cheery—a beautiful warbling that often ends with a buzz. The female occasionally sings a shortened version. Calls are chirp, *like a sparrow;* cheep, *and* veet. *Also a slurred* chee-eep *and* vee-eet.

Below: Eating elderberries. **Next page, top:** Spring migrating pair. **Middle left:** Courtship feeding—the male's way of saying, "I'll take care of you and the babies." **Bottom:** Female in blackberries. Note the ***plain face*** and ***down-curved bill***. Compare with Purple and Cassin's.

Purple Finch (6")

Male Purple Finches are not purple but have a strawberry wash over their entire body.

Of the three similar-looking finches, the House, Cassin's, and Purple, the Purple Finch is the least common in California. They like **moist**, shaded habitat and are found year-round in forests and woodlands, especially in the far north and in the northern Coast Ranges. They are less common in the western Sierras. Some winter in the Central Valley, very few farther south. In season, they eat leaf buds, blossoms, insects, fruits, and seeds. Residents visit feeders; migrants are more shy.

Voice: Songs are sweet warblings similar to but smoother than those of a House Finch. Calls: A sweet warbled Hi there, here-I-am, *and* pic.

Top: Female in crab apples. **Bottom:** Winter, spring males. **Add'l:** P 501.

Cassin's Finch (6.25")

Cassin's Finches are birds of **dryer** coniferous and mixed forests. In the summer, they may be all the way up to the tree line, in the winter, as low as 3,000 feet. They commonly forage in Lodgepole and Ponderosa pine forests and nest in groves of Quaking Aspen.

The Cassin's Finch is similar in appearance to the Purple Finch but note the following differences: The Cassin's bill is more prominent. The male Cassin's red crest stops abruptly at the nape; the Purple Finch's continues down the back of the neck. The female Cassin's has a pale eye-ring; the Purple Finch does not. Also, note the short, sparse, crisp streaks on the breast of the female Cassin's. The differences, especially in the female, can be subtle so habitat can be helpful for identification.

Voice: Songs are beautiful, liquid, fast warblings similar to a House Finch but sweeter. Calls are song segments; one is a slightly raspy cheeri-o.

Top: Female. **Bottom:** Males.

Gray-Crowned Rosy-Finch (6–8")

Gray-crowned Rosy-finches, jewels of the high country, live in seemingly inhospitable habitat near or above the tree line. They are found mostly from Tahoe, in the north, to Olancha Peak, south of Mount Whitney. Gray-crowned Rosy-finches forage on the ground, often at the edges of snowfields and on talus slopes for insects and seeds carried there by the wind. They are occasionally seen at feeders at high mountain resorts.

Good places to look for Rosy-finches are Virginia Lakes, in Mono County; Aspendell, in Inyo County; and Squaw Valley High Camp. They are usually in groups and are very shy if found away from feeders.

Voice: No song. Calls are a buzzy or squeaky chew *and a squawk.*

Top: Subspecies Hepburn lives in the Sierras. **Bottom:** Subspecies Gray-cheeked (eating crabapples) is much less common in California and lives in the Cascades. These are likely males; some birds are duller or brighter.

Lesser Goldfinches and House Finch

Goldfinches

We have three goldfinch species in California. Their diet is almost entirely composed of small seeds, and they typically perch on a plant and pluck seeds from it rather than forage on the ground.

American Goldfinch (5")

American Goldfinches like **moist habitats** and are year-round residents of the northern quarter of the state and along the coast down to Big Sur. They live in valleys and low foothills and nest along water courses, typically in groves of alders, willows, or cottonwoods. For dining, they prefer weedy fields with some trees or tall shrubs nearby. They are especially fond of sunflower, thistle, and dandelion seeds.

In the fall, some American Goldfinches form flocks and fly to Central and Southern California, where they stay near water. The flocks are nomadic and are often found in weedy land around reservoirs, in streamside willows, and in parks with Liquid Ambers, whose seeds they favor. They are less common in the south, arriving late and leaving early. For those that stay in the north, alder and cedar seeds make up much of their winter diet.

Voice: Song is a canary-like musical mixture of warbles, twitters, and chattering with a lot of variation. A common call is a buzzy or nasal zoo-wheet. *Also, a rapid, sweet* tay-toe-chip? *and a soft* ta-chip?

Below: Nonbreeding plumage (August to March); male is on right. Breeding females look similar to nonbreeding males.

354

Jeff Bleam

Jeff Bleam

Jim Cummins

Top row: Two males, left transitioning; right, full breeding plumage. Both photos were taken on April 11.

Middle: Nonbreeding birds can be dull, as on the left, or even brighter than the bird on the right, which may be a first-year bird. Photos were taken on August 20 and September 29.

Bottom: Fledgling/juvenile.

Jeff Bleam

Lesser Goldfinch (4.5″)

The Lesser Goldfinch is California's most common goldfinch and a year-round resident throughout most of the state. They prefer **dryer, semi-open habitat**. Lesser Goldfinches typically avoid the north coast and the high mountains. They are very social and usually seen in flocks.

The species' plumage varies considerably—even in California birds—as the photos show.

Voice: During the spring breeding season, the male's song is a complex, rapid-fire jumble of musical chatter. He's the guy who can play all the instruments in the school band but quickly loses interest in each one. During the rest of the year, the song is sweet, mostly in a minor key, and interspersed with chit-chit-chit. *A common call is the sweetest* twee-ooo *you have ever heard.*

Below: Males eating wild sunflower seeds. Some birds are more green on the back, others more black.

Next page, top, left to right: Young male or bright fall female; dull fall female eating Farewell to Spring blossoms. **Middle:** Bright summer female; light winter female eating Crepe Myrtle seeds. **Bottom:** Dark winter female eating Mulefat seeds; likely a juvenile, note lack of wing bars.

Goldfinches

Lawrence's Goldfinch (4.75")

The uncommon Lawrence's Goldfinch inhabits dryer areas than our other goldfinches. They prefer chaparral, weedy fields, and open woodlands and sometimes join Lesser Goldfinch flocks at a food source.

Lawrence's Goldfinches are nomadic, typically stay in flocks, and follow the seed crops. In the spring, they are found in the dryer foothills, both around the Central Valley and in the south. Lawrence's are especially fond of fiddleneck and that may be the best way to find them. They are also spring regulars at Walker Ranch, near Santa Clarita. In the fall, they retreat to the Colorado River Valley, southern Arizona, or Mexico.

Voice: Song is as sweet and lively as that of any canary in a pet store. Calls include a sweet dweee? *and* dwee-do. *Also, scratchy squeaking.*

Top: Spring male on fiddleneck. **Bottom left:** Spring female. **Right:** September male; females similar but lack black face. Grayer than AMGF.

Christopher Lindsey

Pine Siskin (5")

Pine Siskins are goldfinch-like and even have some yellow color like a goldfinch. They breed in the Sierras and other northern forests, and winter in much of the rest of the state in diverse habitats from grasslands and weedy fields to mixed, open forests and suburban neighborhoods.

Like Lawrence's Goldfinches, Pine Siskins are nomadic and follow the seed crops. They are a good example of how bountifully birds are provided for throughout the year. In the fall and winter, siskins forage for seeds as they ripen in a wide variety of conifers and deciduous trees, as well as seeds of grasses and weeds. In spring and summer, they eat leaf buds and insects. Siskins are almost always in flocks.

Voice: Song is explosive, jumbled, squeaky chattering that rambles on. Calls are a buzzy, rising zreeeeeit?, *a louder* reeet?, *and a squeaky* seeet.

Photos: Some birds show more yellow than others, both as a wash over the body and as patches or highlights on the wings and tail. The patches are usually only seen in flight. Females are darker with little or no yellow.

Grosbeaks

Grosbeaks are finches equipped with huge bills for cracking hard seeds and hard-bodied insects. Although they are chunky birds, most species can hover to pluck insects off the outside leaves of trees.

Black-Headed Grosbeak (8.25")

Winter residents of central and southern Mexico, Black-headed Grosbeaks begin arriving in California in April and leave by mid-September.

These wonderful singers breed in deciduous or mixed forests near water and can be found all over the state where there are large trees, a complex understory, and some elbow room. Black-headed Grosbeaks will even visit spacious residential neighborhoods if trees and bushes are abundant—especially if you have sunflower seeds in your feeder. They are uncommon east of the Sierras and avoid the deserts except during migration.

Voice: Song is cheerful, if not downright jubilant. It is similar to a robin's but is longer, sweeter, and more varied. Call is a soft spik. *Some males will sing through the night if a bright light is left on. (How do I know that?)*

Below: Juvenile.

Next page, top: Male eating willow blossoms—a favorite of many birds. **Bottom:** Female in mesquite.

Grosbeaks 360

Blue Grosbeak (6.75")

These beautiful birds winter in Mexico and Central America and come to the southern half of our state to breed in April. Blue Grosbeaks need a dry habitat and are usually seen away from the coast in large open areas with dense thickets of tall weeds near riparian edges. A good place to find them is in the various preserves where open space is plentiful. They are uncommon elsewhere.

Male Blue Grosbeaks frequently perch in the open on tall weeds like mustard or fennel or on a leafless bush or tree. They forage on the ground for insects and seeds in thickets of weeds and brush. Before heading south in the late summer, Blue Grosbeaks often gather into flocks in dry grain, corn, or alfalfa fields to fuel up for the journey.

Voice: The male sings a rich, musical warbling similar to that of a House Finch but without a buzz. Calls include chink, bzzzt, *and a whispered* sip.

Top: Adult male. **Bottom:** First-spring male.

Above: Breeding male; female on a willow branch.
Young juveniles look like females.

Pine Grosbeak (9")

Pine Grosbeaks are giants among the other finches. They live year-round in the lodgepole pine forests of the Sierras and Cascades between 6,000 and 8,000 feet but are scarce in California.

The best places I know to look for Pine Grosbeaks are around Donner Lake, Bridal Veil Campground in Yosemite National Park, and the Twin Lakes and Minaret Vista areas at Mammoth Lakes. Once found, they are easy to watch because they move slowly and are not shy.

Look for them at the edges of meadows near water. In the spring and early summer, they may be found in the fir trees eating tender needles. In the late summer and fall, they may be in lower plants, eating fruits and berries. In winter, their diet is largely seeds and nuts, and they may be feeding on the ground. Since pine trees and other conifers do not bear cones every year, Pine Grosbeaks are often nomadic, especially late in the year.

Voice: Songs are rich, flute-like warbles. Calls are short phrases of their songs. Some songs resemble a Purple Finch or Black-headed Grosbeak, others are quite unlike those of our other common birds.

Below: This bird is enjoying crab apples, a winter favorite. It could be a first-year male or an adult female with variant, or "russet," plumage.

Next page: The males are red, the females are yellow. **Top pair:** Both photos were taken July 3. **Bottom pair:** Both photos were taken February 7.

Grosbeaks

Evening Grosbeak (8")

Evening Grosbeaks are notoriously nomadic. They live year-round in semi-open mountain forests from the mid-Sierras to the far north of the state, but one never knows where they will be. Evening Grosbeaks usually stay in small groups and are often found because they are noisy. Although cold-weather birds, they move to lower elevations in winter if food becomes limited and will visit feeders, especially for sunflower seeds. Evening Grosbeaks are scarce in California and are most commonly found in the Tahoe Basin.

The massive bill on these chunky birds is for cracking the hard seeds they eat during the winter. In the spring and summer, the Evening Grosbeak's diet consists largely of insects, which they can catch on the wing. They also eat leaf buds, juniper berries, crab apples, and other fruits in season.

Females and immature birds look similar and are mostly gray. As the photos show, plumage colors vary considerably. Some females are yellowish. Note that the bills of some birds are much larger than those of others.

Voice: Song is a buzzing of two notes, the second lower or higher. Typical call is a sweet spear, *which is sometimes compressed. Also chirps.*

Below: April male. **Next Page from top:** Two females; July male.

Peter Pearsall / USFWS

Rob English

Jeff Deam

Gary Weller

Lazuli Bunting (5.5")

Lazuli Buntings get their name from the lapis lazuli gemstone—and what a feathered gem they are! They breed throughout California and other western states and spend the fall and winter in western Mexico. The Lazulis arrive in April or May; most are gone by early September.

These beautiful birds are fairly common in their habitat of dry shrubby and weedy areas that adjoin oak and other woodlands up to about 6,000 feet. East of the Sierras they are found even higher. When not foraging on the ground or in low shrubs for bugs and grass seeds, males often perch out in the open. Lazulis need space so are seldom found in suburban neighborhoods. Females typically remain hidden.

Voice: One song is sweet and similar to a Yellow Warbler's but squeakier. It is usually repeated. Another song is similar to that of a Common Yellowthroat. (See pages 427 and 425.) Calls include a sharp twik *and soft* tisp. *In flight,* zit!

Top: Juvenile. **Bottom:** Females.

Below: Lazuli males. **Top left** is first-year; **right,** breeding bird on mustard.

Indigo Bunting (5.5")

This eastern bird is a rare but regular visitor to California. Pictured below is a male. Females are brownish, similar to Lazulis. Indigos interbreed with Lazulis. The males sing a bright, sweet, happy song. Call is *pik*. One recent spring, we had a young male visit us for a few weeks. He sang his heart out every day. I felt sorry for him because he was the only one of his kind. There was no one to match him.

Red Crossbill (6–7")

As fascinating a bird as you will ever watch, the Red Crossbill is perfectly engineered to efficiently remove pine nuts from cones. They open their crossed bills slightly, place them between the scales of a cone, bite down, and then insert their tongue into the crack created to remove the nut. Their tongue is sticky, the nut sticks to it, and dinner is extracted. (**See photo below**.) Red Crossbills typically forage in flocks both in the trees and on the ground.

The range in California for Red Crossbills includes the far north, the coastal ranges north of Mendocino, and the Cascades and Sierras. They are nomadic and follow the cone crops, and since coniferous trees do not produce cones every year, the crossbills can never be relied upon to be at the same place year after year. Sometimes the combined cone crops in a locality fail. In that case, Red Crossbills travel far and wide to make a living, including into Southern California.

Voice: Calls: jip, cheech-o; *song: squeaky chips, buzzes; in flight:* jeep.

The top three photos below are of birds that were in the same small flock eating tender white fir needles at Bluff Lake in early July. The males are reddish; the females are yellowish. Colors and bill size vary for both sexes. **Bottom photos:** A young female (left) and a juvenile (right).

Tanagers

Tanagers are appropriately placed last in this section of thick-billed seed-eaters because, although they are thick billed, they rarely eat seeds. They are insect eaters but eat buds, fruits, and berries in the cooler months when insects are in short supply.

Western Tanager (7.25")

The beautiful Western Tanager arrives from southern Mexico and Central America in April and leaves in September. They breed in mountain areas close to water throughout the state and prefer the edges of forests and woodlands. During migration, Western Tanagers can be found anywhere in the state, including in desert oases. They are frequently seen in parks that have both mature trees and open space. The sexes migrate separately at times. Many males may be in a tree with no females; at other times, perhaps later in the season, the flocks are mixed.

Western Tanagers glean insects off foliage, moving around a tree or bush slowly. They also forage by sitting still and waiting for their dinner to fly by. When it does, out flies the tanager to catch it in midair.

Voice: Song is robin-like but faster and raspy with short warbled phrases and pauses. Call is a rapid, dry chittering of three to five syllables, ped-i-lick.

Below: Likely a young male.

Next page, top: Male in spring (breeding) plumage, in an alder tree. In late summer, most of the fiery plumage on the male's head turns grayish like that of the spring bird on this page. **Next page, middle and bottom:** Bright and dull adult females. Both are mid-September birds and both are enjoying Catalina Cherries.

Scott Jacobson

Roger Zachary

Roger Zachary

Summer Tanager (7.75")

These beautiful birds spend the winter from central Mexico to central South America and arrive in California in April. Small numbers breed along the Colorado River, in the western foothills of the southern tip of the Sierras, and in oases on the inland side of the high southern mountains. Summer Tanagers breed regularly—but not every year—at Kern River Preserve in the foothills east of Bakersfield, arriving by late April and staying through July. Another good place to find them during the breeding season is at Big Morongo Canyon Preserve, near Yucca Valley. Irregularly, individual birds or pairs visit some Orange County parks in winter, usually in January and usually for just a few weeks.

Summer Tanagers live in the cottonwoods that adjoin open areas and feed mostly on bees and wasps. Yes, bees and wasps. They also eat other insects and, occasionally, berries. Summer Tanagers forage in the treetops and sally forth like a flycatcher to capture their prey in midair. They also hover to pluck insects off leaves.

The similar **Hepatic Tanager** of Arizona is duller overall and is seldom seen in California. In late spring and summer, some may be found in the Mojave National Preserve, between Baker and Needles.

Voice: Songs of the Summer Tanager are short, sweet, robin-like, whistled compositions. Calls include a descending chatter of pit *notes and a rapid, Oak Titmouse-like* pretty-da-bird. T*he male also says* peetick!

Below: Adult male.

Next page: Some female plumage variations. Middle bird is in a silk floss tree enjoying a bee. Immature males are splotchy yellow and red.

Jeff Bleam

Songbirds, II: Thin-Billed Birds

Thrushes

Western Bluebird (7")

These beauties are found throughout most of the state in a wide variety of habitats for at least part of the year. They are nomadic and may leave for a month or more and then come back—but not always at the same time of the year. They are simply following the food supply. In the fall, when insects are not abundant, berries ripen, and the bluebirds form flocks, find the berries, and help themselves. Some favorites are juniper berries in October and mistletoe and pyracantha berries in December. Junipers and some other trees and shrubs don't produce berries every year and insect populations vary greatly, hence the nomadic lifestyle of the birds.

Western Bluebirds make their nests in tree cavities. Since woodpeckers usually use their homes for only one season, in times past that worked out great for the bluebirds. But with the invasion of the European Starling (page 480) and increased development and logging, available tree cavities became scarce and the bluebird populations declined accordingly. (Humans don't need dead trees—birds do.) People came to the rescue of these beloved birds and began setting out boxes for them in parks, and the bluebirds have been pleased to occupy them. Much of the spread of the Western Bluebird in recent decades has been the result of this intervention.

Although they avoid dense suburban neighborhoods, Western Bluebirds are well adapted to our parks, which are like their natural habitat of trees and open space. Their foraging pattern explains this preference. Though they can take off nearly vertically, while foraging, they require much more horizontal distance for takeoffs and landings.

Don't let the cuteness of the Western Bluebirds fool you. They can be as territorial as any bird. I saw a female drive off a Vermilion Flycatcher with a fury unmatched by any other bird I have observed. I have also seen males fighting in what appeared to be mortal combat. So much for the cute look. But overall, their demeanor is like their appearance, which is why they are so loved.

Voice: Song is a sweet composition of warbles with pauses and sounds like a cross between a canary's and a robin's. Some of the notes and short phrases of the song also serve as calls. Calls also include House Sparrow-like chattering of chee-check *or* chee-chee-check, *and a soft, sweet* chew.

Next page, top: Adult male in pyracantha. **Second row:** Females or immature males. Most females look like a dull adult male. **Bottom left:** Early winter bird from colder climates. Entire flocks can look like this bird. **Right:** Juvenile. Some are turquoise.

Mountain Bluebird (7.25")

Some Mountain Bluebirds are year-round residents on the east side of the Sierras and Cascades. Others breed in mountain meadows on the west side, usually above 6,000 feet, and winter farther south, typically in smaller foothill valleys but not near the coast. Winter birds are nomadic but are often found along Highway 25 south of Pinnacles National Park.

These beauties inhabit grassy, open country with few trees and forage for insects from fence perches or by hovering just above the ground and dropping down to grab their prey. They prefer undeveloped land or cattle-grazing areas. Mountain Bluebirds are not nearly as common as Western Bluebirds in California. Winter birds are almost always in flocks.

Voice: Calls include chip, *often repeated, and a sweet* chip-ooo. *Song sounds like a robin with a sore throat. In flight, a soft, down-slurred* pew.

Top: Adult male on a Blue Spruce. **Bottom:** Females or immature males. Most are gray but some are rufous or brown, the light playing a large role on color. Juveniles are spotted and look similar to a Western Bluebird.

Howard Patterson

Jeff Bleam

Jerry Ting

Jeff Bleam: Bluebirds on a snowy day

American Robin (10")

The conspicuous king of park lawns and worm hunter extraordinaire, the stately robin is a harbinger of spring in the mountains, of winter in the deserts, and may be found at any time in the lowlands.

Robins are relatively abundant throughout the state. Even in recent years, in the San Jose area, I have seen flocks of several hundred descend on neighborhoods in the early winter and devour every red berry in sight, then take off in droves for the southern hills. In winter, they are often abundant in desert oases, where they feast on fruits.

The robin's flight is straight and powerful; their foraging, legendary.

Voice is as cheery as they are handsome. Songs are unhurried whistled warbles and usually variations of cheer-up, cheer-up, cheerily. *Call is* peep, chuck, chuck *or* peep, peep, tuk. *Also squeaks and chatters.*

Top: Adult male. **Bottom:** Fledgling; female.

Varied Thrush (9.5")

A robin-like bird of damp forests, the Varied Thrush is secretive and typically stays in the shadows. They are year-round residents in the redwoods of the northwest corner of the state and are fall-to-spring visitors across the northern half of the state, usually where wild fruits or berries are abundant. Migrating birds come from as far as Alaska.

Varied Thrushes are sometimes seen foraging with robins for berries or worms. They often uncover worms and grubs by grabbing leaves with their bill and hopping backward. Like many birds, they eat insects during the warm months and switch to berries and seeds in winter.

In spring and summer, Varied Thrushes are usually alone or in pairs; in fall and winter, they may be seen in small flocks around a food source. They can be found all year in just about any park in Humboldt County.

Voice: Song—if you can call it that—sounds like a test of the Emergency Broadcast System. Calls include chup, chup *and a raspy, short staccato.*

Top: Adult male. **Bottom:** Adult female or perhaps a juvenile.

Hermit Thrush (6.75")

Generally a cool weather bird in the western half of California and a late spring and summer breeder in the eastern mountain forests, Hermit Thrushes are easily identified by their **nervous twitch.** The similar-looking Swainson's Thrush lacks this characteristic.

Hermit Thrushes live at the edges of forests near open spaces. They eat many berries and are particularly fond of California coffeeberries. Hermit Thrushes also forage on the ground for insects and worms like their cousins the robins but are more secretive, usually staying in the shadows or near bushes or fallen trees.

If they know they are being watched, Hermit Thrushes will stare at the observer and nervously twitch or cock their tail and lower it slowly. They are fairly common and are usually seen alone or in pairs.

Voice: Song is a flute-like warble similar to that of a meadowlark but as if out of an echo chamber, so not nearly as beautiful. Calls includes wreeee, *similar to that of a Spotted Towhee, and* chup *or* chek.

Below: Adult in a winterberry bush. (The sexes look alike.)

Swainson's Thrush (7")

About the time most of the Hermit Thrushes leave the western half of the state in favor of the eastern mountains, the Swainson's Thrushes arrive. They begin arriving in California in April and breed in the coastal mountains and in the far north. Their winter homes may be as far away as northern Argentina.

Swainson's Thrushes are found in forests and wet woodlands, especially near streams, and are fairly common in season. Like Hermit Thrushes, they tend to stay **in the shadows** and are easy to overlook.

Voice is quite different from the Hermit Thrush's. The Swainson's song is a warble that has a slight echo. The song of some individuals is more flute-like, some more like a whistle, and some more electronic sounding. They have several calls, including fwip, whit, *and a high* weep! *Also, one high note immediately followed by a short bleating like that of a goat kid.*

Below: The most reliable identifier of the Swainson's Thrush is that it lacks the nervous twitch of the similar-looking Hermit Thrush. Other than that, the Swainson's also has a **bolder eye-ring**.

Jerry Ting

Townsend's Solitaire (8.5")

A slim gray bird with a long tail, the Townsend's Solitaire lives year-round in the forests of the Cascades, the Sierras, and the high southern mountains. They require an **open canopy and a semi-open scrub layer** on the forest floor and often prefer areas with manzanita. In winter, they may move to lower elevations, where chaparral and juniper are dominant and are also found in the Mojave.

Townsend's Solitaires are often solitary, but in the fall and winter may be in small flocks at a food source—typically juniper berries in the fall and a variety of others in winter. In the spring and summer, solitaires eat insects, often capturing them in midair. They forage from the treetops, where they perch in an upright position, sit still, and wait for their dinner to come by. Townsend's Solitaires are not common but in their range and habitat are not scarce either. Good places to find them are at Big Bear, in the south, and at Calaveras Big Trees State Park off Highway 4.

A solitaire looks somewhat like a gray female Western Bluebird but has a longer tail. The bluebird also lacks the solitaire's white stripe on the outer tail feathers and yellow on the wing.

Voice: Song is a collection of sweet warbles, some similar to a California Thrasher's. Calls include a short, high-pitched, hollow whistle of pheep.

Above: Adult. (The sexes look alike.)

Right: Juvenile. First-year birds are tan.

Additional photo is on page 502.

Thrashers

Thrashers do just that—they thrash around in the leaf litter with their long bills looking for insects, larvae, and fallen berries.

The sexes look alike.

Sage Thrasher (8.5")

The well-named Sage Thrasher breeds and nests in sagebrush areas east of the Sierras from May to September. They winter in southern Arizona and Mexico and, during the spring migration (February to April), are fairly common in the deserts and other arid areas of Southern California. For the return trip, in September and October, they are not seen as much and may migrate farther east.

Sage Thrashers eat insects in the spring and summer and fruits and berries in the fall. They have a shorter, straighter bill than our other thrashers and, although they scurry around on their feet a lot, will fly from place to place while foraging more than our other thrashers do.

Voice: Their complex and varying songs are somewhat like those of a mockingbird. Call is chip! *and is usually repeated.*

Below: An adult. The photo was taken in late October, so this bird has a new set of feathers. After the nesting season is over, in the late summer, the adults look worn and pale.

California Thrasher (12")

California Thrashers are common and nearly endemic to California. They live year-round in the western half of the state in areas of chaparral and also in the coastal sage scrub. California Thrashers require thick leaf litter and do not live where it is not present. They avoid most of the Central Valley.

The California Thrasher's long bill is perfect for picking out grubs and bugs in hard-to-reach places in the undergrowth—places inaccessible to towhees and sparrows.

Voice: California Thrashers are great singers with a strong voice, a good vocal range, and an abundant repertoire. Songs are similar to a mockingbird's but are smoother and more pleasant, largely because they are not as repetitious. Some songs are comical. Calls: chep *and* chu-weet.

Below: An adult in quail bush, aka big saltbush. **Spring birds are brown, not grayish like this fall bird.** California Thrashers look similar to, but are lighter than, the Crissal Thrasher on the next page. **Additional photo:** Page 501.

Crissal Thrasher (11.5")

As the Abert's Towhee (page 345) takes the place of the California Towhee in the deserts, so the Crissal Thrasher takes the place of the California Thrasher there. Note the following differences in the Crissal: grayish belly with bright cinnamon under-tail feathers, yellow eyes, and darker, more defined drooping mustache. (The California Thrasher has a light orange belly and under-tail feathers; some much brighter than others.)

Crissal Thrashers inhabit desert washes with thick vegetation as well as riparian thickets. Like most thrashers, they run along the ground more than they fly. Their diet is mostly insects but is supplemented with berries in season.

Look for Crissal Thrashers in their preferred habitats in the early morning and late afternoon anywhere along California's eastern border south of Death Valley. Prime areas for them are along the Colorado River and in the Coachella, Imperial, and Borrego Valleys. The males are easy to locate in the spring when they perch to sing early in the morning.

Voice: Calls and songs are similar to those of the California Thrasher.

Below: Adult in big saltbush.

LeConte's Thrasher (11")

A scarce desert bird, LeConte's Thrasher is similar to, but paler than, Crissal and California Thrashers. They are year-round residents of some of the harshest deserts in the state and in the milder areas adjoining those deserts. Their range extends as far north as Death Valley. Additionally, a small population is found in an isolated pocket southwest of Bakersfield near Maricopa (but that is all private land so access is limited).

LeConte's Thrashers are found in areas of sparse creosote brush and also in saltbush scrub, especially in washes.

Good places to see LeConte's Thrashers are at Harper Dry Lake, near Barstow, and at Cottonwood Campground in Joshua Tree National Park. Look and listen for them in the early morning when they perch to sing. They are found where the vegetation is the thickest.

Voice is similar to that of the California Thrasher.

Note: The bills of young Crissal, LeConte's, and California Thrashers are shorter and not as curved. They achieve close to full length a month or two after fledging.

Bendire's Thrasher (9.75")

Another scarce desert bird, Bendire's Thrasher is nearly identical to the common **Curved-billed Thrasher** of Arizona, New Mexico, and Texas. Although the bill of the Bendire's is slightly shorter and straighter than that of the Curved-billed, the most noticeable difference between the two may be their voice. The ranges of the two species overlap.

During the spring breeding season, Bendire's Thrashers can be found east of Joshua Tree National Park in brushy areas, often with yuccas. They winter in southern Arizona and Mexico.

The Bendire's habits are similar to those of other thrashers.

Voice: The Bendire's has a large repertoire of songs that are a cross between a California Thrasher's and a mockingbird's. Like a mockingbird, the Bendire's can become a little annoying because of repetition. Perhaps that is the best way to differentiate them from the Curved-billed Thrasher. You don't have to analyze this—after a while you are either annoyed or you're not.

Below: The Bendire's looks somewhat similar to the Sage Thrasher (page 384) but, among other differences, the Bendire's has a longer, slightly down-curved bill.

Northern Mockingbird (10")

Northern Mockingbirds are common or abundant year-round residents in most of California except in the forests and mountains. They seem to prefer living around people.

The white patches on the mockingbird's wings flash when they fly, which produces a strobe-light effect. Many birds have this feature, including Willets, shrikes, and several woodpeckers, to name a few. The design may be to confuse predators. **Juvenile mockingbirds are spotted like a robin** (see page 379).

Mockingbirds eat mostly insects, worms, and the like. When fruit is available, so much the better.

Voice: Mockingbirds are silent during the nonbreeding period but more than make up for it the rest of the year. They are incessant singers that practice their craft, not for the joy of life but to announce ownership of territory. Their songs are many and varied and can differ greatly between individuals. Many of their voicings mimic other bird species' or, for that matter, even my mother-in-law's alarm clock. Identifying them by voice is easy: they almost always repeat their songs a few times before they go on to the next tune.

I have often wondered how the males have time to make a living, given that they are so occupied with filling the airwaves. As if their day job isn't enough, they often sing into and even through the night.

***

Some people have found the mockingbird's continual "singing" irritating, including my wife's aunt Mattie Sue, who lived in rural Louisiana. Mattie Sue kept a shotgun on her back porch. One day, when my wife was young and was visiting, a mockingbird was doing its thing, and Mattie Sue excused herself, went to the back door, opened it, and fired off a round. The singing stopped—whether because of a willful decision of the bird or otherwise is unknown.

***

Next page: This is "Fritz," our neighborhood mockingbird. He's showing off from the top of our neighbor's Italian Cypress tree. Each spring, he perches on top of the tree and does gymnastics, jumping up and down and strutting his stuff, all the while making as much noise as he can. The purpose of his efforts is apparently to attract a female.

I've never seen a female pay attention to Fritz, but he must be successful because young mockingbirds keep showing up in the neighborhood.

Loggerhead Shrike (9")

The Loggerhead Shrike is a bird of semi-open country with a hawk-like bill designed for tearing apart grasshoppers and other prey. It hunts from low perches such as fence posts and low, bare branches.

Loggerheads are usually present in grassland where grasshopper-like insects are plentiful and are seldom found elsewhere. The birds are widespread throughout California all year except in the high mountains and driest deserts.

Although the Loggerhead's bill is like that of a raptor, they lack the raptor's strong feet. To hold their prey, they stick it on a thorn or cactus spine. In winter, when insects are in short supply, they take small birds, mice, lizards, and just about anything else that moves. If food is abundant, they store it—impaled on a barbed wire fence or a thorn—thus earning the nickname "butcherbird." (Photo on page 508.)

Voices include a Steller's Jay-like, scratchy, single-note call; a short, electronic-sounding buzzeet!; *and liquid, two-note calls that end with a piercing* deet! *One of the latter sounds similar to a Brown-headed Cowbird. Sometimes the sounds are jumbled together into a song and can be repetitious, especially in the spring.*

Below: Adult on a cattail. **Inset:** Fledgling

Northern Shrike (10")

The Northern Shrike breeds in northern Canada and Alaska and is a rarity in California except in the far north during winter. They seldom travel farther south.

Habitat for the Northern Shrike is like that of the Loggerhead. Their winter diet is songbirds and small mammals such as mice.

Northern Shrikes are readily distinguished from Loggerheads by their scaly breast feathers and narrower dark face mask. Northerns are also a little larger, and their voice is different.

Voice: One call is a raspy, jay-like jack, *usually repeated; another is a buzzy* beeek. *One song is a sweet, wooden, four-syllable trill of mid-range notes; another is a sliding whistle similar to that of a Brown-headed Cowbird. Northern Shrikes sing all year.*

Below: Adult. The sexes look similar. Many Northern Shrikes are brownish, as though they had been dipped in muddy water. These are probably younger birds.

Additional photo is on page 508.

Mick Thompson

Wrens

Wrens have long, slender, slightly curved bills for probing narrow spaces for insects. All California wrens live solitarily or in pairs, and each species is perfectly suited for the habitat in which it lives.

The sexes look alike; juveniles look like adults but colors are muted.

Marsh Wren (5")

Marsh Wrens live in the cattails and bulrushes (tules) throughout the state, and because they forage in dense foliage, they are more often heard than seen. They are common but shy birds, and they flit almost continually.

Marsh Wrens that summer in mountain areas migrate downslope or as far south as Mexico in winter.

Voice: Song is energetic. It begins with chit *or* chit-chit, *followed by raspy, scolding, almost mechanical-sounding chatter. The chatter is composed of about five distinct voicings separated by short pauses, and they can keep it up for a while. Calls are* chit, *expressed as a single note or as chatter; a soft* chip; *a scratchy* churr; *and a buzz.*

Below: Plumage brightness varies.

Jerry Ting

House Wren (4.75")

House Wrens are common and can be seen all over California at one time of the year or another. They breed in the northern half of the state and are year-round residents in southern coastal areas. Many that breed farther north spend the winter in the Colorado River Valley or in Mexico. Migrating birds can be heard and seen throughout the south.

These tiny, energetic birds nest in tree cavities, in birdhouses, and in other confined spaces. They are comfortable in a wide variety of habitats, as long as they are near a water source, and do particularly well around human dwellings. Give them some small trees and shrubs planted close together, and they are happy to move in. Bold and often aggressive, within a short time House Wrens will let you know who really owns your backyard.

Voice: The joyful song of a House Wren varies but usually has three or four parts. It often begins with jumbled chattering, then bubbly trills, and ends with a warble. It can be performed rapidly or staggered. Calls include a raspberry buzz and rapid, scolding chatters and rattles. The songs are sweet; the calls are not.

Below: Some individuals are rufous colored to one degree or another, others are more brown or grayish.

Bewick's Wren (5.25")

Longer and thinner than a House Wren, Bewick's Wrens are common year-round residents throughout most of the state. They live in a wide variety of habitats but prefer dryer areas than those favored by the House Wren. Oak woodlands with a brushy understory, desert scrub, and dense chaparral are favorites. Typically, the more tangled the vegetation, the more the Bewick's call it home.

Voice: Bewick's Wrens are avid protesters and will let you know in a variety of scolding tones if they are the least bit offended by you. Their songs, thankfully, are not so, and they have a wide assortment of them. In the spring, the males sing sweet, high-pitched songs that include piping notes, trills, and buzzes. Some of the songs can easily be mistaken for the songs of a Song Sparrow. The Bewick's calls are mostly raspy and include a raspberry buzz that is more pronounced than that of a House Wren.

Below: Adult on Red Flowering Eucalyptus. Bewick's Wrens are easily identified by their **bold white eyebrow** and bolder voice.

Pacific Wren (4")

The tiny Pacific Wrens are fairly common all year in the humid forests along the coast in Northern California. They are also found in the Sierras and Cascades, usually in mature forests on the west side of the divide. In the winter, some inhabit coastal forested areas as far south as Point Conception. Many of these migrating birds probably breed north of the state and leapfrog over the locals.

Pacific Wrens live near streams in shady areas with abundant ferns. They usually stay low to the ground and are not shy.

The movements of the Pacific Wren are mouse-like, and they are commonly seen looking for bugs on decaying logs. These wrens often cling to a tree trunk like a Brown Creeper, but their movements are quite different.

Until recently, the Pacific Wren was considered a subspecies of the **Winter Wren** of the eastern states.

Voice: These little guys know how to belt out a song! During the breeding season, the males sing a sweet, rapid, complex ballad. It lasts about five seconds—much longer than the songs of our other wrens. They also sing shorter songs that are just as sweet. Volume is such that their songs can easily fill the forest. Call is usually chet *or* chet, chet *and is also expressed as chatter, a staccato burst, or a trill. Volume and tempo vary.*

Below: Pacific Wrens are easily identified by their small size, their song, and their short, cocked tail.

Rock Wren (6")

Well-named birds, Rock Wrens forage on boulder piles and talus slopes in arid and semi-arid habitats from the coast to the high mountains and deserts. They are usually seen alone or in pairs and are relatively common in their habitat.

Rock Wrens are typically year-round residents, but birds that summer in the mountain areas may winter in the foothills or near the coast.

While scampering over piles of rock, probing here and there, Rock Wrens will also fly out a short distance to snag flying insects in midair.

Voice: Songs are composed of sweet musical trills and piping notes with buzzing and electronic noises thrown in. After listening for a while, you realize the bird is singing a medley of other birds' songs and wonder if there is any song he can't sing. Calls include an explosive high buzz and a sweet pit *followed by a dry, squeaky buzz, perhaps* pit-zeeeeeeep!

Below: Adult; the orange-pink wash on the belly, barely visible here, is more pronounced on juveniles.

For more than a decade, we have watched the bird in the photo, and perhaps its parents and grandparents, work the same 200 yards of cliff face at Crystal Cove State Park.

Canyon Wren (6")

Another well-named bird, the Canyon Wren, is found in canyon areas throughout much of California except along the north coast. They are not common but typically remain all year where they occur, including in the deserts and in the mountains up to about 7,000 feet.

Canyon Wrens forage for insects and spiders in rocky areas and eroded cliff sides where vegetation is relatively sparse. They prefer arid environments and steeper terrain.

These beauties are much shyer than a Rock Wren, or at least forage more frequently in constricted spaces, but like a Rock Wren, they will eventually hop up on a rock or boulder to have a look around.

Canyon Wrens are more often found in Southern California. Good places to look for them are around Big Bear, in the San Bernardino Mountains; in the Kern River Canyon, east of Bakersfield; and at Morro Rock on the coast.

Voice: Song is a beautiful, liquid whistling that descends in pitch and slows at the end. Perhaps tsee-tsee-tsee-tsee, tsu, tsu, tsu. *Sometimes it ends with a buzz. Call is a* zeep *or* tseep, *sometimes repeated rapidly.*

Below: Note the rufous plumage and longer and more curved bill than that of the Rock Wren.

Cactus Wren (8.5")

By far our largest wren, and another well-named bird, the Cactus Wren lives year-round in the southern deserts, where it is fairly common. Like so many birds, they are easier to find in the spring when the males sing.

Cactus Wrens are also found, but not commonly, in remote areas of dry brushland closer to the coast in Orange and San Diego Counties. They are usually seen around prickly pear and cholla cactus. (A cholla cactus is on the next page.)

I took the **top photo** of the bird on the next page and then watched as it went to get something on the ground close by. Suddenly, another wren appeared and flew right into the cactus! Eventually, I discovered the nest they were building. One of the wrens saw me, got nervous, and took up its post on a nearby Joshua tree (**this page, below**).

What can cause injury or even death to predators is the Cactus Wren's protection. Safe within their fortress, the wrens will raise their young and continue on.

Voice: The song of the desert birds sounds like a rusty starter motor on an old car. Coastal birds drop the rusty. The most common call is a raspy chuck, chuck, chuck, chuck, *which is the first part of the starter motor. In late winter and early spring, Cactus Wrens are easily found by their voice.*

Wrentit (6.5")

Neither a wren nor a tit but similar to both, the Wrentit inhabits dense tangles of shrub and chaparral all along our coast and in the hills adjacent to the Central Valley. In the north, they are frequently found in blackberry thickets; in the south, in chaparral and coastal sage scrub.

Wrentits are common year-round residents of most brushy habitats but are more often heard than seen. In the spring, the males come out briefly, but most of the time these birds stay hidden. They are usually seen as single birds or as pairs, but in the winter small groups (perhaps families) or flocks will forage together.

Most Wrentits live in a small area of perhaps 20 acres for their entire lives.

Voice is commonly a sweet, descending pit *or* chip *with a unique pattern. The pattern sounds like two or three bounces of a basketball, and then the bouncing becomes increasingly rapid, as if you pushed your hand to the floor making the ball bounce faster and faster. Some birds don't seem to get it quite right. At times, segments of the same. Call is a short chittering.*

Below: Adult on Laurel Sumac. The tiny, encrusted seeds are a favorite winter food for many bird species, ranging from Bushtits to quail.

Oak Titmouse (5.75")

A cute little guy, and nearly endemic to California, the Oak Titmouse is a year-round resident of the oak woodlands throughout the state. They are abundant, vocal, not shy, stay in flocks, and their crest is usually up, so they are easy to find and identify.

Oak Titmice are cavity dwellers that move into abandoned woodpecker houses. They are omnivores and forage for insects, berries, and leaf buds in the trees and for insects and seeds on the ground. Titmice also eat acorns, which they hold with their feet on a branch and pound away at like a woodpecker until the shells break open. (See page 290.)

Recently, the **Plain Titmouse** was split into two species: the Oak Titmouse and the **Juniper Titmouse**. The Juniper is grayer and inhabits the dry, desert-like areas east of the southern Sierras. The Oak Titmouse stays on the west side of the Sierras. Otherwise the two differ very little.

Voice: Titmice have a large vocabulary. Songs are composed of sweet and scratchy notes and are usually three to five syllables. Common voicings include a sweet, very rapid chitty-bird, chitty-bird; *a slower but still rapid* chee-bird, chee-bird; *a sweet* dweet-dweet-dweet-dweet; thu-weet; *and a scratchy* did-it, did-it. *They also chatter in a scratchy, squeaky, sometimes scolding voice and can mimic a Steller's Jay. Call is a soft* tseep.

Jeff Bleam

Ruby-Crowned Kinglet (4.25")

These bold little bundles of energy breed in the mixed forests of the Cascades and Sierras and winter in the temperate areas of the state.

The red crown of the male is usually hidden (**bottom left photo**) but appears when the bird is excited and sticks up when he's really excited.

In the summer, Ruby-crowned Kinglets nest high in the trees, flit almost continually, and often flick their wings to flush gnats from foliage. While foraging, they frequently hover to pluck insects from the outer leaves of a tree or shrub. In the winter, they eat seeds and berries and forage close to the ground. During colder weather they may sit relatively still for quite a while. They are often seen in flocks, especially in the fall and winter.

The Ruby-crowned Kinglet looks similar to the Hutton's Vireo (page 405) but has an additional black wing bar. The Hutton's also has a hooked beak; the kinglet does not. The kinglet is the more common.

Voice: Song is jumbled, rapid, and usually begins with soft, thin, high-pitched notes, followed by a sweet twittering or warble, and ends with up-and-down notes or chatter. Call is a rapid, disjointed chittering of jit and jidit.

Top: Adult male on a Cryptomeria. Note that the bird is in shadow but the crown glows. **Bottom, left to right:** Note the faint red crown; winter adult.

Golden-Crowned Kinglet (4")

Golden-crowned Kinglets are residents of the coniferous forests of the north coast and the Cascades and Sierras. In winter, mountain birds move to lower elevations and migrating birds from as far as Alaska may appear in small numbers in coastal areas farther south.

Although common in their range and habitat, Golden-crowned Kinglets are tiny and, in the summer, often prefer treetops, so they can be difficult to find. In the fall and winter, they tend to feed close to the ground and are easier to see. Golden-crowns frequently flock with other small birds, especially chickadees. Like chickadees, they often hang upside down while foraging in the trees. Like warblers, they can hover while feeding.

Both sexes have a golden crown. The male also has an orange crown, but it is often at least partly concealed. Note the white eyebrow.

Voice is thin and difficult to hear. Song begins with high-pitched tsee *notes that accelerate and go higher in pitch—like a hearing test. Sometimes it ends in a warble. Call is creeper-like, a thin, squeaky* tsee, *often repeated.*

Top: Female on a Douglas fir. **Bottom:** Male and juvenile. **Add'l:** P. 504.

Vireos

The name vireo comes from the Latin word meaning "green." Vireos are little olive-green to grayish birds about the size of warblers. Some individuals, even of the same species, are much greener than others. All are duller by mid-summer. Vireos lack the bright colors of most warblers, and their beaks are hooked, not pointed like a warbler's. The hook on the beak is for tearing off the wings of the insects they capture.

Vireos also differ from warblers in how they forage for insects. Most warblers flit around in a tree or bush; vireos move around methodically. After watching them for a while, one can often anticipate with some accuracy where a vireo will move next.

Each species has its own particular range and niche. The sexes look alike.

Hutton's Vireo (4.75")

Hutton's Vireos are usually associated with oak woodlands and forests but also thrive in a wide variety of other woodland and forest habitats. They are found throughout the state up to about 5,000 feet. Most are full-time residents but some move to warmer areas in the winter. They are common in the hilly areas of California and can almost always be found in areas of heavy acorn moth infestation. Depending on the bugs, they may also be in the cottonwoods, willows, or sycamores. Hutton's Vireos will not be far from water but avoid the flat wet areas on the coast.

The Ruby-crowned Kinglet (page 403) looks similar to a Hutton's Vireo but is brighter in color, has a black bar behind the second white wing bar, and often hovers to feed, which the vireo does not do.

Voice is commonly a buzzy zoo-weet *and* tsee-ooo, *both repeated many times. Also,* chit, *chitting chatter, and nasal gnatcatcher-like squeaking.*

Below left: Winter adult with fresh feathers. **Right:** Juvenile. **Add'l:** P ix.

Melissa Kung

Warbling Vireo (5")

From spring to late summer, Warbling Vireos are found throughout much of California in deciduous woodlands and mixed forests near a water source. They often live in groves of aspen, alder, sycamore, cottonwood, and willow. These tiny greenish birds are fairly common in season but like to stay in the top half of tall trees and blend in with the foliage, so they can be a challenge to see. Warbling Vireos are easily identified, however, by their beautiful song, their **long white eyebrow**, and their lack of wing bars.

Warbling Vireos specialize in caterpillars and pupae but also fly out to grab moths, butterflies, and other insects in midair.

In the fall, with their new young ones in tow, they head back to Mexico and Central America.

Some people describe Warbling Vireos as plain looking. But if you've looked at them carefully, I think you will disagree. Unfortunately, they are often parasitized by cowbirds (see page 477).

Voice: Songs are sweet, House Finch-like warbles that vary considerably. Warbling Vireos have three common calls. One is grating and sounds similar to a Steller's Jay's buzzy eeaak! *Another is* vit. *The third is a scratchy, squeaky trill that rises, then falls in pitch and lasts for about a second. At times, all three of these calls together. (For precise definitions of warble, trill, twitter, and staccato, see Glossary, page 510.)*

Below: Late spring adult. Early spring birds are brighter; summer birds, duller. **Inset:** Likely a first-year bird. The photo was taken on June 22.

Jeff Bleam

Cassin's Vireo (formerly **Solitary Vireo**) (5")

These secretive birds prefer oak and mixed coniferous-oak forests and woods. They arrive from western Mexico in the early spring to breed along the coast, in the far north, and in the Sierras and Cascades. Migrants are often seen in live oak woodlands. Cassin's are not as common as Hutton's or Warbling Vireos and are gone by late summer.

Although their geographical ranges and preferred habitats overlap significantly, and they forage for the same bugs, the foraging location preference of the Cassin's Vireo differs from those of the Hutton's and Warbling Vireos. The Hutton's likes to stay low and toward the outside of trees and shrubs; Warbling Vireos take the treetops; and the Cassin's stays low in the trees and often takes the interior. They are all methodical (see the introduction to vireos on page 405).

Based on DNA findings, in 1997, the Solitary Vireo was split into three species: Cassin's, of the West Coast; Plumbeous, of the Great Basin; and Blue-headed, of the eastern states. Differentiation of the three can be difficult, especially in the late summer when the birds are grayer.

Cassin's Vireos are identified by a thick white eye-ring, a white line extending from the eye to the bill, and the black line under it.

Voice: Songs are a collection of bright, whistle-like, and slightly buzzy notes or phrases with pauses. A common call is a buzzy squeak.

Below: Adult. Juvenile looks similar.

Jeff Bleam

Plumbeous Vireo (5")

The Plumbeous Vireo is similar to the Cassin's but lacks the greenish color. Until recently, both were considered subspecies of the Solitary Vireo. During the breeding season, Plumbeous Vireos are found along the eastern border of the state from the Mono Basin to the south end of Death Valley National Park. Most of these birds leave California in the late summer and head to Mexico, but some stay all year.

Due to their limited range in California, Plumbeous are the least common of the vireos found here. They are much more common to the east of the state and down into Mexico.

Like all vireos, Plumbeous Vireos are methodical and deliberate in their foraging, as if they think out every move.

Voice: Songs are similar to Cassin's but more elaborate. Hearing them reminds you of being in a pet store. Calls vary. Some calls are parts of their songs, others are grating, raspy, or like a kingbird.

Below: The hanging nest is woven of catkins, or long, rope-like clusters of male flowers. The tree appears to be a Silver-leaf Oak.

Stephanie Lee Smith

Bell's Vireo (4.75")

These songsters winter in Mexico and Central America, arrive in Southern California in April, and stay for the summer. They nest mostly in willow thickets and cottonwoods and, where such habitat remains, are fairly common in a wide swath of land along the coast up to Point Conception. Bell's Vireos also nest in the Colorado River Valley and in that dryer inland area are often seen in mesquite thickets. They are never far from a water source.

Bell's Vireos like to sing but usually stay hidden in the middle of a tree or thicket, so they are more often heard than seen.

Due to cowbird parasitism and removal of thicket habitat, Bell's Vireos continue to decline in population.

Voice: Song is a cute and cheery cheedeldeedeldee, cheedeldeedeldoo *or variations thereof. Common calls are a buzzing similar to a Bewick's Wren's and a raspy* churt.

Left: Adult in Sweet Acacia, March 31. **Top right:** Most birds are gray, like this May 21 juvenile, and turn dull gray by mid-summer. **Bottom right:** Some are brownish, like this molting one. Photo taken August 9.

Lois Manowitz

Can you find the birdie?

See page 415

Nuthatches

Nuthatches get their name from their practice of jamming acorns and pine nuts into cracks in the bark of a tree, then hammering away at the acorns to get the meat out. In spring and summer, their diet is mostly insects and insect larvae and eggs; in winter, they rely on the nuts and acorns they have stashed.

All three California nuthatch species are at least fairly common where they occur, and all forage primarily on tree trunks, large branches, or on the ground. They often forage with other small birds, including titmice and chickadees, and are not shy in the least.

White-Breasted Nuthatch (5.75")

Often hyper and always inquisitive, the White-breasted Nuthatch lives in mature oak woodlands throughout California. They usually do not inhabit a forest where conifers are predominant—that is the territory of their red-breasted cousins, but there is some overlap. Although year-round residents where they occur, sometimes they all disappear for a while. I don't know where they go but I assume it is to another food source.

White-breasted Nuthatches typically forage down tree trunks and are usually seen with their mates.

Voice: Songs are a nasal waa-waa-waa-waa *that is deeper than you would expect from a small bird, and a higher* dwee-dwee-dwee-dwee *at the same tempo. Call is a buzzy* yink, *or maybe* yack, *repeated.*

Below: The classic pose of a nuthatch.

Below: I watched this pair for quite a while as they went in and out of their home in the cavity of a willow tree, taking food to their little ones. How she collected all those flies in her bill at the same time, I'll never know. (The female is duller overall with a gray cap.)

Red-Breasted Nuthatch (4.5")

The beautiful Red-breasted Nuthatch is a year-round resident of the coniferous forests throughout the state. They avoid the oak woodlands, which are the habitat of their White-breasted cousins, except in cold weather when those in the mountains may come down to lower elevations for a short time.

Their primary food is insects, supplemented with conifer seeds and nuts, which they store for the winter in tree-bark crevices. The Red-breasted Nuthatch's foraging pattern is more random than that of the White-breasted. Like other nuthatches, the Red-breasteds commonly forage with small birds of other species. Amazingly, they all get along well, even though they appear to be after the same foods.

Voice: Call is a nasal yank, *or* YANK!, *with evenly spaced repeats. They also draw that same sound out longer—like a southern drawl. Song is essentially the same but much faster and a little higher, a staccato without the drawl.*

Below: Adult male. Female is duller.

Jerry Ting

Pygmy Nuthatch (4.25")

Pygmy Nuthatches are year-round residents of the Jeffery and Ponderosa pine forests throughout the state. They are also found in many of our other forests but avoid the damp far north coast.

Our smallest nuthatch, the Pygmy, forages for nuts, seeds, and bugs mostly on cones and needle clusters, often on the outside of the tree. They also forage on the ground. Insect eggs, like the one **the bird in the photo** has, are a common food.

Pygmies are highly social and are almost always found in small flocks of 10 to 30 birds that are usually quite talkative. Flocks are often joined by chickadees and other small birds.

Voice: Pygmy Nuthatches chatter when foraging together. The sound is of peeps and pips as single notes, trills, or various squeakings. At times, the peeping becomes shrill and sounds like a rubber ducky.

Below: Adult male. Female is duller.

Brown Creeper (5.25")

Brown Creepers live in the forests along with the nuthatches. While the White-breasted Nuthatch typically forages down a tree trunk, the creeper forages upward. The creeper also favors the underside of tree branches, while the nuthatch favors the top side. Although they eat the same bugs, there does not appear to be a conflict between the two. Both are specialists. The creeper starts at the bottom of a tree and works its way up, then drops to the ground and goes up another tree close by. They work the branches the same way: they start at the trunk and work their way out, then fly back to the trunk and take another branch out.

The Brown Creeper is fairly common but camouflages well and is easy to overlook (**see page 410**). If you want to find a creeper, the easiest way may be to look closely where nuthatches are foraging.

Voice: Call is a soft, high frequency tsee *that is easy to miss. In the spring and early summer, the males sing a high-pitched, rapid "trees, trees, beautiful trees." The "trees" are the call note but are much louder.*

Photos: Colors vary due to region or morph (see p. 510), not age or sex.

Chickadees

We have three species of chickadees in California. They live year-round where they are found, thrive in their own special habitats, and each species has its own way of enunciating its name, chick-a-dee. Some imagination may be required to hear the name.

Chickadees are the birder's best friend: they are always in flocks, are not shy, and other small birds are comfortable foraging with them. So when you see chickadees, be on the lookout for kinglets, warblers, nuthatches, and any number of other bird species.

Although chickadees are highly social, they respect each other's personal space and keep a certain distance from one another while foraging.

The sexes look alike and juveniles look much like adults.

Mountain Chickadee (5.25")

As the name implies, Mountain Chickadees inhabit the higher mountains of the state. They prefer coniferous and mixed forests and often use aspen groves for nesting. Some migrate short distances to lower elevations in winter. They are abundant and are always in flocks.

Voicings include a wide variety of songs and calls. Songs include a high, clear fee, fee, bee, bee *with the* fees *higher than the* bees. *They also sing a sweet, compressed* prettybird *that is often repeated or combined with a fast, scratchy* lookoverhere. *Their* **namesake call is scratchy**. *They also chatter, ending it with a buzzy squawk. Also, a soft* seep.

Below: Adult on an incense-cedar.

Chestnut-Backed Chickadee (4.75")

The beautiful chickadee of the coastal forests from Big Sur to the Yukon, the Chestnut-backed Chickadee also inhabits the west side of the Cascades and northern Sierras but is less common there. They are highly social birds, are always in flocks, and other species of birds are usually found with them.

Chestnut-backed Chickadees have regional plumage variations in California. These are shown in the **photos below**. Birds in the far north tend to have black caps and chestnut sides; around San Francisco Bay, they tend to have brown caps and gray sides; and those of the Central Coast tend to have black to brown caps with gray sides.

Voice: Chick-a-dee *can be clear and sweet, squeaky, or buzzed. Also, a wide variety of high-pitched, short, squeaky notes and phrases.*

Keith Carlson

Melissa Kung

Jerry Ting

Black-Capped Chickadee (5")

Although by far the most common chickadee in North America, the Black-capped's range in California is limited to the forests in the northwest tip of the state. They are readily found there all year. Inquisitive and lively birds, they are as cute as any bird, perhaps because of their large, round, baby-like head.

Like all chickadees, Black-caps are highly social. They are almost always seen together and usually with other forest birds.

In fall and winter, they eat berries and seeds; in spring and summer, mostly insects.

Voice: Like all chickadees, Black-caps have a lot to say. One common call is a high, sweet **cheese bur-ger** *with the* bur-ger *a little lower. The same call can be made about an octave lower. Another call is a scratchy chattering that some people say sounds like* fries-wid-dat, *or a longer version may be* wouldjalikesome fries-wid-dat—*but that may be stretching it a little. Its namesake call,* **chick-a-dee**, *is usually scratchy-sounding, similar to a Mountain Chickadee's, and is often more like* chick-a-dee-dee-dee. *Short calls include* seep, *which can be expressed as a soft call, a trill, or a very high-pitched and thin call that is almost inaudible.*

Below: Adult enjoying rose hips.

Jim Cummins

Warblers

"The butterflies of the bird world," warblers are tiny, colorful, and constantly flitting about. All are primarily insect eaters, but some species are treetop specialists, some make a living close to the ground, and some forage in between. The most common species are listed first.

Almost all of our warblers migrate and most travel at night. Many migrate in mixed flocks, probably because populations of some species are historically low. All are spring beauties. By the time they head south in the late summer, they are duller in appearance than they were in the spring.

The songs of several species are similar or have similar components. They are of two parts: a few rapid, identical *seet* or *sweet* notes followed by a short warble. Positive ID by voice is not easy because both parts can vary.

Yellow-Rumped Warbler (4.75–5.5")

The adaptable Yellow-rumped Warbler thrives in a wide variety of habitats and is the most abundant warbler in California from fall to spring. They are seen in flocks except when breeding. Yellow-rumps breed in the Sierras and Cascades and northward into Canada and have one or two broods a year. In the south and the lower elevations, they usually leave for their breeding grounds when the Yellow Warblers arrive in the spring.

Two different-looking birds make up this species, the Myrtle and the Audubon's. The Myrtle is a bird of the damp northern forests; the Audubons' are more widespread. **The Myrtle has a white throat patch; the Audubon's is yellow.** Sometimes the patch is yellow and white, making identification difficult. No other California warbler varies as much and determining the age and sex of nonbreeding birds can be very difficult.

When perched, the yellow on their rump is often hidden by their wings and may not be visible until the bird flies.

In the winter, Yellow-rumps commonly forage on the ground for seeds and insects and often hover to pluck insects out of the air. In the spring and summer, they typically forage in the treetops for insects. They are expert fly catchers.

Yellow-Rumped Warbler, Myrtle subspecies
Voice: Call is a soft chep *or* chek. *Song (spring and summer only) is a repeat of the same* seet *note four times, at times followed by a short, soft warble.*

Next page, top: Breeding male (April to August; female is duller). **Second row:** Males. Both are December birds. **Third row:** Females, November and September birds. **Bottom:** First-winter female.

Warblers 420

Yellow-Rumped Warbler, Audubon's subspecies

Voice: Calls are a sharp whit, whet, *and* wheet. *Song, heard only in breeding season, is* sweet-sweet-su-we-chu. *Varies but usually ends with* u.

Photos show a wide variation of plumage in this subspecies. **Below, top:** Two March males. **Bottom:** November adult males. **Next page, top two:** April male; November female. **Third row:** Adult October female (left); first-winter female. **Bottom:** First-year; fledgling. **Add'l photo:** Page 504.

Jim Cummins

Jeff Bleam

Orange-Crowned Warbler (5")

A common warbler of many habitats throughout California, the Orange-crowned Warbler is rarely identified by its orange crown because it is seldom seen. Some are year-round residents along the coast; others breed in the north and winter in the south.

Orange-crowned Warblers are low-level foragers and prefer shrubs and small trees at the edge of a clearing. They often forage with birds of other species and frequently fly out to catch prey in the air. Orange-crowns are not shy, so our suburban neighborhoods are suitable to them.

This species has a lot of plumage variations as well as seasonal changes. The **dark line through the white eye-ring** is almost always present but is more prominent on some birds. Sometimes, when bathing or frazzled, the bird shows orange down that is hidden under its body feathers.

Voice: Call is tisp, *at times very soft. One song is a descending trill that ends with a warble or fade-out; another, a sweet warble with a trill mid-way.*

Below, top: Adult on April 4. **Bottom:** Some birds, perhaps younger, are lighter. The photo was taken on April 27. In the fall, the birds turn darker and duller and remain so until midwinter or spring.

Next page, from the top: September adult; November bird on coyote brush; two January birds. Sexes similar. **Additional photo:** Page 496.

Peter Pearsall/ USFWS

Eric Ellingson

Roger Zachary

Common Yellowthroat (4.75")

Common Yellowthroats inhabit just about every marsh in the western half of California where reeds of any kind are present. In warmer areas, they stay all year.

The male is easy to identify because of his bandit mask. Immature males have only a partial black mask. The females can be confused with female Yellow Warblers (see page 428), as both vary considerably, but Yellowthroats are typically less yellow overall and ***muddy on the back***.

Foraging can be systematic—going up one bulrush stalk, then starting at the base of another—or can appear entirely random.

Voice: Calls are chuck, *a staccato version of the same, and scolding chatter. Songs are warbles that vary but have similar components. The most common songs are* witcheywa, witcheywa, witcheywa *and* chut-chut-chew, *usually repeated three times.*

Below: Light spring female in cow parsnips. Some are much yellower than others.

Next page, top: Spring male. **Middle:** Dark and light spring females. **Bottom:** Juvenile (left) and fall female.

Note: This warbler is not to be confused with the Yellow-throated Warbler of the eastern states, which looks unlike any California bird.

Yellow Warbler (5")

As beautiful a bird as you will ever see, the Yellow Warbler is another common California warbler but is often overlooked because it is so small and usually stays in the treetops. They winter in the tropics and breed in willow thickets from northern Baja to Nome, Alaska.

Like most warblers, Yellow Warblers often migrate at night to conserve energy. Along the migration route, they stay in flocks and are commonly found in the tops of cottonwoods and tall willows. Flocks, usually of 20 to 80 birds, start arriving in Southern California by early April. In the fall, the migrating birds have finished passing through by mid-October.

Yellow Warblers are frequently parasitized by cowbirds, and their population continues to slowly decline. (See *Cowbirds*, page 477.)

The **white eye-ring** varies in intensity and sometimes is not visible. Note the **dark and light streaking on the wings** in the photos.

Voice: Song is seet-seet-seet, so-o-sweet. *Varies. Wilson's and Yellow-rumped songs are similar. Common calls are* chip *and a whispered* tink.

Below: A breeding male on Desert Senna. The nonbreeding adult male has brown, not red, streaking on the breast.

Next page, top: First-fall female. **Middle:** Adult late summer female in crab apples. Adult females may have *light* red streaking on the breast. **Bottom:** Pale spring female on an alder. Many spring females are brighter yellow; fledglings and juveniles are much lighter, like this bird's belly.

Wilson's Warbler (4.25")

The tiny warblers with the black hats, the Wilson's, arrive from Mexico and Central America in the early spring. They breed in willow, alder, and aspen thickets mostly along the north coast, in the far north, and in the Sierras. Wilson's Warblers are somewhat common and during migration can be seen throughout the state. Migration peaks in April and September.

Their small size notwithstanding, Wilson's Warblers are relatively easy to find because they are not terribly shy and are often seen in the open and on the lower branches of trees and shrubs.

Voice: Call is chip *or* tsik *and can sound like a loud kiss; song is sweet and resembles a Yellow Warbler's but is shorter and choppier.*

Top: Male. **Bottom:** Female (brown cap); fledgling. **Add'l photos:** P 507.

Townsend's Warbler (4.75")

Townsend's Warblers breed in Oregon, Washington, and British Columbia. Some of these birds winter along our central coast, where they are found in mixed forests and in the oaks. Many more winter as far south as central Mexico. The birds migrating to and from Mexico can be seen in almost any habitat. In the spring, they migrate through the interior and are common in desert oases in the south and in the live oaks and manzanita farther north. In the fall, many travel through the mountains.

Its distinctive face makes the Townsend's Warbler easy to identify. For a warbler, they are fairly common.

Voice: Calls are a sharp tsip *or* chip *and a stuttering chipping similar to that of a Bushtit. Songs are a **very high-pitched** tsee-tsee-tsee dzoo zumba and weezy, weezy, weee-zeet. Both songs vary and **both are buzzy**.*

Top: Male on a Silver-leaf Oak. **Bottom:** Female. Immatures are similar but paler.

Stephanie Lee Smith

Melissa Kung

Black-Throated Gray Warbler (4.75")

The Black-throated Gray Warbler winters in Mexico and arrives in California early in the spring to breed, mostly in dry, open wooded areas of oak, juniper, and pine. On their trip north, they are often seen in desert oases and in willow thickets along streams. Like many other species, post-breeding Black-throated Grays often move to higher elevation forests before they depart in the late summer or early fall. As the lower vegetation dries out, the bugs decrease and the birds are forced to go higher.

Black-throated Grays are relativity easy to find because they are not shy and commonly forage toward the outside of a tree. They search for insects on branches, fly out to catch them in midair, and pick them off leaves while hovering. Black-throated Gray Warblers often forage with birds of other species.

These birds superficially resemble Mountain Chickadees because of their small size and similar colors. However, the warbler has a different color pattern, does not have the shape of a chickadee, has wing bars, and has a *yellow spot in front of the eye*.

Voice: Calls include chip *and a faint* tink. **Songs are buzzy**, *some more than others. A common song is a high-pitched* zee-del, zee-del da-deechee, *which can be soft or loud and piercing. Another begins with a few* tsee *notes followed by a blurred warble. As with other warblers, songs vary.*

Below: Male. **Next page:** Male in a birch; female in willows. **Add'l:** P 515.

Jerry Ting

Jeff Bleam

Nashville Warbler (4.25")

Unmistakable due to their ***broad-rimmed white spectacles***, Nashville Warblers were first discovered by Europeans in Nashville, Tennessee, hence the name. But actually, they merely migrate through the area.

In California, Nashville Warblers breed in the far north and in the Sierras at lower elevations. They winter from central Mexico to Central America and are seen briefly during the spring and fall migrations throughout the state. In the spring, look for Nashville Warblers feeding in the live oaks and in the tops of willows, bottlebrush, and other trees with bright blossoms that attract insects. In the nesting areas, look among the black oaks and pines where the understory is brushy. There, they feed in the understory or low in the forest canopy. Nashvilles may move to higher elevations late in the season. They are not common in California.

Voice: Call is tisp. *One common song is a sweet ditty of two notes and about ten syllables. The first note is a rapid* seet, seet, seet, seet, seet. *It is followed by a smoother and faster* swee-swee-swee-swee-swee *that is sometimes shortened. Another is* chipa-chipa-chipa-see-swee-sweet; *a third song is softer but starts the same and ends with a short, descending trill.*

Top: Male. **Bottom:** Female. Immature males look similar. (Comp. p. 492.)

MacGillivray's Warbler (5")

This bird with the ***distinctive white eyelashes*** winters in the tropics and is present in California from mid-spring to early fall. Some MacGillivray's Warblers breed in the Sierras and Cascades and along the coast from Big Sur to the Oregon border. However, like the Nashvilles, most of these birds breed much farther north and are just passing through. They are not common in California.

MacGillivray's Warblers almost always stay hidden in thick brush or in streamside thickets of alder, willow, or aspen. They also favor healed clear-cuts and burn areas and are usually identified only by their unmistakable voice. To call this bird, kiss the back of your hand.

Voice: One call is a sparrow-like chep *or* chek. *Another,* tisk. *Both can be soft or much louder. Song, sung from inside the brush in April and May, is commonly* tseet-tseet-tseet, churry churry. *It varies but is of two parts.*

Top: Male in an alder. **Bottom row:** Adult female; first-summer bird.

Hermit Warbler (5.5")

The Hermit Warbler is not more solitary than most warblers but is usually seen with birds of other species. Due to their lack of numbers, they often join mixed flocks during migration. Most Hermit Warblers we see in California are traveling from their winter homes in Central Mexico to breed in western Oregon and Washington, but some breed along our north coast and in the Sierras and Cascades. A relative few winter along our coast from Marin to Point Conception.

The migration path of Hermit Warblers is similar to that of many other songbirds—northward through the lowlands in the spring and southward through the mountains in the late summer or early fall. This is probably because of the availability of insects.

Hermit Warblers nest in coniferous forests but are often found in the oaks and other deciduous woods during migration. During the breeding and nesting season, they prefer the interior of the tops of tall trees, so they are difficult to see unless you are in steep terrain where you can look out on them instead of up.

The foraging methods of Hermit Warblers help us find them. They start at the trunk of a tree and work out to the end of a branch, then fly back to the trunk and go out on another. They also hover while feeding.

Good places to find Hermit Warblers during the breeding season are in the Donner Pass area and at McArthur-Burney Falls State Park.

Voice: Hermit Warblers have two song types, both **piercingly high-pitched** *and buzzy. One is very similar to a Townsend's; the other, more like a Black-throated Gray's. Call is a soft* chip.

Below: First-winter female in a pine. Photo was taken January 10.

Adult male in an alder tree; photo taken May 21. Adult females are duller. By mid-summer many are molting and look splotchy.

Lucy's Warbler (4.25")

A bird of the hot Sonoran Desert, the tiny Lucy's Warbler lives in the driest habitat of any warbler found in the United States. From April to mid-August, they are fairly common in the washes and tributaries that lead into the Colorado River. Lucy's prefer areas of mesquite, cottonwoods, and willows. Surprisingly, they are often found far from water.

Most Lucy's Warblers spend the nonbreeding season along the west coast of central Mexico. Strays are seen sporadically in coastal areas as far north as San Francisco, usually from October to March.

Voice: Song is composed of a sweet trill followed by one of at least a few warbles. One ending warble is two or three lower-pitched, longer, smooth notes. Perhaps tsee-tsee-tsee-tsee, swee, swee. *The trill is faster than the beginning of other warblers' songs. Calls are a soft* tisp *and a faint* tsip.

Below: Adult male on Velvet Mesquite. Both males and females have a rusty patch on the rump but only the males have the rusty cap. The females and male juveniles are duller and look plain.

Greg Lavaty

Virginia's Warbler (4.75")

The comparatively dull-looking Virginia's Warbler is found on the dry mountain slopes of the eastern border of California between Lake Tahoe and Las Vegas. Their preferred habitat is pinyon-juniper forests with brush and chaparral, but they are also found in aspen groves in the higher elevations.

Virginia's Warblers arrive in early spring and leave by late August to winter in Mexico. They are uncommon in California but are much more common east of the state within the Great Basin. A good place to look for them is in the aspen groves near Monitor Pass. They are tail pumpers and flickers, and that movement can give away their location.

Voice: Virginia's song is sweet and of two parts. The first part is like that of a Yellow Warbler, sweet-sweet-sweet-sweet. *The second part can be much faster than, but similar to, a Yellow Warbler's, and it can sound jumbled. Calls are* chip *and a faint* tisp.

Below: An adult female in a fig tree. Juveniles are similar but may lack the yellow. The male is slightly brighter and sometimes shows a red crown. Note the **white eye-ring**.

Frank Salmon

Palm Warbler (5.25")

Palm Warblers are scarce in California and are usually seen here as individuals or with flocks of other birds. The western subspecies we see in California is not as colorful as the Palm Warbler of the eastern states. The western birds breed in or near Alberta and winter along the West Coast. A small number consistently come as far south as Marin County. They are rarely seen in the south. The bird in the **lower left photo** was a celebrity when it stayed one winter in Orange County.

In winter, Palm Warblers are as brown as a sparrow. Furthermore, they behave like a sparrow, foraging mostly on the ground in weedy areas or in low shrubs. But they walk instead of hop, and their sharp, pointed bills and thinner bodies are sure indications they are not sparrows. Like other warblers, they can sally out and snag an insect in midair.

Voice: Call is a short, thin seep. *Their song is a buzzy trill like that of a Chipping Sparrow and is mostly reserved for the breeding grounds.*

Top: Photo was taken in December. **Bottom left:** March 10. This bird is molting. Note the pin feathers on its head. **Right:** Breeding adult, May 5.

Yellow-Breasted Chat (7")

Hardly a warbler, but not fitting elsewhere taxonomically, the large Yellow-breasted Chat winters in the tropics and breeds all along our coast and in the northern half of the state. They are found in a variety of shrubby habitats where water is present and vegetation is dense.

The chats arrive in the south in early April and sometimes stay only two or three months. Since they are capable of having two broods a year, some may have one brood in the south and another farther north. Regardless, shortly after their young fledge, many move on, and I assume it is to the north where it is wetter.

Yellow-breasted Chats feed on insects and berries in thickets. When satisfied, the males frequently perch on a treetop to sing or give an oration. They are prolific singers and speakers.

Voice is a combination of whistles, clucks, squawks, catcalls, pops, gurgles, mews, and caws, often strung together in mockingbird fashion.

Along with the mockingbird, the California Thrasher, and a few others, the chat is among a small group of common California birds with a wide repertoire that sing loudly out in the open. Like the thrasher, the chat can sound comical. One tune sounds like forced laughter.

Below: Adult male; females are duller. **Additional photo** is on page 508.

Gnatcatchers

Blue-Gray Gnatcatcher (4.5")

An abundant bird, and by far the most common gnatcatcher in California, the Blue-gray is a year-round resident along the southern coast in riparian thickets, chaparral, and other undisturbed brushy habitats. During breeding season or migration, it is found in most of the rest of the state but usually not in the desert territory of the Black-tailed Gnatcatcher and not in the high mountains or dense forests. In the south, the population explodes in winter as migrating birds join permanent residents. They are not shy in the least.

Gnatcatchers are well-named birds. They flit almost continuously and flick their tails to flush gnats and other insects from foliage.

I once saw a Blue-gray lying on its back, floating in a large cloud of gnats. The bird was expending little effort to stay aloft and was enjoying a rich feast. It was suspended, I suppose, largely by the swarming action of the gnats, something I have never read about but saw that day. How many such things have been witnessed by birders!

Voice: Calls are squeaky, buzzy, and sometimes nagging. Song is like a meal made up of leftovers of other birds' songs with plenty of squeaky sauce added to hold it together.

Below: Winter male in coastal goldenbush. Note the black-and-white pattern on the underside of the tail.

Roger Zachary

Below, top: Spring male in the willows. Note the blue tint and dark eyebrow of this breeding bird. They are brightest from March to July. **Bottom:** September female in Mulefat. **Juvenile photo:** Page 503.

Black-Tailed Gnatcatcher (4.5")

A common year-round resident of the Sonoran Desert in the southeastern part of the state, the tiny Black-tailed Gnatcatcher lives in a wide variety of desert habitats, sometimes far from water. In the waterless places, it is assumed that they get their hydration from the insects they eat.

Watching these gnatcatchers flit while foraging on a cactus or thorn bush is a real head scratcher. How they can do that and not get hurt, I don't know. Maybe no one else does either.

The Black-tailed's flight pattern is undulating, like that of goldfinches.

Voice: A harsh, short, scolding buzz; chits; scratchy chittering; and a buzzy squeal. When agitated, all are put together as a rant.

Top: Spring (breeding) male on Honey Mesquite. **Bottom left:** Non-breeding male. Compare the black-and-white pattern on the underside of the tail with that of the other gnatcatchers. **Right:** A fluffed female.

California Gnatcatcher (4.5")

Until the late 1980s, the California Gnatcatcher was classified as a subspecies of the Black-tailed, which is nearly identical. The Black-tailed is found mostly in the Sonoran Desert; the California is a bird of the coastal scrub in a narrow strip of land from southern Baja California to Los Angeles. Little coastal scrub remains in this part of California, but where it does, California Gnatcatchers make use of it. Most of the California population winters in Baja.

Compare the black-and-white pattern on the underside of the tail with the patterns of the Black-tailed and Blue-gray Gnatcatchers.

Voice is buzzy and kazoo-like squeakings in a few varieties, commonly like the mew *of a cat. It differs significantly from the Black-tailed's.*

Top: Fall (nonbreeding) male in big saltbush. Breeding female is similar. **Bottom left to right:** Spring (breeding) male; winter female. The male wears his ***black cap from February to July***.

Flycatchers

A lot of birds catch flies, but some are specifically designated as flycatchers. In many cases, their voices are the key to identification.

In this section, the sexes look alike or similar unless stated otherwise.

Brown-Crested Flycatcher (8.75")

Brown-crested Flycatchers are Mexican birds that breed in the Colorado River Valley and in isolated sites in the Mojave Desert. They typically arrive here in May and leave in August.

These birds are much more common in southern Arizona, where housing is more abundant in the form of woodpecker holes in Saguaro cacti. In California, they live among the tall cottonwoods and sycamores by streams and in desert washes and oases.

Brown-crested Flycatchers are scarce in California but can usually be found in the late spring at Big Morongo Canyon Preserve near Yucca Valley.

Voice: Unlike the docile Ash-throated Flycatcher on the next page, the Brown-crested is usually loud and raucous. Calls include a sharp and comparatively soft whit.

Below: The Brown-crested Flycatcher is an ***enlarged version*** of the common Ash-throated Flycatcher on the next page. The Brown-crested also has a ***longer and stouter bill*** and is easily differentiated by voice.

Nick Pulcinella

Ash-Throated Flycatcher (8.25")

The beautiful, pastel-painted Ash-throated Flycatchers begin arriving in California in March. They breed all over the state in a wide variety of arid habitats, ranging from desert mesquite and willows to Joshua trees and yucca, and from pinyon-juniper forests to woodlands of cottonwoods, oaks, and sycamores. A relative few Ash-throated Flycatchers are year-round residents of the Colorado River Valley; the rest head back to western Mexico and Central America in September.

These birds are cavity dwellers and such housing is scarce in California, so although Ash-throated Flycatchers are common here, they are not abundant.

Voice: Song is a high-pitched, squeaky, disjointed sputtering. Calls are segments of the song and include a soft pip, *a cricket-like* pippip, *and a louder* ki-pick *and* pip-peer.

Below: Ash-throated Flycatchers usually perch erect, as in the photo, and often tilt their heads to the side as if to say, "I'm so cute." And so they are. **Photo of a fledgling** is on page 504.

Olive-Sided Flycatcher (7.5")

Olive-sided Flycatchers winter in South America and arrive in California beginning in mid-April to breed near clearings in mountain forests. A small number breed along our coast, but most go to the Sierras, the far north of the state, or as far north as Alaska. They have usually left California by the end of September.

These somewhat common birds are easy to identify by their piercing voice and by the pale yellow stripe on the breast that makes them look like they are wearing an **unbuttoned vest.**

Olive-sided Flycatchers forage by darting out from a high perch, snagging their prey in midair, and returning to the same perch to resume their erect posture.

During migration, they are often seen in the desert sitting still out in the open at the top of a bare branch, as if oblivious to Cooper's Hawks.

Voice: Call is a high, sharp pip, pip, pip. *Sometimes, the middle syllable is slurred. Song is a whistled, piercing, three-syllable* what-PEEVES-you. *Also, an emphatic* Quick, free beers!

Below: Adults and juveniles look alike. The back of an Olive-sided Flycatcher looks almost identical to that of the pewee on the next page. Note the faint eye-ring.

Western Wood-Pewee (6.25")

The Western Wood-Pewee is another bird that winters in South America and comes to California to breed. They breed in forests and woodlands and are commonly found in ponderosa pines, cottonwoods, and aspens, often near streams. Range and habitat are similar to the Olive-sided Flycatcher's. During migration (late April and May; September and early October) both can be seen just about anywhere in the state.

Foraging is from a low (or relatively lower) perch and precise: sit still and wait, sally out horizontally to snag an insect in midair, and return to the same perch. They are patient but occasionally give up on a perch and choose another close by or a little farther away.

Voice is a buzzy, piercing PAY-wee! *Sometimes it is preceded by a few sweet piping notes followed by a short twitter, then* PAY-wee! *At times, it is much softer. Also,* bzEEET! *and* beez-eet.

Below: Western Wood-Pewees look similar to Olive-sided Flycatchers but are much smaller and their vest is not as clearly defined. The pewee's **eye-ring is faint or lacking**. They can be confused with the smaller Willow Flycatcher (page 451), but note the **paler wing bars** on the pewee. Also, the pewee's voice easily identifies it.

Pacific-Slope Flycatcher (5.5")

The Pacific-slope Flycatcher winters along the west coast of Mexico and breeds along the Pacific coast from the Mexican border to southern Alaska. They also breed on the west side of the Sierras and Cascades.

In California from April through September, these beauties are commonly found along streams in forests and woodlands.

Pacific-slope Flycatchers are distinguished by their olive color above, yellowish color below, **teardrop eye-ring** that flares at the back, sweet call, and—most of all—by their unsurpassed cuteness.

In 1989, what was known as the **Western Flycatcher** was split into two species: the Pacific-slope and the **Cordilleran**, which is found east of the Sierras.

Voice: The male's call is a crisp sue-WEET!; *the female's is a soft* tsip. *Song is a crisp and sweet* pid-it, seet, sue-WEET, *often repeated. Sometimes the sequence is:* seet, sue-WEET, pid-it.

Below: Adult on a redwood. Juveniles look pale.

Melissa Kung

Empidonax Flycatchers

I purposely avoided using Latin taxonomic names in this book, but with Empidonax Flycatchers there is no avoiding it. The term comes from the ancient Greek, empis, meaning "gnat," and anax, meaning "master." Identifying Empidonax Flycatchers can be like straining gnats.

The first Empidonax Flycatcher, the Pacific-slope, is much easier to identify than the others because of its cute baby face and clearly different song, which is why I put it on the previous page, before the rest.

The other Empidonax Flycatchers commonly found in California—the Willow, Dusky, Hammond's, and Gray Flycatchers—can look nearly identical in the field and are usually differentiated by voice. With the exception of the Willow, that's not easy.

All have a partial molt in the spring and a nearly complete molt in the late summer or fall, so birds of the same species can look quite different. Adding to the complexity, their ranges overlap, often making field identification impossible if you do not hear them.

Whether the crest is up or down, or partly up or down, means nothing when it comes to identification. The photos on the next pages were selected to show how different the birds may appear.

Perhaps the most helpful clue for identification, besides voice, is the eye-ring: the Willow has little or no visible eye-ring; the Hammond's is flared, mostly at the back, as is the Dusky's; and the Gray's is obvious but is not flared at the back like the Hammond's and Dusky's. At least that is how they usually appear.

Identifying the Empidonax Flycatchers on the following pages as separate species is slicing the salami pretty thin, and the field guides that attempt to do so can contradict one another. I'll keep it simple: if the bird is in a coniferous forest and the eye-ring is clear, it's likely a Hammond's; if it's in the scrub or a dryer forest and the eye-ring is clear, it's likely a Dusky; if it's in the willows and the eye-ring is faint, it's likely a Willow; and if it's gray, in the sage, and the eye-ring is clear, it's likely a Gray.

Almost all these birds winter in Mexico. They come to California to breed, and they time their arrival with the beginning of spring at their destinations. Their return trip is also staggered. Overall, the spring migration starts early in the spring, and the fall migration is over early in the fall.

Like many other birds their size, the lifespan of Empidonax Flycatchers is typically three to four years.

In season, and in their habitats, all these birds are common in California.

Willow Flycatcher (5.75")

This bird winters along the coasts of Central America and southern Mexico. A relative few breed in the Sierras and Cascades, but most we see in California are migrating to or from the Pacific Northwest. We can infer that because their populations in the state are much greater during the migrations in the spring and in the late summer.

As the name implies, their preferred habitat is willow thickets, which are always near water. That helps make the Willow one of the easiest of the Empidonax Flycatchers to identify. In the spring, they are fairly common in the willows through the length of the state. In Orange County, we typically see them for a few weeks in both May and September. There are fewer in the fall, I suppose because more are traveling farther inland.

Willow Flycatchers have little or no eye-ring, which, with their voice and habitat, sets them apart.

Voice: A common call is whit, *like a Yellow-rumped Warbler's but sweeter. Typical song is something like* bzzzip! fitzz-bew! *Sometimes the second part is warbled. Also, a buzzy* fitzz-bew.

Below: Both photos are of the same bird and were taken in late May.

Hammond's Flycatcher (5.5")

The Hammond's Flycatcher winters in Mexico and Central America and breeds in the cool coniferous and mixed forests of the Sierras, Cascades, and Coast Ranges as far south as Geyserville. They are usually found where firs are present. Spring arrives late, and the weather fluctuates more in the mountains, so the Hammond's may have extended spring and fall migrations and be seen along the way in many habitats.

Note the *flared eye-ring*. The adult bird has a distinctive "vest" that may or may not be slightly streaked. The Hammond's looks similar to a Western Wood-Pewee, but the pewee either has no eye-ring or it is faint. The spring Hammond's is brighter, usually olive on the back and yellowish on the belly; fall birds are typically grayer overall.

Voice: Calls include a sweet pip!, pee-ooo, pooh, *and a short squeak. Song is a soft, clear* see-eeet, *a short pause, then a grinding, rapid* tsrt, *usually repeated. Sequence may be reversed. Also,* pip, pip, pee-ooo.

Below: Both photos are of the same bird and were taken in mid-April.

Dusky Flycatcher (5.75")

In California, the Dusky Flycatcher is a summer bird of the mountains. They breed in the Cascades and to a lesser degree in the Sierras and high southern mountain ranges. The Dusky Flycatcher's favorite habitats include scrub, chaparral, aspen groves, and open forests with few trees. They also do well in healed-over burn areas and in power line corridors.

Duskys winter in Mexico and begin crossing the border into California in early April. Many of the birds we see here are just migrating through to places as far away as northern British Columbia. Judging by the birding reports, most of the migrating birds likely travel the length of the state in a week or two. The Duskys are gone by September.

Like our other Empidonax Flycatchers, Duskys typically have one brood a year.

Voice: Call is whit, *like a Yellow-rump Warbler's. Song is three sounds: a sharp, high, sweet* pseet, *a rising* pa-zit, *and a buzz. The sequence varies.*

Below: Duskys are virtually indistinguishable from a Hammond's except by voice. (See introduction on page 450.)

Gray Flycatcher (6")

This bird winters in Mexico and is seen in California, mostly east of the Sierras where it breeds. During the spring migration, they are found in desert washes and oases between these locations, less so in the fall.

The Gray Flycatchers' primary nesting habitat is Big Sagebrush, which shelters them from the winds that sweep the Great Basin. They also inhabit pinyon-juniper forests and are fairly common in both habitats.

These birds are (you guessed it) grayer than the other Empidonax Flycatchers, with less green or brown tint than the others.

Unlike the Willow Flycatcher's, **the Gray's eye-ring is obvious but is not flared at the back** as is the Hammond's and Dusky's.

Voice is somewhat like a House Sparrow's—a slightly buzzy cheeping and something like chu-lip, chu-lip. *Also, a sharp* pew! *and softer* whit.

Top: Photo, May 5. **Bottom left**: September 22. **Right:** Likely a juvenile.

Vermilion Flycatcher (5.5")

A more beautiful bird you will never see. I've said that before, haven't I? Maybe that's because the most beautiful bird is the one you're watching at the time.

The Vermilion Flycatcher is a Mexican bird that has increased its range into Southern California in recent years. We first saw them in parks and other open areas in Orange County around 2005. They arrived in December and stayed a month or two. Now a few breed here and may be seen throughout the year. Vermilion Flycatchers are not common in California, but the males are not shy and are easy to find where they occur, which can be in just about any open habitat in the south but not in the high mountains.

Vermilion Flycatchers can almost always be seen at the San Joaquin Marsh in Irvine from late December through January and at Big Morongo Canyon Preserve, near Yucca Valley, in the spring.

Their foraging pattern is similar to that of a Black Phoebe but Vermilions frequently use higher perches. They sally forth a short distance to snatch an insect in the air, then gracefully return to the same perch.

Voice: Call is a sharp, high peet. *Song starts with stuttering* pits *and ends with a fast warble. Perhaps* p-p-pit ca-zee-ooo. *They often snap their bills while foraging but not as loudly as a Black Phoebe does.*

Below: Adult female.

Next page, top: Adult male. **Middle:** Juvenile female; first-year male. **Bottom:** Juvenile male.

Black Phoebe (6.75")

Black Phoebes are abundant year-round residents of the coastal half of California. They are found in semi-open habitats near a water source as high as the lower elevations of the Sierras. Residential neighborhoods and parks suit them just fine.

Expert flycatchers, Black Phoebes usually forage from a perch only a few feet off the ground. They sit upright, pump their tails, and wait for their prey to appear. When it does, they swoop down, snap their beaks on it, which makes a popping sound, and then return to the same perch in a short graceful arc. Black Phoebes can hover and pick insects out of spider webs, and watching them is great backyard entertainment. Sometimes they hunt at night, taking advantage of our insect-attracting porch lights.

Black Phoebes build their nests of grasses and mud and often place them under eaves and bridges. Their flight is direct and buoyant.

Plumage varies from black to dark brown.

Voice: Twee-deet, twee-doo, *or one half of that. Varies. Call is* tsip.

Left: Adult. **Right**: Juvenile. Sexes look alike. **Add'l photos:** Pp. xi, 501.

Say's Phoebe (7.5")

Say's Phoebes are common year-round residents in the southern half of the state in arid, open, or semi-open habitats, especially grassland. In winter, their population explodes along the coast.

Masters of hovering, the Say's usually perform just above the ground.

The wisdom behind the design of this bird's guidance system, which enables it to safely and repeatedly land on thorny bushes, is beyond our comprehension. Consider the mathematical calculations required for the last-second adjustments made on each landing.

Voice is a high-pitched pity-ooo (*the* pity *compressed, the* ooo *drawn out);* pee-ooo; *and a raspy, buzzy* bdeeet!, *like a referee's whistle.*

Top: An adult on a Russian thistle or tumbleweed. **Bottom, left to right:** A juvenile and adult. Some adults are bright, some are duller. Both photos of the adults were taken in late November.

Cassin's Kingbird (9")

Bold, noisy, and entertaining, the sociable Cassin's Kingbirds are year-round residents of a narrow coastal strip south of Ventura. Some birds also come up from Mexico in the spring to breed farther up the coast and on the east side of the coastal mountain ranges as far north as the Bay Area.

Kingbirds like open areas with a few tall trees. They are flycatchers by trade, and they hover to snag insects in midair. Their typical foraging method is to sally forth from high in a tree and go up to snag an insect rather than down. When flying from one perch to another, they often do so in a fluttering, hovering manner, slowing the flight and enabling them to forage along the way. If the bugs are low, they'll perch on a fence post.

The Cassin's is distinguished from the Western Kingbird by its contrasting white chin and voice. See *Western Kingbird*, next page.

Voice sounds like a **squeaky toy** *(at least two voicings). Call is* ch-KEER!

Below: Adult on Curly Dock.

Western Kingbird (8.75")

A close relative of the Cassin's Kingbird, the Western Kingbird has a broader range in California. They breed in the lower elevations throughout the state, usually inland from the coast, and winter in southwestern Mexico and Central America. They begin arriving in March and are gone by October.

Behavior and habitat are much like the Cassin's Kingbird's. Both prefer open grassland with tall grasses and some tall trees nearby. They can then forage from low perches for low flying insects or from high in a tree for the high ones. The ranges of the two kingbirds overlap some and they appear to get along reasonably well.

When Western's feel threatened, they may display an otherwise hidden red crest. I have never seen it, but some books mention it.

Voice is a collection of sharp, high-pitched, sputtering, squeaky twitterings. Call is a high-pitched squeaky kit. *Unlike the Cassin's, the Western's voice, although squeaky, does not instantly make you think of a squeaky toy.*

Below: Compare the ***muted white mustache*** with that of the Cassin's.

Bushtit (4.5")

A happier bunch of little socialites you will never meet. Bushtits just love to do everything together. If you see one Bushtit, you will likely see 20 or more. Even the nest, which looks like a long sock, often houses not only the pair and their brood but also helpers that may be older offspring.

Bushtits are abundant year-round residents throughout most of California up to about 8,000 feet. They typically avoid the deserts, at least during the hottest months, and the higher mountains during the coldest.

These tiny birds bounce through the air waving their long tails in back of them like a banner. They live mostly on small insects but also eat seeds in winter.

Few things in life are more awe inspiring than sitting still in the midst of a flock of foraging Bushtits that don't mind your being there. Being allowed to participate in their joyous lives is a wonderful gift.

Voice: Bushtits keep up a chatter that ties the flock together. The chatter varies. It may consist of high-pitched, squeaky notes; a staccato of four or five syllables; or wispy chipping notes.

Below: A coastal female. Note the yellowish eye; males have black eyes.

Next page, top: Nest in a fir tree. **Bottom:** Some inland flocks are whitish like the flock that included this bird seen in the Kern River Gorge east of Bakersfield. Birds of coastal areas are brown or brown-gray.

Sherrie Stahl

Verdin (4.5")

The tiny Verdins are fairly common year-round residents of the Southern California deserts. They forage in any kind of shrub or tree but nest in thorny varieties to keep predators away.

Verdins are mostly insect eaters and forage in the manner of Bushtits and chickadees. However, they are solitary or live in pairs or with their young; they are not seen in flocks like Bushtits and chickadees.

Voice: Song is a rapid three- or four-syllable whistle; the first note is often softer and a little lower than the others that are the same note—maybe tse, seet-seet. Call is a scratchy chip or cheep with a slight lisp.

Top: Adult on Mexican Honeysuckle. **Bottom:** Juvenile in mesquite.

American Pipit (6.5")

These are birds of bare fields, short grassland, and mudflats that can be mistaken for sparrows until you see them walk or notice their needle-like bills. American Pipits wag their tails as they walk and bob them while foraging, neither of which are done by a sparrow. With closer observation, you will also notice their legs are longer than a sparrow's, and their bodies are more streamlined.

Some American Pipits breed in alpine meadows between Lake Tahoe and Yosemite, but most that we see throughout the state are fall and winter residents that breed in British Columbia and Alaska. The migrating birds are common and are always in flocks, usually of 40 to 200 birds. They arrive with the first heavy, cold rain. As with other migrating birds, after the flocks leave in the early spring some stragglers often stay behind.

Voice: Call is a soft, high-pitched pip-it *or* sip-it. *Song, if you can call it that, is a rapid continual repeating of its name.*

Top: Photo was taken October 6. **Bottom left:** March 3. **Bottom right:** April 13. The sexes look alike but colors and streaking can vary greatly. Some breeding birds may be redder on the breast.

American Dipper (aka **Water Ouzel**) (7.5")

The songbird that acts like a duck, the American Dipper, lives year-round along rushing streams in the northern coastal mountains and in the Sierras and Cascades. A few are reported in the higher elevations of the Southern California mountain ranges, but they must be visitors because, practically speaking, there are no year-round mountain streams south of the Kern River, and the Kern is muddy and therefore not dipper habitat.

American Dippers fearlessly forage for insect larvae at the water's edge and in the water. Sometimes they even jump into the torrent. They can swim under water like a loon and even walk along the bottom of a streambed to forage for food. Dippers are easily distinguished from Brewer's Blackbirds by their behavior and by their short tails, which they habitually bob up and down.

American Dippers build their nests along streamsides, commonly under bridges. Breeding pairs need about a half-mile of stream for foraging and are very territorial, so it is highly unlikely to see more than a few in one place.

Although generally uncommon, dippers can often be found in less crowded areas of Yosemite National Park and Pfeiffer Big Sur State Park.

Voice: Song is pleasant and complex, made up of whistles, cheeps, and short warbles. Calls include a soft chip *that carries. I have heard it from 50 yards away despite the loud noise of rushing water. Also, a louder* zeet.

Photos: Plumage color varies from light to dark gray, but that may depend upon how the light is shining on the bird. The bird below looked light or dark depending on the shadows. It also looks like it just woke up from a nap. It did.

Jeff Bleam

Jeff Bleam

Cedar Waxwing (7.25")

Winter residents that sometimes stay well into spring, Cedar Waxwings are social birds that like red berries. They can eat an astonishing number of them and usually swallow them whole. Waxwings also eat leaf buds in the spring when berries are not available. In addition, they are masterful fly catchers, usually flying up from a perch to catch their prey in midair.

Most of the Cedar Waxwings we see breed north of California. In early winter, large, hungry flocks descend on our state anywhere berries are plentiful. They are common in the suburbs thanks to the planting of pyracantha and other ornamental berry bushes. Usually, when the berries are gone, so are the waxwings.

Flocks of waxwings often fly in close ranks in meandering fashion. They have strong, continual wingbeats and keep up a constant peeping.

These beauties, as much as any, made a lifelong bird-watcher out of me. As a child I watched the winter flocks from our living room window with great fascination and each year looked forward to their arrival.

Voice is a high-pitched, soft squeak or whistle. They can also trill the same note and make a high, insect-like buzzing noise. Like Bushtits, they often keep up a chatter that seems to glue them together socially.

Below: The feathers of waxwings have a silky appearance that is unlike that of any of our other songbirds. The males and females look alike.

Phainopepla (7.75")

Phainopeplas are common residents of arid oak and sycamore woodlands, chaparral, and desert washes and woodlands mostly in the southern half of the state. They are nomadic, especially in winter, and follow the ripening of sumac, mistletoe, and juniper berries, as well as elderberries. They also dine on insects, which they capture flycatcher-style in midair.

Phainopeplas have an especially strong symbiotic relationship with mistletoe. In the late fall and winter, the berries are their main food source, and as they excrete waste, they plant the seeds on tree branches, thus spreading the mistletoe.

In flight, their white wing patches flash. Many birds have this feature.

Voice: Song is an unusual, complex combination of whistles, buzzes, and warbles reminiscent of, but softer than, a Red-winged Blackbird's. Calls include a hard trill, a cat-like mew, *and a soft, sweet* wurp *that somehow carries over a much greater distance than one would expect.*

Top: Female in mistletoe. **Bottom:** Male. **Additional photo:** Page 496.

Western Meadowlark (9.5")

Meadowlarks can be found, at least for part of the year, all over California wherever spacious meadows and grasslands exist. From late September to March wintering flocks can be numerous in the lowlands, especially near cattle. In season, they eat insects, weed seeds, and grain.

Meadowlarks built their nests on the ground in thick, matted grass. I learned that the hard way as I was walking across a grassy area in search of a calling meadowlark. I got closer and closer, and eventually realized I was standing right on top of the poor bird. It must have been a young one that didn't know when to keep quiet.

Voice: There is not a more cheerful voice in all of birddom than the sweet flute-like warble of a meadowlark.

Top: Spring (breeding) plumage. **Bottom:** Fall plumage. The sexes look alike; juveniles look like nonbreeding birds.

The spring bird was a sentry watching over a flock. The fall bird was in a field full of meadowlarks, all evenly spaced, quiet, and not moving much. They could all have easily gone unnoticed.

Horned Lark (7")

Birds of dry, flat, open space with sparse, low vegetation, Horned Larks are year-round residents throughout the state. There are many subspecies, one formerly called the California Horned Lark.

Horned Larks do not migrate in the usual sense of the term, but birds in the higher elevations go lower in winter, and those in the north commonly travel south a short distance. They resemble sparrows in habits and diet and are easily overlooked due to excellent camouflage.

These common birds are often found on seemingly bare ground where you wonder how they find anything to eat. In such places, they also make their nests, which are surprisingly well hidden.

Voice is a sweet sparrow-like peeping, commonly ending in a warble.

Top: A female. **Bottom:** Males with and without "horns" showing.

Blackbirds, Cowbirds, and Starlings

Brewer's Blackbird (9")

Once seen mostly in fields and meadows, Brewer's Blackbirds are now common in shopping center parking lots and on park lawns, where the males strut around like roosters. They are as abundant and as tame as any native bird in California.

Brewer's Blackbirds are social, even during the nesting season, and work together marvelously to protect their young. They will mob any intruder, even if it's just me trying to take out the garbage.

In winter, Brewer's Blackbirds gather into large, nomadic flocks that are often seen in agricultural fields, especially grain fields.

The iridescence of the male can be spectacular, as it is with **the poor guy below** that was dazzled by the abundance of food at Mono Lake.

Voice is chuck, chuck, shaREEE! *with the last note rising. The last part is a whole-body exercise in which the bird fans its tail, ruffles its feathers, and bows in order to get the sound out. Another call is* quit!

Top: Adult male. **Bottom left:** Female. **Right:** Variant male.

Tri-Colored Blackbird (8.5")

Almost exclusively a California species, Tri-colored Blackbirds inhabit marshes of cattails or bulrushes (tules) and forage in flooded pastures, mostly in the Central Valley. In winter, during the nonbreeding season, they stay in tight flocks and often mix with the similar-looking and much more common Red-winged Blackbirds. In winter, both species frequent cattle feedlots; the Tri-colored may prefer dairies.

Although similar in appearance to the Red-winged Blackbirds on the next page, Tri-colored males have white instead of yellow below the red patch on the wing and Tri-colored females have a bluish tint instead of a rusty tint. The Tri-colored's voice is also different.

Voice is like that of a Red-winged Blackbird that is choking to death. They also make a noise like a rusty teletype machine.

Top: April female; April male in mustard. **Bottom:** October flock.

Red-Winged Blackbird (8.5")

Red-winged Blackbirds are the common blackbird of marshes, fields, and pastures throughout California.

Like many other birds, Redwings are nomadic and follow the food supply. Males migrate separately from females, both in flocks. During the spring and summer breeding season, when they feed on insects, they are seen in loose flocks. When insects are scarce in the fall and winter, they eat seeds and grain and form large, tight flocks that congregate wherever cattle are present. At the cattle feedlots especially, the flocks are often mixed with other blackbirds, grackles, and starlings.

With the arrival of the breeding season, the males begin to sport their bright-red shoulder patches. These they inflate while belting out a song in order to impress the ladies and claim territory. The fall molt dulls, and all but removes, the red patches. The males take three years to fully develop their colors. In the Central Valley especially, some males do not have the yellow-orange band under the red patch as others do. Females look like large sparrows, except for the pointed bill.

Voice: Calls are chit *and a faint* cheet. *Red-wings have many songs and they vary considerably. One common song is* conk-a-lor-EEE!, *which starts muffled and low and ends higher. Once heard, never forgotten.*

Below: Breeding (spring) adult male.

Next page, top, left to right: Fall adult male; young male getting his colors. **Middle:** First-year bird, sex unknown; spring adult female. **Bottom:** A winter flock of females; fledgling. **Male flock:** Page 517.

Jerry Ting

Yellow-Headed Blackbird (9.5")

Yellow-headed Blackbirds inhabit marshes and forage in wet fields. They are year-round but nomadic in the Central and Colorado River Valleys, breed along our eastern border from the Klamath to Mono Basins, and may visit anywhere else with suitable habitat. Yellow-headed Blackbirds are not nearly as common as our other blackbirds. They are summer residents of the marsh at South Lake Tahoe and many winter in Mexico.

The behavior of Yellow-heads is much like that of other blackbirds. They often follow farm tractors to dine on exposed grubs and grain.

Voice is usually unpleasant. Song begins with a few grating chups that are followed by a loud, nasal rusty gate hinge noise. Another song is a raspy, squeaky chip, chip, chip chee-oo. *Calls include a very raspy jay-like* squawk; *a growled* chup; *a scratchy* chid-it; *and a sweet five-syllable trill.*

Below: Male; female on cattail. **Next page:** Males, with some red-wings.

Brown-Headed Cowbird (7.5")

These birds are year-round residents in temperate areas throughout the state and also breed in the mountains and deserts. They associate with all the California blackbird species, have the same diet, and share many of the same mannerisms—except one.

Brown-headed Cowbirds are parasites. The female lays her eggs alongside a host's eggs—one in each of several nests of smaller songbirds. When the eggs hatch, the cowbird chick is larger and takes all the food that the hosts bring to the nest. The hosts' own chicks then starve to death, and not infrequently the host pair, not being gifted with discernment, are exhausted, sometimes to death.

If that is not bad enough, the cowbirds' habitat has expanded greatly. They prefer the edges of woodlands, while the host birds live in thick woods and thickets. Because woods and thickets have been removed for development, for grazing land, and for logging, there is now more habitat for cowbirds and less for their usual hosts.

The most common birds preyed upon by cowbirds are warblers, vireos, and small flycatchers. Female cowbirds can often be seen foraging with their prospective hosts. Some species and some individual birds have more discernment than others and are not fooled by the cowbird. They will often abandon a nest entirely if they cannot throw out the offending egg. Whether they abandon their nest or serve as host, the victims rarely reproduce. The female cowbirds, since they don't spend their energy taking care of their own responsibilities, spend their time breeding. As a result, a female cowbird will commonly lay 30 to 40 eggs in a season—each in a different nest.

Nearly everywhere that land has been cleared, the cowbird's range has increased. Consequently, in the last 150 years, their population has exploded in California and elsewhere. Because of the destruction of habitat for the smaller host birds, those populations have seen a sharp decline. For this reason, cowbird traps are sometimes installed in places of compromised habitat. Where the traps are maintained, the vireo, warbler, and flycatcher populations have a chance to rebound. But without a vigilant effort to control the cowbirds, their hosts have no chance. War is never pleasant, but it is necessary at times if we are to preserve something that is precious.

Voice: Common calls are a soft, high-pitched, sliding whistle, seeep; *a squeaky gurgle followed by* seeep; *and popping chitting, and chattering. Most are unusual sounds. Perhaps the only calls resembling that of a host are the Lesser Goldfinch-like chatter and* twee-ooo, *which are not sweet.*

Next page, top: Female with a couple of suitors. Juvenile is like female but is streaked below. **Bottom:** Yellow Warbler feeding a cowbird chick.

Stephanie Struckman

European Starling (8.5")

European Starlings were brought to the United States in 1890 by a well-meaning, but not clear-thinking, individual and have since spread across the country. They are abundant, can live almost anywhere, have displaced many other bird species, and are destructive to fruit and grain crops.

Starlings are year-round California residents and are common in the suburbs most of the year. They stay in tight flocks and in season eat insects, fruit, seeds, and grain. Starlings are often seen feeding on park lawns together. When someone gets within about 60 feet of them, they move in unison to another spot on the lawn or to a tree. In the fall and winter, large flocks are numerous in farm country, especially around cattle feedlots. The winter murmurations of starlings (the swooping, twisting, and changing direction of large flocks in flight) are fascinating and are commonly seen in cattle country and around the feedlots.

Starlings place their nests in any kind of cavity, including bird boxes, tree cavities, holes in cliff faces, and nooks and crannies on buildings or other man-made structures.

Voice is a variety of clucks, whistles, warbles, chatters, smooth notes, and rattles. They also mimic a large number of birds, including meadowlarks and jays. In the trees, starlings have a lot to say and seem to all talk at once.

Below: Nonbreeding adult (September to January). The sexes look alike.

Next page, top: Adult mostly in breeding plumage. The iridescence of breeding adults can be spectacular. **Middle:** One that left the nest too early; nest site. **Bottom:** Juvenile.

Orioles

Orioles are large, slender songbirds with long, sword-like bills. They are primarily fruit eaters, and the males are much brighter in color than the females. We have three species in California.

Hooded Oriole (8")

Hooded Orioles breed in the lowlands of the western half of the state as far north as Santa Rosa. They begin arriving from Mexico in late March and begin their return in August.

These beautiful birds dine on insects, fruit, and nectar and are especially fond of palm fruits. They are treetop birds and are also commonly found in cottonwoods, willows, and sycamores.

With little fear of people, Hooded Orioles are no strangers to parks in the suburbs. They are also attracted to hummingbird feeders and (sliced) oranges but won't touch grapefruit.

*Voice: Song is a **squeaky, jumbled** warble with chatter mixed in that varies considerably. Calls include a harsh* chuck*, often repeated; the same as a trill; a sparrow-like* seet!*; and a short buzz.*

Below: Breeding male (March–Aug.); most are more yellow than orange.

Next page, top: Female. **Middle:** Male. **Bottom:** Fluffed female; first-spring male.

Note the long, curved bill; the Bullock's Oriole's is straight.

Bullock's Oriole (aka **Northern Oriole**) (8.5")

Bullock's Orioles begin arriving in California in late March to breed. Most return to Mexico in August but some stay much longer. They are more widespread in the state than their Hooded cousins and breed farther north. The Bullock's commonly nest in cottonwoods and sycamores and feed in the tops of tall trees, especially willows, along streams.

Like our other orioles, the Bullock's eat insects, fruit, and nectar, so look for them on flowering trees such as magnolias, orchids, and willows. In two of the photos here, they were eating nectar from willow blossoms, which no doubt were garnished with small insects.

Note the **black streak through the eye**. It is less prominent on the female but distinguishes the Bullock's from a Hooded Oriole. Also, the Hooded has a longer, curved bill.

Voice: Song is a **cheerful** *mix of rapid chattering and warbled and whistled phrases. It varies greatly but often is* chit-chachit-chee-choo *followed by a sweet warble. Calls include a scratchy* chup *and harsh chatter; sometimes a rapid, complex outburst of different sounds.*

Below: Breeding male in Pacific Willow.

Next page, from top: First-year male in mesquite, female in willows, nest in a California Sycamore; fledgling (note shorter bill).

Jeff Bleam

Scott's Oriole (9")

The beautiful Scott's Oriole breeds in the Mojave Desert, where Joshua trees or yuccas are present, and winters mostly in western Mexico. They avoid harsher deserts and are usually found singly or in pairs. They begin arriving in California by mid-February and stay until at least mid-July.

Scott's Orioles are a study in the symbiotic nature of the desert. They live on insects, fruit, and nectar and depend largely on Joshua tree fruit. In return, the orioles propagate those trees by excreting the seeds wherever they go. Scott's Orioles also collect nectar from yucca and agave blossoms and, in doing so, pollinate those plants. The blossoms are commonly covered with small insects, and the nectar and insects together provide the orioles with a rich diet while they keep the insect populations in check. Marvelous!

Voice: Song is a warble of melodious whistles similar to that of a meadowlark; calls are a nasal chuck *and* peep.

Below: Female. The juvenile looks similar and both look like a Hooded Oriole that was dipped in muddy water.

The adult male has a white shoulder patch, which is often hidden, as it is in this photo. Both birds shown are on Joshua trees.

Established Exotic Imported Species

While there are many escaped or released exotic birds in California, the ones included in this section are well established here.

Mandarin Duck (18")

Imported from western China, these flashy dressers have become established in Sonoma County and, to a lesser extent, in other places throughout the state. In most places, they may be more feral than truly wild, as they are more commonly found in parks than in wild areas.

For decades, we have seen Mandarin Ducks from time to time at Irvine Regional Park in Orange County in the summer and at San Joaquin Marsh in the winter. But they are unpredictable, as are the parrots on the next page.

Voice: Unknown. I've never heard them say anything.

Top: Breeding pair (June). **Bottom:** Nonbreeding male (October).

Red-Crowned Parrot (12")

The Red-crowned Parrots we see in Southern California are natives of the forests of northeastern Mexico that have become established here by escaping captivity or by being released. In about 2005, we saw a pair in our neighborhood for the first time. The next year, we saw 6 parrots. The following year, we saw 13; the year after that, 27. The next year, I counted 64; and the following year, more than 120. Since then, the population has leveled off, and we seldom see more than a few dozen at any one time.

Ironically, due to the pet trade, these parrots are probably more numerous in California and Texas than they are in their native land, where they are said to be endangered.

The birds come and go throughout the year according to the ripening of various fruits in the neighborhoods. Loquats and Magnolia blossoms are favorites; sycamore buds are less desirable but will do in a pinch.

Voice consists mostly of loud squawking. If a dozen or more get going at the same time, some people call that irritating. Anyway, I do know it is better not to be in the middle of an important phone call when they decide to have a social gathering nearby.

Photo: Several species are similar, including the Lilac and Yellow-crowned. Some birds are probably hybrids.

Pin-Tailed Whydah (4.5")

Tiny imports from sub-Saharan Africa, Pin-tailed Whydahs are established in many neighborhoods in Southern California.

The males grow their long tails during the breeding season. To impress the ladies, they dance in the air jumping up and down while hovering with their tails churning like an egg beater below them.

In flight, Whydahs bounce through the air like a House Finch, the breeding males waving their long tails behind them. The tail feathers may be stiffened (as on the next page) or relaxed.

Whydahs are social birds; several breeding pairs may nest in the same tree. They have been in our neighborhood in every season and sometimes breed here, but they come and go. We first saw them in about 2010, and since then they have become fairly common.

Voice: Squeaky twittering unlike any native bird; occasionally warbles.

Below, top: Adult female. **Bottom:** Juvenile or nonbreeding female; nonbreeding male. **Next page:** Breeding male on horseweed.

Nutmeg Mannikin (aka Scaly-Breasted Munia, Spice Finch) (4")

This bird is an import from Southeast Asia that since the 1980s has become established in many California neighborhoods. They stay in flocks and are found in wet areas, including marshes and parks.

Voice: Whistled peeps and House Sparrow-like chirping.

Top: Adults with juveniles at center. **Middle left:** Some adults are brown, not red as in the top photo. **Middle right and bottom:** Juveniles. I've seen entire flocks of juveniles that looked like these birds.

Japanese White-Eye (aka **Swinhoe's White-Eye**) (4")

Japanese White-eyes are almost always seen in small flocks of 10 to 30 birds. Like Bushtits, they are quite vocal, but unlike Bushtits, they tend to stay under cover in the middle of a tree and are difficult to see until they fly away.

These beauties feed in trees on blossoms, nectar, fruits, and small insects. Warblers, often single birds, frequently forage with them.

Released on Oahu in 1929, Japanese White-eyes are now the most abundant land bird on the Hawaiian Islands. Escaped or released birds have recently become established in many Southern California neighborhoods. I first saw them in our neighborhood in about 2008; now they are common all over town.

Voice differs from any native bird. Calls are sweet and include a pneumatic tsee, tsee-eet, *a soft* tisp, *and a sweet trill. Flocks chatter.*

Photo: This bird was part of a flock of about 15 birds that were feeding on the blossoms of a carob tree. A Townsend's and an Orange-crowned Warbler were mingled in among them. When a flock of Yellow-rumped Warblers arrived, all the smaller birds left. I observed the same thing the next day at the same location—a shopping center parking lot. Several dozen carob trees were in bloom there, but the birds preferred the same three trees both days.

Epilogue

I hope you have enjoyed our birding outing together.

What a joy birds are! What a gift!

It is out of appreciation for the gift of the birds and for the joy they have brought me, that you have this book in your hands. Truly, the one who made the heavens, the earth, and all that are in them did not leave Himself without a witness.

The perfection of the creation speaks loudly of the attributes of the Author of Life. His wisdom, majesty, orderliness, bountiful nature, faithfulness, goodness, love, and power are all clearly seen.

It is more than great poetry when the 19th Psalm proclaims:

> The heavens declare the glory of God,
> And the sky shows His handiwork;
> Day unto day utters speech,
> And night unto night reveals knowledge.
>
> There is no speech nor language
> Where their voice is not heard;
> Their line has gone out through all the earth,
> And their words to the end of the world.

God bless you all!
Tim Stanley

Donna Pomeroy

Appendix 1: Molting Photos

Below, top: Female Mallard's wing showing "pin" feathers. (Page 76.) The feather casings will fall off. **Bottom left:** Lesser Goldfinch (page 355). I don't know if that's Gramps or not, but he sure looks like him. **Bottom right:** Male House Finch (page 347).

Next page, top: A tired out male House Sparrow (page 339) and a Bushtit (page 461) with worn out tail feathers. **Middle:** Male Phainopepla (page 468), perhaps a first-year bird; sparrow growing new tail feathers. **Bottom:** Greater Roadrunner (page 258) and Orange-crowned Warbler (page 423).

For more about molting, see the preface.

Molting Photos

Top left: Western Bluebird (page 375). This one is likely transitioning into first-year plumage. The photo was taken on August 24.

Top right: Nuttall's Woodpecker (page 283).

Bottom left: California Scrub Jay fledgling getting his juvenal feathers. (Page 264). Note the short bill. The photo was taken on June 14.

Bottom right: Another California Scrub Jay, this one lacking tail feathers.

Molting Photos

Top left: Female House Finch (page 347).

Top right: Anna's Hummingbird female or juvenile male. (Page 271.) The photo was taken on April 25.

Bottom left: Adult male Spotted Towhee (page 343). The photo was taken on January 18 when these birds are the brightest.

Bottom right: Spotted Towhee. The photo was taken on September 16 when the birds are dullest. Both sexes turn duller after the nesting season but this bird is probably a female or a juvenile male.

Appendix 2: Helpful Silhouettes

Top to bottom, left to right: Blue Grosbeak, Pacific-slope Flycatcher, Purple Martin, American Robin, Marbled Godwit, Reddish Egret.

Silhouettes

Top to bottom, left to right: Western Bluebird, Black Phoebe, Pigeon Guillemots, Hummingbird (story on page 269), Red-tailed Hawk, Bushtit.

Appendix 3: Uncommon Variants

Birds of the same species can look very different. Some are called variants.

Top row: A brown Black Phoebe and a yellow Purple Finch. (Pages 457 and 349.) I have seen only one photo like the phoebe and one like the finch.

Bottom left: A leucistic California Thrasher (page 385). The condition (partial albinism), is somewhat rare but I've taken similar photos of a wren.

Bottom right: A male Anna's Hummingbird (page 271) with what appears to be a brood patch. A brood patch is bare skin that forms on the underside of a nesting bird to increase warmth for the eggs. Anna's Hummingbird females are said to tend the nest alone, but apparently not in this case.

Some common or fairly common variants are on pages 340, 363, 377, and 471.

Top left: A blue juvenile Townsend's Solitaire. They are typically brown as on page 383. Note the yellow patch and streaking on the wing.

Top right: A gray juvenile Red-tailed Hawk. Photo was taken near Bodie State Park in Mono County. Typical Red-tails are on pages 200-202.

Bottom: A black Great Blue Heron (page 167). The color is probably from an abundance of pigment, a condition the opposite of albinism.

I have never seen a similar photo of any of the three birds shown here.

Appendix 4: Fledglings and Juveniles

Fledglings, and to a lesser extent, juveniles, can present identification challenges. As always, it comes down to a process of elimination. The definition of a juvenile on page 509 is helpful for this section.

Top left: Blue-gray Gnatcatcher (page 441). Note the bill, eye-ring, and tail feathers.

Top right: Horned Lark juvenile (page 470). Note the longer, pointed bill and plumage that does not look like any of our sparrows.

Bottom left: Savannah Sparrow juvenile (page 319).

Bottom right: Juvenile Song Sparrow at Arcata Marsh. (Pages 315 to 317).

Fledglings and Juveniles

Top left: House Finch fledgling. This one was foraging with a flock of Lesser Goldfinches and looked like a giant among them. Note that the bill is too large for that of a goldfinch. (Pages 347 and 355.)

Top right: A Yellow-rumped Warbler fledgling that was with an adult. Note the bill, tail feathers, and eye-ring. (Pages 419-422.)

Bottom left: A Golden-crowned Kinglet fledgling/juvenile that was with an adult. (Page 404.)

Bottom right: Ash-throated Flycatcher fledgling/juvenile. (Page 446.)

Top left: Black-headed Grosbeak juvenile. (Page 359.)

Top right: Chipping Sparrow juvenile. (Page 325.) Compare the bill size, eye stripe, and tail feathers with the grosbeak.

Bottom left: Cassin's Finch juvenile. (Page 350.)

Bottom right: Mountain Bluebird juvenile. (Page 377.) Note the lack of spots on the back. The Western Bluebird juvenile (page 376) has spots on its back.

Top Left: Anna's Hummingbird fledgling. (Page 271).

Right: Northern Rough-winged Swallow juvenile. (Page 305).

Bottom Left: Violet-green Swallow juvenile. (Page 299.)

Right: Tree Swallow juvenile. (Page 297.) Compare the definite line under the eye with that of the Violet-green.

Appendix 5: More Photos with Interesting Stories

Top: During the early winter molt, some warblers, like this Yellow-rump, sport a black comb or coarse whiskers around their bills.

Middle: A gull's worn wingtips can appear as spots at a distance.

Bottom: One of six Wilson's Warblers that joined our pelagic trip after we were out several miles from land. They had no fear of us whatsoever and landed on us as readily as on anything else on the boat. We were out of Dana Point, and I assume they were headed to Catalina Island; we were not, so after a while they left us.

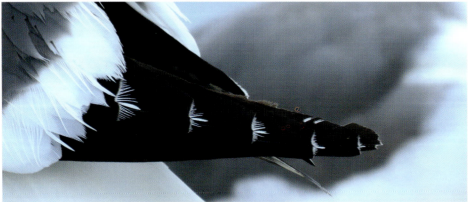

The Value of Birds

The value of birds to human beings cannot be overstated. Besides the enjoyment we derive from seeing and hearing them—and what we can learn by observing them—birds perform at least two much needed services: they pollinate plants and scatter seed, covering the land with beautiful trees and other vegetation, and they eat bugs and other animals that, if not kept in check, would soon make the earth uninhabitable.

Glossary

Beak. A short bill.
Brood. A group of baby birds in a nest. Specifically, birds that don't have enough feathers yet to keep themselves warm.

Cavity dweller. A bird that lives in holes—in trees, buildings, etc.
Central Valley. The Sacramento and San Joaquin Valleys. It extends approximately from Redding in the north to Bakersfield in the south.
Chaparral. A region of dry summers and moist winters characterized by shrubs with hard, thick leaves that remain all year. The term also refers to the shrubs themselves.
Coastal sage scrub. Coastal plants with soft leaves that fall off during the dry season. Sometimes called soft chaparral.
Continental shelf. The relatively shallow area of sea between the (continent's) coast and the deep ocean.
Coverts. From "to cover." The small, contoured feathers that cover the base of other larger feathers. For example, the wing coverts cover the base of the flight feathers on the wing.

Delta (of the Sacramento and San Joaquin Rivers). Lowland east of San Francisco Bay that is, or historically has been, often flooded.
Drake. A male duck.
Endemic. Restricted to a particular region (such as California).
Estuary. The wide area where the mouth of a river meets the tide.
First-year. (or first-summer or winter bird). See discussion at *juvenile*.
Fledgling. A young bird ready to leave the nest, able to fly somewhat but usually not yet able to fend for itself.
Gizzard. A muscular organ in a bird's digestive tract for grinding up seeds. Birds swallow pieces of sand that stay in the gizzard to aid the process.
Great Basin. The landmass between the Sierras and Cascades and the Rockies that has no drainage outlet to the ocean.
Habitat. The type of environment suitable for a species.
Headland. A landmass that juts out into the sea. A point.
Iridescence. The rainbow or prism-like effect (on bird feathers) caused by the refraction of light on microscopic feather structures.

Juvenile. A bird wearing its first set of feathers after shedding its downy feathers. For a songbird, these juvenal feathers, as they are called, remain for only a few weeks before they are replaced by other feathers. The bird is then called a first-year bird. The appearance of the bird changes dramatically between these two sets of feathers and, to a lesser degree, when they get their adult feathers. (Photos, p. 328.)
Mandible. The lower portion of the bill. Generally, both halves.
Marsh. A wet area with reeds and rushes. In contrast, a swamp predominately has trees; a bog has peat (mosses).

Mixed flocks. Flocks comprised of more than one species.
Molt. The complete or partial replacement of feathers in a relatively short time.
Montane. Mountainous area dominated by coniferous forest.
Morph. A plumage variation of a bird that is not related to age or sex and that is retained for life. For example, some species of hawks and seabirds have a light and dark morph.
Nape. The back of the neck.
Niche. An ecological or multidimensional space to which a species is restricted by competition from other species or by other factors.

Passerine. A songbird.
Peep. A general name for the smallest sandpipers.
Pelagic. The deep ocean waters (and birds that inhabit them.)
Pin feathers. Developing feathers encased in (usually white) sheaths.
Point. See *headland*.
Preening. The grooming and cleaning of the feathers.
Primaries, primary feathers. The largest feathers on a bird's wing.

Raft. A tight group of (usually) ducks on a body of water.
Range. A geographical limitation.
Raptor. A bird of prey, such as hawks, eagles, and owls.
Riparian. The bank of a stream or other watercourse or lake.
Rump. The low back (of a bird).
Savannah. Grassland.
Secondaries, or secondary flight feathers. The short, straight feathers on the inner edge of the wing close to the body but not as close as the smaller tertial feathers.
Shorebird: Any bird that frequents the shore.
Staccato. Rapid, short, usually evenly-spaced detached sounds.
Tree line. The elevation at which trees no longer grow. About 10,500 feet in the south; 8,200 feet on Mount Shasta in the north.

Trill. A rapid alteration of two adjacent notes.
Tubenose. See introduction to shearwaters on page 17.
Twitter. High-pitched quivering chatter that is usually repetitious.
Vent. The opening for excrement and, yes, for egg delivery too.
Wader: Any wading bird.
Warble. To sing melodiously with rapid modulations in pitch.
Wing bar. A contrasting color line on the wing that runs perpendicular to the feathers.

Woods, woodland. A habitat dominated by trees but without the dense canopy of a forest. The oak-studded hills throughout California are a good example of woodland. The willows, cottonwoods, and walnut trees that grow along creeks are examples of riparian woodlands as are the aspen groves in the ravines of the high mountains.

Bibliography

Brockman, C. Frank. *Trees of North America.* Racine, WI: Western, 1979.

Clark, Gary. *Book of Texas Birds.* College Station, TX: Texas A&M University Press, 2016.

Dunn, Jon L. and Johnathan Alderfer. *National Geographic Field Guide to Birds of Western North America.* Washington DC: National Geographic, 2008.

Evens, Jules and Ian Tait. *Introduction to California Birdlife.* Berkeley and Los Angeles, CA: University of California Press, 2005.

Gaines, D. *California Wildlife Habitat Relationship System, CDFW, California Interagency Wildlife Task Group, Gray-crowned Rosy-finch.* Sacramento, CA: CWHRS, 1988-1990.

Garrett, Kimball L., Jon L. Dunn and Brian E. Small. *Birds of Southern California.* Olympia, WA: R.W. Morse, 2012.

Hansen, Keith, Edward C. Beedy, Adam Donkin. *Birds of the Sierra Nevada.* Berkeley, CA: Heyday, 2021.

Hochbaum, H. Albert. *Magnificent Voyagers: Waterfowl of North America.* Charlottesville, VA: Thomasson-Grant, 1988.

Jaramillo, Alvaro. *American Birding Association Field Guide to Birds of California.* New York: Scott & Nix, 2015.

Kaufman, Kenn. *Kaufman Field Guide to Birds of North America.* New York: Houghton Mifflin, 2000.

Kaufman, Kenn. *Lives of North American Birds.* New York: Houghton Mifflin, 1996.

Kemper, John. *Southern Oregon's Bird Life.* Medford, OR: Outdoor Press, 2002.

Little, Elbert L. *National Audubon Society Field Guide to Trees, Western Region.* New York: Alfred A. Knopf, 1980.

Lukas, David. *Wild Birds of California.* Santa Barbara, CA: Companion Press, 2000.

Peterson, Roger Tory. *Peterson Field Guide to Birds of North America.* New York: Houghton Mifflin, 2008.

Quady, David E., Jon L. Dunn, Kimball L. Garrett, and Brian E. Small. *Birds of Northern California.* Olympia, WA: R.W. Morse, 2015.

Schram, Brad. *A Birder's Guide to Southern California.* Ashville, NC: American Birding Association, 2007.

Sibley, David Allen. *The Sibley Guide to Bird Life and Behavior.* New York: Alfred A. Knopf, 2001.

Sibley, David Allen. *The Sibley Guide to Birds.* New York: Alfred A. Knopf, 2014.

Stallcup, Rich and Jules Evens. *Field Guide to Birds of the Northern California Coast.* Berkeley, CA: University of California, 2014.

Tyrrell, Esther Quesada. *Hummingbirds, Their Life and Behavior: A Photographic Study of the North American Species.* New York: Crown, 1985.

Udvardy, Miklos D. F. *The Audubon Society Field Guide to North American Birds, Western Region.* New York: Alfred A. Knopf, 1977.

Willson, Mary F. and Katherine M. Hocker. *American Dippers: Singers in the Mountain Streams.* Juneau, AK: Cinclus Press, 2010.

Wyatt, Betty, Audrey Stoye, and Cecily Harris, editors. *Birding at the Bottom of the Bay,* 2nd ed. Cupertino, CA: Santa Clara Valley Audubon Society, 1990.

Major websites consulted:
www.allaboutbirds.org
www.audubon.org
www.calflora.org
www.crystalcovestatepark.org
www.ebird.org
www.flickr.com
www.ipm.ucanr.edu
www.nathistocbio.uci.edu
www.natureinstruct.org/piranga
www.newportbay.org

Acknowledgments

Writing a book—and this is my fifth—is always a humbling experience. In every case, I know what I want to produce, but to accomplish it I need the help and cooperation of many people. I'm talking about an average of sixty or more people. And because small volume books (and especially full-color books) are money losers, almost no one is getting paid. These people help out of kindness, out of a love for the subject, and because they see value in sharing what they have. Nevertheless, while working on a book, I am constantly reminded not only of my own inadequacies but also of the need to ask for help again and again.

Although I have taken photos of the great majority of the birds discussed in this book, many of mine did not depict what I needed to express or were not of publishable quality. So I am greatly indebted to the 63 photographers who allowed use of their images. Their names are on their photos throughout the book. Photos without a credit line are mine.

A special thanks to Jeff Bleam (www.byjcbphoto.com) and Jerry Ting (https://www.flickr.com/people/jerryting/), who contributed nearly 200 images between them. Their knowledge of the subject—and love for it—shows in their work. Several other photographers have but one or two photographs in the book, but they were the right ones to use where they were placed, and without these photographers, the book would be of lesser quality. The majority of the photographers fell between these extremes and many of them have vast experience and expertise. Thank you all again!

I learned a tremendous amount from these and other photographers. By studying their images and reading their comments, I was able to round out my own understanding. Field guides, along with our own observations, only get us so far. The articulated observations and stories of others were especially helpful in compiling this book. So, thank you to all of you who commented on your photographs.

Thank you to all those who handled some of my many questions. A special thanks to Jeff Bleam, who graciously helped with some tough identification puzzles, and to Roger Zachary for his help with several of the plant names. Petra Schaaf, Tom Benson, Howard Patterson, Lois Manowitz, Stephanie Smith, Ethan Winning, Gail West, Hemant Kishan, Len Blumin, Marlin Harms, Melissa Lu, Sherrie Stahl, Steve Jones, and Donna Pomeroy also provided some missing pieces to the puzzle. Our combined effort made the book.

Thank you to Flickr, the photo-sharing website, and to all who post their photos there, and especially to those who comment on them. I have learned a great deal from all of you.

Thank you to the Cornell Lab of Ornithology for their *eBird* and *All About Birds* websites and to all who contributed to them. What a tremendous work! This book could not have been completed without you.

Thank you to the Audubon Society for their work and online guide and to all who contributed to it. Another wonderful resource.

A big thank you goes to my dear wife, Deborah, who has been a huge help in all my writing endeavors. Her support has been invaluable, as has her technical expertise and her patience with me, especially when I got up so many mornings in the wee hours to write something down or to go on a birding outing. Without her help, patience, and understanding, you would not be holding this book in your hands.

It is well for me to mention my folks at this juncture. Dad instilled in all his children a love for the outdoors. He was always taking us into the mountains and forests, usually up the coast into the redwoods or to the Sierras. Mom loved the birds. She introduced us to a game called Bird Lotto by which we learned the names of many birds and we watched for them in their seasons. She also instilled in us a love for books and learning. It's not a coincidence that none of us developed much of a taste for television; we wanted to be outdoors or reading. Thank you so much, Dad and Mom, you did a great job!

To my early editor, Annie Jo Smith, who took on the project with great zeal and skill, what can I say other than without you my best efforts at writing are woefully short of what is needed for a publishable book. Thank you, Annie. To my proofreader, Skye Loyd, thank you for your careful work. And, after I expanded the book considerably, I wanted a fresh set of skilled eyes to look at it and Polly Kummel, you did a magnificent job! Thank you. Any remaining errors or awkwardness are mine.

Thanks to our son, James, to my brothers, John and Ron, and sisters, Tricia and Susan, and to so many friends. Your insightful comments, questions, and encouragement helped more than you know. Writing is a lonely occupation, and all of you helped make it less so.

To all who have purchased one of my books, especially to those who have written to thank me for writing, to add additional insight, or to point out an error, I owe a special debt of gratitude. Your help and encouragement have been invaluable, and without you I never would have attempted this book. Thank you all.

Last, but really first, thanks to God. What a wonder are all Your works! What perfection and what love are shown in all of them!

515

Author's Apology

I have lived in California all my life, both in the north and in the south, and from my youth have traveled enough in the state to know I did not need to go elsewhere to find all the beauty I could handle. Birds have always been of particular interest to me and at a certain point I became frustrated with all my bird books and other resources that told me so much about birds I will never see and not enough about those I do see or want to see. So I set out to compile as comprehensive a book as I could that matches my interests, which are birds that are at least somewhat commonly found in California.

My method would be to gather the best information I could from reliable sources, check it for accuracy as it pertains to California, combine it with my own experience, and put it all in one comfortably sized volume. I also determined to include an adequate number of relevant photographs for the birds normally found in our state. In order to fit the required number of photos and show the birds at a good size, the book would have to be larger than a field guide. It would be a hybrid of a coffee table book and a guide.

How hard could that be?
Harder than I thought.

So now, although the separation anxiety is great, it's time to stop. Even though this work is not in all respects what I hoped it would be, I have come to the point where I've given what I can and if this book is ever going to print, it needs to go now.

But how can you write about perfection without having your own imperfections magnified? When I was about three years into the project, I realized that in my 80,000 words I was making about 30,000 statements. That was alarming, to say the least, and was underscored on my many birding outings after that time, during which I observed things that caused me to make modifications in the manuscript. To my surprise, after I had read through the manuscript carefully another dozen times or so, I discovered that the number of adjustments, clarifications, corrections, and additions was increasing instead of decreasing. And so it continued for many more passes. Eventually I realized it would ever be so. The subject is too wonderful. So with all the book's shortcomings and imperfections here it is.

While working on the book, and even more so now, I have often felt like Job, who, when challenged with the creator's perfection, could only say, "I have uttered what I did not understand, things too wonderful for me, which I did not know."

Donna Pomeroy, Red-winged Blackbirds

Voices Index

Many birds have a large vocabulary, subtle differences in intonation, or both. The voicings listed are among the most common. Most are from the text. Source: Author's field notes compared with notes and recordings by others.

aaah-weetick! (*weetick compressed*)	Eared Grebe, breeding	105
ah-ooo-gah (*horn, but staticky*)	Sandhill Crane	181
baboon (*bad human imitation of*)	Roadrunner, female	258
baby's cooing, but deeper	Pelagic Cormorant	61
banjo string, loose	Forster's Tern	46
bark, loud, nasal, varies	Pileated Woodpecker	288
bark, raspy	Scaup, females	92
bark, raspy or nasal	Black Skimmer	51
bark, squeaky	Gila Woodpecker	285
bark of clack or chuck, *repeated*	Ridgeway's Rail	163
barking of a little dog	Black Tern	48
barnyard full of chickens and ducks	Heerman's Gull, flock	35
beeek (*buzzy*)	Northern Shrike	392
beep, beep, beep (*truck backing up*)	Northern Saw-whet Owl	231
beer (*nasal*)	Common Nighthawk	237
bicycle horn	Canada Goose	67
bloody-murder scream	Ring-billed Gull	37
blowing over the top of a bottle	Sooty Grouse, male (spring)	253
boatswain's whistle	Black-bellied Plover	119
bumblebee-like sound	Calliope Hummingbird	278
burping, muffled	Double-crested Cormorant	59
burst of steam (*carpet cleaning*)	Cassin's Auklet	8
buzzeet! (*electronic sounding*)	Loggerhead Shrike	391
buzzy gurgling	Rough-winged Swallow	305
bzEEET! (*piercing*)	Western Wood-pewee	448
bzzzip! fitzz-bew!	Willow Flycatcher	451
canary-like voice	American Goldfinch	353
canary-like voice	Lawrence's Goldfinch	357
cartoon-like noises	Yellow-billed Magpie	261
cartoon-like whistles	Great-tailed Grackle	268
cartoon-like squawking	Acorn Woodpecker	279
cat, fussy	Short-eared Owl	226
cat (*tail stepped on*)	Spotted Towhee	343
cat (*tail stepped on, serious*)	Rough-legged Hawk	207
cat calls	Yellow-breasted Chat	440
cat-like mew, *buzzy*	California Gnatcatcher	444
cat-like mew, *soft*	Phainopepla	468

cat's meow, *kazoo-like*	Green-tailed Towhee	346
caw *(raspy, in varying pitches)*	American Crow	259
caw, caw, caw *(crow-like but nasal)*	Pinyon Jay	265
cellophane being pulled apart	Wood Duck	77
chat	Yellow-breasted Chat	440
chatter, buzzy	Bank Swallow	306
chatter, mechanical-sounding	Marsh Wren	393
chatter, musical	Lesser Goldfinch	355
chatter, scolding, buzzy	Mountain Plover	121
chatter, scolding, dry	Common Yellowthroat	425
chatter, scolding, raspberry	House Wren	394
chatter, scratchy	Black-capped Chickadee	418
chatter, shrill, scraping	White-throated Swift	310
chee-bird, chee-bird *(rapid)*	Oak Titmouse	402
cheech *and* cheech-up	House Sparrow	339
chee-check *and* chee-chee-check	Western Bluebird	375
cheech-o	Red Crossbill	369
cheedeldeeldee, cheedeldeeldoo	Bell's Vireo	409
chee-eep *(slurred)*	House Finch	347
cheep *(squeaky; also, fading staccato)*	Ladder-back Woodpecker	284
cheer *(repeated with short pauses)*	Scrub Jay	264
cheer-ear-ear-ear-ear *(rising, fades)*	Osprey	211
cheeri-o *(slightly raspy)*	Cassin's Finch	350
cheer-up, cheer-up, cheerily	American Robin	379
cheese bur-ger *(very high, sweet)*	Black-capped Chickadee	418
chee-up *(sharp, high-pitched)*	Semi-palmated Plover	118
chet *(sharp, squeaky, nasal)*	Black-backed Woodpecker	289
chet *or* chet chet	Pacific Wren	396
chew *(second syllable of a sneeze)*	Short-eared Owl	226
chew *or* chee-chew	Purple Martin	307
chew-chew-chew *(see tu-tu-tu)*	Greater Yellowlegs	133
chew, *and a sweet* cheep	White-tailed Kite	213
chi-CA-go	California Quail	247
chick-a-dee *(scratchy)*	Mountain Chickadee	416
chick-a-dee *(sweet, squeaky or buzzed)*	Chestnut-backed Chickadee	417
chick-a-dee-dee *(usually scratchy)*	Black-capped Chickadee	418
chicken-like cackling	Sage Grouse	251
chicken-like clucking	Least Bittern	178
chicken-like noises but nasal tones	Common Gallinule	162
chip *(sharp; often as staccato)*	Nuttall's Woodpecker	283
chip, chip, chip chee-oo *(very raspy)*	Yellow-headed Blackbird	475
chipa-chipa-chipa-see-swee-sweet	Nashville Warbler	433

chip-ooo *(sweet; also, chip)*	Mountain bluebird	377
chips, chits, and gurgles	Tree Swallow	297
chirk, chirk, chirk *(squeaky chicken)*	Mountain Quail	250
chirt *(squeaky, sharp)*	Black-backed Woodpecker	289
chit and chit-chit	Marsh Wren	393
chit-chachit-chee-choo	Bullock's Oriole	483
chit-chit-chit *(cute as can be)*	Lesser Goldfinch	355
chit-chitty bird *(very rapid)*	Oak Titmouse	402
chits and chips, sometimes twittered	Vaux's Swift	311
chitting chatter	Hutton's Vireo	405
ch-KEER!	Cassin's Kingbird	459
chorpel-chorpel	Allen's Hummingbird	273
chuck	Fox Sparrow	323
chuck, chuck, chuck *(raspy)*	Cactus Wren	399
chuck, chuck, shaREEE!	Brewer's Blackbird	471
chuckchuckchuckchuck *(nasal)*	Least Bittern	178
chup *(sharp, high-pitched)*	Semi-palmated Plover	118
chup, chup	Varied Thrush	380
chup, chup, chup, chup; chup	White-tailed Kite	213
chur *(nasal)*	Cliff Swallow	301
churt *(buzzy)*	Rough-winged Swallow	305
chut-chut-chew *(repeated 3x)*	Common Yellowthroat	425
clack, clack, clack *(barked)*	Ridgeway's Rail	163
comical songs (some)	California Thrasher	385
comical voice at times	Yellow-breasted Chat	440
conk-a-lor-EEE!	Red-winged Blackbird	473
cricket-like buzzing (that slows, drops)	Brewer's Sparrow	336
crow gargling	Canvasback, female	96
crow-like but higher-pitched, nasal	Clark's Nutcracker	267
did-it, did-it *(scratchy, rapid)*	Oak Titmouse	402
donkey, braying	Black-footed Albatross	11
dropped ping-pong ball	Black-chinned Sparrow	334
dropped ping-pong ball	Wrentit	401
drops of water in a deep well	American Bittern	177
duck quacking through a kazoo	White-faced Ibis	179
dweee? and dwee-do	Lawrence's Goldfinch	357
dwee-dwee-dwee-dwee	White-breasted Nuthatch	411
dweet-dweet-dweet *(squeaky or scratchy)*	Bewick's Wren	395
dweet-dweet-dweet-dweet *(sweet)*	Oak Titmouse	402
electronic noises	Rock Wren	397
Emergency Broadcast System test	Varied Thrush	380
fee, fee, bee, bee *(high and clear)*	Mountain Chickadee	416

Voices Index

fitzz-bew!	Willow Flycatcher	451
flute-like warble, out of an echo chamber	Hermit Thrush	381
flute-like warbles	Pine Grosbeak	363
flute-like warbles	Western Meadowlark	469
fries-wid-dat *(compressed chattering)*	Black-capped Chickadee	418
gargling	Brants, flock of	69
greeet! *(often repeated with pauses)*	Scrub Jay	264
gruk	Merganser: Com and RB	108
gurgle, squeaky, followed by seeep	Brown-headed Cowbird	477
gurgles	Yellow-breasted Chat	440
gurgles, sweet	Tree Swallow	297
gurgling, buzzy	Rough-winged Swallow	305
ha-ha-ha-ha *(scratchy or squeaky)*	Herring Gull	31
hank-hank-hank *(loud, nasal)*	Pileated Woodpecker	288
hawk-like scream, cry-ah	Williamson's Sapsucker	295
He didn't see me *(compressed, melancholy)*	Oregon Junco	341
hearing test (high notes, nearly inaudible)	Golden-crowned Kinglet	404
Here Comes the Bride *(melancholy)*	White-throated Sparrow	326
Hi there *(can be scratchy or sweet)*	Purple Finch	349
Here-I-am *(sweet, warbled; often with above)*	Purple Finch	349
hog	Brandt's Cormorant	57
hog-like croak	Com. Golden-eye (female)	93
horsefly-like buzzing	Rufous Hummingbird	275
Housefinch-like *warbles without the buzz*	Blue Grosbeak	361
Housefinch-like *warbles, but higher*	Warbling Vireo	406
Housefinch-like	Japanese White-eye	492
howling wolf	Common Loon, breeding	113
hwaah, hwaah *(raspy)*	Eurasian-collared Dove	244
I'm so tired *(slow)*	Golden-crowned Sparrow	329
insect-like buzz	Spotted Towhee	343
insect-like tszeeeee	Grasshopper Sparrow	337
insect-like trill (sweet, trails off)	Chipping Sparrow	325
jeep, jeep	Red Crossbill (in flight)	369
jeka-jeka-jeka *(or* weka, *squawking)*	Acorn Woodpecker	279
jip *(often followed by cheech-o)*	Red Crossbill	369
jit *and* jidit *(disjointed chittering of)*	Ruby-crowned Kinglet	403
kackkackkack *(yelping, continues)*	Prairie Falcon	183
ka-ka-ka-ka, kow-kow-kow, kalup	Yellow-billed Cuckoo	257
kak-kak-kak *(scratchier than Cooper's)*	Peregrine Falcon	185
ka-rah *and* ka-rack *(nasal croaks)*	Caspian Tern	43
kar-eeek!, *or* eeek! *(grating)*	Elegant Tern	45
kazoo, soft note	California Gnatcatcher	444

kazoonta *(raspy; repeats w pauses)*	Acorn Woodpecker	279
kear *or* kear-ah *(piercing, 3x min.)*	Red-shouldered Hawk	203
keeeeeaar *(clearer than RT Hawk)*	Swainson's Hawk	205
keeeeeaar *(piercing, fades into static)*	Red-tailed Hawk	199
keer! *(higher pitched than RT Hawk)*	Northern Flicker	296
keer! *or* peer! *(a gull-like scream)*	Marbled Murrelet	9
kek-kek-kek *(inflection changes)*	Pileated Woodpecker	288
keow! *(a classic gull scream)*	Herring Gull	31
keow-keow-keow *(nasal)*	Glaucous Gull	33
kereep! *(a piercing scream)*	Western Grebe	101
kiddie cartoon show, intro tune	Great-tailed Grackle	268
kik *(nasal, squeaky)*	Cooper's Hawk	193
ki-ki-ki-ki *(high-pitched, 10-20x)*	Northern Goshawk	191
kik-kik-kik-kik-kik *(monkey-like)*	Cooper's Hawk	193
kill-deer *(high-pitched, repeated)*	Killdeer	117
kil-up *(squeaky, compressed)*	Least Tern	49
klee-klee-klee-klee *(high-pitched, rapid)*	Kestrel	187
kleep *(high-pitched)*	Wandering Tattler	140
kleep-kleep *(sharp, high-pitched)*	Solitary Sandpiper	143
kleet, kleet, kleet! *(high-pitched)*	Avocet	123
kraaw *(croaking)*	Common Raven	260
kreek *(raspy, squeaky)*	Least Tern	49
kreekreekree *(continues)*	Prairie Falcon	183
krreee *(electronic, raspy, or buzzy)*	Dunlin	145
kuck *(nasal, repeated sporadically)*	Green Heron	166
kuk-kuk-kuk *(nasal)*	Sooty Grouse, female	253
Lesser Goldfinch-like sounds (several)	Golden-crowned Sparrow	329
Lesser Goldfinch-like chatter	Pine-siskin	358
Lesser Goldfinch-like twee-ooo *(but sour)*	Brown-headed Cowbird	477
little dog barking	Black Tern	48
lookoverhere *(rapid, compressed)*	Mountain Chickadee	416
machine gun-like bursts	Allen's Hummingbird	273
mechanical-sounding chatter	Marsh Wren	393
minor key (often sings in)	Lesser Goldfinch	355
monkey in the jungle	Pileated Woodpecker	288
monkey-like chatter	Burrowing Owl	234
moo *(like a cow, but comically)*	Rhinoceros Awklet	7
Morse code	Anna's Hummingbird	271
Morse code	Costa's Hummingbird	276
mournful crying	Mourning Dove	239
mouse-like squeak	Harlequin Duck	97
No hope	Inca Dove	243

Oh, dear me *(can be rapid or slow)*	Golden-crowned Sparrow	329
Oh, you really scared me *(high, fast)*	Willet, alarmed	132
ooo WEE-ooo, woo, woo, woo	Mourning Dove	239
orator (the bird talks)	Yellow-breasted Chat	440
orrr-weet or orr-wee-it (whistled)	Snowy Plover	120
Ow! *(high-pitched, as if being hurt)*	Ring-billed Gull	37
PAY-wee! *(buzzy, piercing)*	Western Wood-pewee	448
peek *(squeaky; often staccatoed)*	Downy Woodpecker	281
pee-ooo *(high-pitched)*	Say's Phoebe	458
pee-ooo *(compressed)*	Hammond's Flycatcher	452
peep, chuck, chuck	American Robin	379
peep, peep, tuk	American Robin	379
peer *(hawk-like but mild, ends abruptly)*	Rufous-crowned Sparrow	324
peet *(sharp, high-pitched)*	Vermilion Flycatcher	455
peet and peet-up	Dowitcher, Long-billed	135
peetick!	Summer Tanager, male	373
pheep *(high-pitched, hollow)*	Townsend's Solitaire	383
pick-pick-pick *(also, pick)*	California Quail	247
pid-it, seet, sue-WEET	Pacific-slope Flycatcher	449
pig-like grunt, raspy	Band-tailed Pigeon	245
pig-like snort	Cinnamon Teal, male	83
pip and pip-peer!	Ash-throated Flycatcher	446
pip, pip, pee-ooo	Hammond's Flycatcher	452
pip, pip, pip *(high, sharp)*	Olive-sided Flycatcher	447
pip-it *(soft, high-pitched)*	Pipit	464
pit! *(can be fussy or not)*	Wild Turkey	255
pit-zeeeeeeep! *(squeaky buzz)*	Rock Wren	397
pity-ooo *(pity is compressed)*	Say's Phoebe	458
poit *(compressed, high-pitched)*	Mountain Plover	121
poor-willup or poor-willa	Common Poor-will	238
p-p-pit ca-zee-ooo	Vermilion Flycatcher	455
ped-i-lick *(compressed, sputtering)*	Western Tanager	371
pretty-da-bird	Summer Tanager	373
prettybird *(sweet, rapid, compressed)*	Mountain Chickadee	416
pumping nosie: rapid, low and raspy	Pied-billed Grebe	104
pump-like noise: rhythmic, buzzing	Black-chin Hummingbird	277
que-ar! *(rapid, high, squeaky)*	Mountain Quail (spring male)	250
radio static	Bank Swallow	306
radio static (dense)	Burrowing Owl	234
raspberry buzz	House Wren	394
raspberry buzz	Bewick's Wren	395
reee *(shorter than Spotted Towhee)*	Hermit Thrush	381

Voice	Bird	Page
reeeeeee *(ringing staccoto)*	Spotted Towhee	343
reeet?	Pine Siskin	358
referee's whistle (often with pity-ooo)	Say's Phoebe	458
referee's whistle (somewhat like)	Pigeon Guillemot, alarm	5
rheeek (repeated, drawn out)	Peregrine Falcon	185
rheeek!	Spotted Towhee	343
rick rack (raspy, fussy)	Cattle Egret	172
robin-like, but clearer	Summer Tanager	373
robin-like, but faster and raspy	Western Tanager	371
robin-like, but longer, more varied	Black-headed Grosbeak	359
robin-like, but with a sore throat	Mountain bluebird	377
rubber ducky (shrill peeping)	Pygmy Nuthatch, excited	414
rusty gate hinge, nasal, loud	Yellow-headed Blackbird	475
saw blade being sharpened	Northern Saw-whet Owl	231
scolding chatters	House Wren	394
scolding chatters	Bewick's Wren	395
scream, muffled, like a crazy person	Flammulated Owl	233
screaming lunatics	Common Loons, breeding	113
screech, raspy	Barn Owl	229
see-eeet, tsrt	Hammond's Flycatcher	452
seet (5x), swee (5x); 2nd part faster	Nashville Warbler	433
seet-seet-seet-chu-chu-chu	Nashville Warbler	433
see-eeet (rising)	Pine Siskin	358
shack-shack-shack (scolding)	Steller's Jay	263
sheck (scolding)	Steller's Jay	263
sheck (very similar to Steller's)	Scrub Jay	264
shek-shek-shek (scratchy)	Yellow-billed Magpie	261
shook-shook-shook (rapid-fire)	Steller's Jay	263
sick rooster crowing	Ring-necked Pheasant	256
sip (soft)	Fox Sparrow	323
sip-it	Pipit	464
siren-like sound, hollow, nasal	Redhead, spring male	95
sneeze, explosive, low, raspy, muffled	Green Heron	166
sputtering (squeaky)	Ash-throated Flycatcher	446
squeak, grating	Cliff Swallow	301
squeaky chicken	Mountain Quail	250
squeaky chittering	Rufous-crowned Sparrow	324
squeaky toy	Cassin's Kingbird	459
squeaky, nasal two-syllable bark	Parasitic Jaeger	13
squirrel-like squeal	Northern Saw-whet Owl	231
starter motor on a car, rusty	Cactus Wren	399
starter motor on machinery	Pied-billed Grebe	104

stip	Oregon Junco	341
sue-WEET!	Pacific-slope Flycatcher	449
sweet, sweet, so sweet	Yellow Warbler	427
sweet-sweet-su-we-chu	Yellow-rumped Warbler	421
tay-toe-chip?	American Goldfinch	353
tea kettle, first whistle of	American Wigeon	77
tea kettle, sputtering	Dowitcher, Long-billed	135
teletype machine	Virginia Rail	164
thook *(loud, deep, hollow; blowing over a bottle)*	Sooty Grouse, male (spring)	253
thuck-thuck *(nasal)*	Shoveler, male	85
tic *or* tic-it *(at times like Morse code)*	Costa's Hummingbird	276
tink *(faint)*	Vesper Sparrow	321
tisp *(sharp, almost* chip*)*	Calliope Hummingbird	278
tisp *(high-pitched)*	Savannah Sparrow	319
tisp *(faint)*	Vesper Sparrow	321
tisp *(faint, sharp)*	Chipping Sparrow	325
toad-like trill (7 seconds or more)	Lesser Nighthawk	235
trees, trees, beautiful trees (very high)	Brown Creeper	415
truck backing up (beep, beep, beep)	Northern Saw-whet Owl	231
tsee, seet-seet *(whistled)*	Verdin	463
tsear *and* tsrt *(buzzy)*	Bank Swallow	306
tsee-eet, *and* tsee-weet	Japanese White-eye	492
tsee-ooo *(buzzy)*	Hutton's Vireo	405
tseet-tseet-tseet, churry churry	MacGillivray's Warbler	434
tsee-tsee-tsee dzoo zumba *(high, buzzy)*	Townsend's Warbler	430
tsee-tsee-tsee-tsee, swee, swee	Lucy's Warbler	437
tsee-tsee-tsee, tsu, tsu, tsu *(slows, fades)*	Canyon Wren	398
tu-tu-tu *(descending, piercing)*	Greater Yellowlegs	133
tu *or* tu tu *(mellow)*	Lesser Yellowlegs	134
tu-tu, tu-tu-tu *(sweet, rapid)*	Dowitcher, Short-billed	135
twee-deet, twee-doo	Black Phoebe	457
tweek *(high-pitched; often staccato)*	Hairy Woodpecker	282
twee-twee-twee-twee-twee *(rapid)*	Oregon Junco	341
twee-ooo *(sweetest you ever heard)*	Lesser Goldfinch	355
urr *(gutteral)*	Common Murre (in colony)	3
vee-eet *(slurred)*	House Finch	347
waa-waa-waa-waa *(nasal, low-pitched)*	White-breasted Nuthatch	411
weck? *(nasal, squawking)*	Black-billed Magpie	262
weeoo *and* weeoo-ah	Gray Jay	266
weer? *(nasal, squawking)*	Black-billed Magpie	262
weet! *(1 or 2x, high-pitched, whistled)*	Spotted Sandpiper	149
weezy, weezy, weee-zeet	Townsend's Warbler	430

wek-wek-wek-wek *(nasal, continues)*	Northern Flicker	296
weka-weka-weka *(squawking)*	Acorn Woodpecker	279
wuk-wuk-wuk *(rhythm changes)*	Pileated Woodpecker	288
what-PEEVES-you *(piercing whistle)*	Olive-sided Flycatcher	447
whinny (like a horse but higher)	Sora	165
whinny, descending	Black-backed Woodpecker	289
whinny, kacking	Lesser Nighthawk	235
whistle, boatswain's	Black-bellied Plover	119
whistle, high, sweet and repeated	Spotted Sandpiper	149
whistle, high, thin, sliding	Brown-headed Cowbird	477
whistle, high-pitched	Pigeon Guillemot	5
whistle, piercing: what PEEVES you!	Olive-sided Flycatcher	447
whistle, sharp: tsee, seet-seet	Verdin	463
whistle, shrieking, high-pitched	Great-tailed Grackle	268
whistle, soft, wailing	Black Scoter	100
whistle, two-note descending	Yellow-billed Magpie	261
whistles, (many, varying)	Euorpean Starling	479
whistling in a minor key	Golden-crowned Sparrow	329
whit	Yellow-rumped Warbler	421
Who cooks for you?	White-winged Dove	241
who-up	Common Ground Dove	242
whoo, h-whoo, whoo, whoo *(muffled)*	Great Horned Owl	224
witcheywa, witcheywa, witcheywa	Common Yellowthroat	425
wock? *(nasal, squawking)*	Black-billed Magpie	262
wound-out motor	Allen's Hummingbird	273
wreee *(shorter than Spotted Towhee)*	Hermit Thrush	381
wurp *(soft, sweet)*	Phainopepla	468
yank *(or YANK!)*	Red-breasted Nuthatch	413
yeeb *(subdued, hoarse)*	Mallard, male	76
yeow! *(a classic gull scream)*	Herring Gull	31
yup, yup *(high yelping)*	Long-eared Owl	225
zee-del, zee-del da-deechee	Blk-throated Gray Warbler	431
zeee-chuppity-chuppity	Allen's Hummingbird	273
zoo-weet *(buzzy)*	Hutton's Vireo	405
zooweet *(may be compressed)*	Dowitcher, Short-billed	135
zreeeeeeit? *(rising)*	Pine Siskin	358
zweet	Dowitcher, Short-billed	135

Index
Names of plants are in italics.

Acacia, Sweet 409
Accipiters 191
Albatross
    Black-footed 11
    Laysan 12
Alder 371, 427, 435
Alder, red 231, 427
Algae, red 142
Alkali weed 78, 135
Aspen, Quaking 191, 226
Auklet
    Cassin's 8
    Rhinoceros 7
Avocet 123
Birch 431
Bittern
    American 177
    Least 178
Blackberry 247, 329
Blackbird
    Brewer's 471
    Red-winged 473
    Tri-colored 472
    Yellow-headed 475
Bluebird
    Mountain 377
    Western 375
Bottlebrush 433
Brant 69
Bulrushes 60, 178, 303
Bunting
    Indigo 368
    Lazuli 367
Bushtit 461
Butterfly bush 343
Carob tree 492
Cattail 475
Ceanothus, Greenbark 407
Cedar, Western Red 227
Channel Islands 1
Chat, Yellow-breasted 440
Cherry, Catalina 371

Chickadee
    Black-capped 418
    Chestnut-backed 417
    Mountain 416
Chicken-like birds, marshes 161
Cholla cactus 314, 399
Condor, California 220
Continental shelf 1
Coot, American 161
Cormorant
    Brandt's 57
    Double-crested 59
    Pelagic 61
Cottonwood 230, 284
Cottonwood, Black 193
Cow parsnips 425
Cowbird, Brown-headed 477
Coyote brush 423
Crab apples 349, 363, 427
Crane, Sandhill 181
Creeper, Brown 415
Creosote bush 276
Crepe Myrtle 353
Crossbill, Red 369
Crow, American 259
Cryptomeria 403
Cuckoo, Yellow-billed 257
Curlew, Long-billed 129
Curly Dock 338, 459
Cypress, Italian 389
Desert Deerbrush 336
Desert Peach 331
Desert Senna 427
Dipper, American 465
Douglas fir 404
Dove
    Common Ground 242
    Eurasian Collared 244
    Inca 243
    Mourning 239
    Rock 246
    White-winged 241

Dowitcher
    Long-billed............................135
    Short-billed...........................135
Duck
    American Wigeon...................77
    Barrow's Goldeneye...............94
    Black Scoter.........................100
    Bufflehead.............................88
    Canvasback...........................96
    Common Goldeneye 93
    Gadwall 79
    Greater Scaup 92
    Harlequin................................97
    Lesser Scaup..........................91
    Mallard 76
    Mandarin..............................487
    Northern Pintail 80
    Northern Shoveler 85
    Redhead 95
    Ring-necked...........................90
    Ruddy 89
    Surf Scoter............................98
    White-winged Scoter 99
    Wood.....................................77
Ducks..75
Dunlin 145
Eagle
    Bald 217
    Golden..................................215
Egret
    Cattle....................................172
    Great....................................173
    Reddish................................175
    Snowy..................................174
Elderberries 347
Eucalyptus, Blue Gum 219
Eucalyptus, Red Flowering.....395
Falcon
    Peregrine..............................185
    Prairie 183
Farallon Islands 1
Farewell to Spring...................353
Fiddleneck 355
Fig 438
Filaree....................................244

Finch
    Cassin's 350
    Gray-crowned Rosy - 351
    House...................................347
    Purple 349
    Spice 491
Fir 461
Fir, white 370
Flicker, Northern 296
Flight pattern xiv
Flycatcher
    Ash-throated.......................446
    Brown-crested 445
    Dusky 453
    Empidonax 450
    Gray 454
    Hammond's 452
    Olive-sided..........................447
    Pacific-slope.......................449
    Vermilion 455
    Willow.................................451
Flycatchers 445
Fuchsia..................................423
Fulmar, Northern 15
Gallinule, Common 162
Gnatcatcher
    Black-tailed 443
    Blue-gray............................441
    California 444
Godwit, Marbled...................131
Goldfinch
    American 353
    Lawrence's.........................357
    Lesser..................................355
Goose
    Brant 69
    Canada 67
    Crackling 68
    Egyptian 74
    Greater White-fronted 73
    Ross's 70
    Snow 71
Goshawk, Northern 191
Grackle, Great-tailed 268
Grebe

Clark's 101
  Eared................................... 105
  Horned 106
  Pied-billed 104
  Red-necked 107
  Western 101
Grebes 101
Grosbeak
  Black-headed 359
  Blue 361
  Evening 365
  Pine 363
Grouse
  Blue 253
  Dusky 253
  Greater Sage 251
  Ruffed 254
  Sooty 253
Guillemot, Pigeon 5
Gull
  Bonaparte's 41
  California 29
  Glaucous 33
  Glaucous-winged 33
  Heermann's 35
  Herring 31
  Mew 39
  Ring-billed 37
  Western 27
Gulls 25
Harrier, Northern 197
Hawk
  Cooper's 193
  Ferruginous 209
  Marsh 197
  Red-shouldered 203
  Red-tailed 199
  Rough-legged 207
  Sharp-shinned 195
  Sparrow 187
  Swainson's 205
Hawks 183
Heliotrope, Alkali 500
Hemlock, Western 191
Heron

  Black-crowned Night 171
  Great Blue 167
  Green 166
  Little Blue 169
  Tri-colored 170
Honeysuckle, Mexican 463
Horseweed 489
Hummingbird
  Allen's 273
  Anna's 271
  Black-chinned 277
  Calliope 278
  Costa's 276
  Rufous 275
Hummingbirds 269
Ibis, White-faced 179
Ice plant 57
Incense-cedar 416
Jaeger
  Parasitic 13
  Pomarine 14
Jay
  California Scrub 264
  Canada 266
  Gray 266
  Pinyon 265
  Steller's 263
  Western Scrub 264
Joshua tree 265, 399, 485
Junco
  Oregon 341
  Slate-colored 342
Juniper 264, 343
Kelp, Giant 33
Kestrel, American 187
Killdeer 117
Kingbird
  Cassin's 459
  Western 460
Kingfisher, Belted 182
Kinglet
  Golden-crowned 404
  Ruby-crowned 403
Kite, White-tailed 213
Kittiwake, Black-legged 26

Knot, Red 137
Lark, Horned 470
Loon
    Common 113
    Pacific 114
    Red-throated 115
Magpie
    Black-billed 262
    Yellow-billed 261
Mallow 318, 439
Mannikin, Nutmeg 491
Maple, Big Leaf 299
Martin, Purple 307
Meadowlark, Western 469
Merganser
    Common 108
    Hooded 111
    Red-breasted 109
Merlin 189
Mesquite 463
Mesquite, Honey 443
Mesquite, Velvet 437
Migration xv
Mockingbird, Northern 389
Molting .... xii, 495
Moorhen 162
Mud Hen 161
Mulefat 318, 353, 441
Munia, Scaly-breasted 491
Murre, Common 3
Murrelet
    Ancient 10
    Marbled 9
Mustard 319, 367
Nighthawk
    Common 237
    Lesser 235
Nutcracker, Clark's 267
Nuthatch
    Pygmy 414
    Red-breasted 413
    White-breasted 411
Oak, Coast Live 247
Oak, Silver-leaf 408, 430
Oriole
    Bullock's 483
    Hooded 481
    Northern 483
    Scott's 485
Osprey 211
Owl
    Barn 229
    Barred 227
    Burrowing 234
    Flammulated 233
    Great Gray 222
    Great Horned 223
    Long-eared 225
    Northern Pygmy 232
    Northern Saw-whet 231
    Short-eared 226
    Spotted 228
    Western Screech 230
Owls 221
Oystercatcher
    American 122
    Black 122
Palm, California Fan 223
Parrots, Red-crowned 488
Peeps 150
Pelican
    Brown 53
    White 55
Pennywort, Water 155, 179
Penstemon 276
Pewee, Western Wood- 448
Phainopepla 468
Phalarope
    Red 159
    Red-necked 157
    Wilson's 155
Pheasant, Ring-necked 256
Phoebe
    Black 457
    Say's 458
Pickleweed 119, 170
Pigeon
    Band-tailed 245
    Rock 246
Pine 267, 369

Pinyon Pine	265
Pipit, American	464
Plover	117
Black-bellied	119
Mountain	121
Semipalmated	118
Snowy	120
Poorwill, Common	238
Pride of Madeira	278
Puffin, Tufted	6
Pyracantha	376, 467
Quail	
California	247
Gambel's	249
Mountain	250
Quail bush	385
Rail	
Clapper	163
Ridgway's	163
Virginia	164
Raven, Common	260
Redwood	217, 449
Roadrunner, Greater	258
Robin, American	379
Ryegrass	299
Sagebrush, Big	321, 346, 456
Saltbush	273
Saltbush, Big	385, 386, 444
Saltwort	163, 319
Sand Verbena	49
Sanderling	147
Sandpiper	
Least	150
Pectoral	144
Rock	142
Solitary	143
Spotted	149
Western	151
Sandpipers	127
Sapsucker	
Red-breasted	292
Red-naped	293
Williamson's	295
Sapsuckers	291
Sea lettuce	140
Sea rocket	120
Seabirds	1
Shearwater	
Black-vented	18
Sooty	17
Shrike	
Loggerhead	391
Northern	392
Silk floss tree	373
Siskin, Pine	358
Skimmer, Black	51
Snipe, Wilson's	139
Solitaire, Townsend's	383
Sora	165
Sparrow	
American Tree	338
Bell's	332
Black-chinned	334
Black-throated	333
Brewer's	336
Brush	331
Chipping	325
English	339
Fox	323
Golden-crowned	329
Grasshopper	337
House	339
Lark	335
Lincoln's	317
Rufous-crowned	324
Sagebrush	331
Savannah	319
Song	315
Swamp	322
Vesper	321
White-throated	326
White-crowned	327
Sparrows	314
Spike rushes	179
Spruce	266
Spruce, Blue	377
Starling, European	479
Stilt, Black-necked	125
Storm-petrel	
Ashy	20

Index

    Black 19
    Fork-tailed 20
    Leach's 21
    Wilson's 21
Sumac, Laurel 329, 401
Sunflower, Coast 425
Sunflowers, wild 353
Surf grass 37, 132
Surfbird 141
Swallow
    Bank 306
    Barn 303
    Cliff 301
    Rough-winged 305
    Tree 297
    Violet-green 299
Swan
    Tundra 66
    Whistling 66
Swift
    Chimney 311
    Vaux's 311
    White-throated 310
Swifts
    Black 313
Sycamore, California 203, 483
Tanager
    Summer 373
    Western 371
Tattler, Wandering 140
Teal
    Blue-winged 81
    Cinnamon 83
    Green-winged 82
Terms used xi
Tern
    Black 48
    Caspian 43
    Elegant 45
    Forster's 46
    Least 49
    Royal 44
Terns 42
Thermal column 36
Thimbleberry 380

Thistle 351, 356
Thistle, Russian 458
Thrasher
    Bendire's 388
    California 385
    Crissal 386
    LeConte's 387
    Sage 384
Thrush
    Hermit 381
    Swainson's 382
    Varied 380
Titmouse
    Juniper 402
    Oak 402
Towhee
    Abert's 345
    California 344
    Green-tailed 346
    Spotted 343
Tubenose 15
Tumbleweed 458
Turkey, Wild 255
Turnstone
    Black 153
    Ruddy 154
Verdin 463
Vireo
    Bell's 409
    Cassin's 407
    Hutton's 405
    Plumbeous 408
    Solitary 407
    Warbling 406
Vireos 405
Vulture, Turkey 219
Walnut, California 339
Warbler
    Black-throated Gray 431
    Hermit 435
    Lucy's 437
    MacGillivray's 434
    Nashville 433
    Orange-crowned 423
    Palm 439

    Townsend's 430
    Virginia's 438
    Wilson's 429
    Yellow 427
    Yellow-rump 419
Warblers 419
Water Ouzel 465
Waterfowl 65
Waxwing, Cedar 467
Whimbrel 130
White-eyes, Japanese 492
Whydah, Pin-tailed 489
Wild oats 367
Wild radish 319
Wild rose 418
Willet 132
Willow 199, 229, 411
Willow, Arroyo 292
Willow, Black 203
Willow, Pacific 483
Winterberry 381
Woodpecker
    Acorn 279

    Black-backed 289
    Downy 281
    Gila 285
    Hairy 282
    Ladder-backed 284
    Lewis's 286
    Nuttall's 283
    Pileated 288
Woodpeckers 279
Wren
    Bewick's 395
    Cactus 399
    Canyon 398
    House 394
    Marsh 393
    Pacific 396
    Rock 397
Wrens 393
Wrentit 401
Yellowlegs
    Greater 134
    Lesser 133
Yellowthroat, Common 425

Also by Tim Stanley:

The Last of the Prune Pickers: A Pre-Silicon Valley Story

Not long before the Santa Clara Valley of California was known for silicon, the valley was largely covered with orchards. There were orchards of pears, apricots, cherries, walnuts, and the king of them all: prunes. Most of the orchards were part of small family farms, and there were thousands of them. This is the story of what preceded those farms, how they came into being, and how they thrived. It is also the story of one of the last of those farms, of the farmer, and of some of the young boys and girls who had the privilege of working for him.

239 pages with 50 photos, soft cover

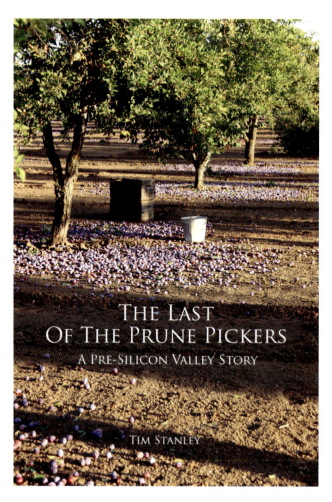

Order online at www.2timothypublishing.com or send a check for $24.00 to:
2 Timothy Publishing, P.O. Box 53783, Irvine, CA 92619
(Shipping and handling included; CA mailing addresses add $1.55 sales tax)

Some Good Birding Places, North

North Coast
Crescent City: Harbor, Point Saint George
Klamath River Estuary
Prairie Creek Redwoods State Park
Patrick's Point State Park
Arcata Marsh

Northeast
Tule Lake National Wildlife Refuge
Burney Falls State Park

Central Valley, Delta
Sacramento National Wildlife Refuge, near Willows
Grizzly Island Wildlife Refuge, south of Fairfield
Colusa National Wildlife Refuge
Merced National Wildlife Refuge

Sierras
Calaveras Big Trees State Park
Yosemite National Park, Wawona Meadow
Yosemite NP: Glacier Point Road, Tioga Pass
Sequoia National Park, Mineral King
Donner Lake, Donner Party Picnic Area

Sierras, East
Sierra Valley, Sierra Valley Preserve
Tahoe Basin: S. Lake Tahoe marsh, Paige Meadows
Mono Lake: South Tufa Area, Mono Lake Park
Bodie area: Bodie Road, State Park
Virginia Lakes, Lundy Canyon

Bay Area
Point Reyes National Seashore, Limantour Beach
Bolinas Lagoon, County Park
Palo Alto Baylands, Shoreline Park
Santa Cruz: Municipal Wharf, West Cliff Drive
Año Nuevo State Park, Waddell Beach, N of S. Cruz
San Jose, Alum Rock Park
Fremont, Coyote Hills Regional Park

Monterey Area
Monterey, Ocean View Blvd.
Carmel, Carmel River State Beach
Point Lobos State Park
Andrew Molera State Park
Pinnacles National Park, Panoche Road, west